AUSTERITY, COMMUNITY ACTION, AND THE FUTURE OF CITIZENSHIP IN EUROPE

Edited by Shana Cohen, Christina Fuhr
and Jan-Jonathan Bock

First published in Great Britain in 2017 by

Policy Press
University of Bristol
1-9 Old Park Hill
Bristol
BS2 8BB
UK
t: +44 (0)117 954 5940
pp-info@bristol.ac.uk
www.policypress.co.uk

North America office:
Policy Press
c/o The University of Chicago Press
1427 East 60th Street
Chicago, IL 60637, USA
t: +1 773 702 7700
f: +1 773-702-9756
sales@press.uchicago.edu
www.press.uchicago.edu

© Policy Press 2017

British Library Cataloguing in Publication Data
A catalogue record for this book is available from the British Library

Library of Congress Cataloging-in-Publication Data
A catalog record for this book has been requested

ISBN 978-1-4473-3103-2 hardcover
ISBN 978-1-4473-3108-7 ePub
ISBN 978-1-4473-3107-0 Mobi
ISBN 978-1-4473-3104-9 ePdf

The right of Shana Cohen, Christina Fuhr and Jan-Jonathan Bock to be identified as editors
of this work has been asserted by them in accordance with the Copyright, Designs and
Patents Act 1988.

Cover design by Hayes Design Ltd
Front cover image: iStock
Printed and bound in Great Britain by CPI Group (UK) Ltd,
Croydon, CR0 4YY
Policy Press uses environmentally responsible print partners

In Memory of Matt Teather, friend and colleague

Contents

Acknowledgements

This book would not have been possible without the generous support of the Templeton World Charity Foundation and an anonymous donor. They provided the funding for both the initial roundtable event 'Austerity and Our Social Future', that brought the authors together, and for the research that informed the Introduction and the Conclusion by Shana Cohen and Jan-Jonathan Bock, as well as Christina Fuhr's chapter on solidarity.

As the editors, we would also like to thank our host institution, the Woolf Institute in Cambridge, and several individuals working there, who either contributed to the pan-European research project on 'Trust and Community Building' or helped with the organisation of the roundtable event, or both. They are Claire Curran, Samuel Everett, Ed Kessler, John Lyon, Tina Steiner, Jessica Tearney, Matt Teather, Austin Tiffany and Miriam Wagner.

We would also like to thank the editors at Policy Press – Rebecca Tomlinson, Ruth Wallace and Laura Vickers – who were very helpful and supportive throughout the process, particularly since the volume involved a number of authors from different backgrounds and countries.

Finally, we are grateful to the authors and to those they interviewed, who shared their life experiences and the challenges they have faced during times of hardship. Throughout the book, both those who provide help and those who receive it have indicated the importance of solidarity and community for achieving any kind of positive change.

Acknowledgements

Notes on contributors

Christopher Baker is Director of Research for the William Temple Foundation and William Temple Professor Religion and Public Life at the University of Chester. He has written and researched extensively on the role and contribution of religion to public life in the UK and Europe and engages with a wide variety of perspectives: theology, political philosophy, critical human geography, sociology of religion and social policy. The themes of his work include ideas of spiritual and religious capital and the post-secular city.

Amardeep Bansil is a Senior Adviser with the Lead on Research and Campaigns at Greenwich Citizens Advice Bureau. He has been actively involved in various charities such as Victim Support and Havering Citizens Advice Bureau of which he was Chair of Trustees from 2012 to 2015.

Jan-Jonathan Bock has a PhD in social anthropology from the University of Cambridge, and is currently a Junior Research Fellow at the Woolf Institute in Cambridge, UK. He is studying intercultural initiatives and the production of trust in heterogeneous communities in Berlin and Rome.

Shana Cohen is Deputy Director of the Woolf Institute in Cambridge, UK and Associate Researcher with the Sociology Department at the University of Cambridge. She led on a comparative analytical project exploring local responses to austerity in Europe.

Patrick Diamond is University Lecturer in Public Policy at Queen Mary, University of London, and Vice-Chair of the Policy Network think tank. He has served as a special adviser in the UK government and as an elected official in the London Borough of Southwark.

Gabriella Elgenius is Associate Professor of Sociology at the University of Gothenburg and Associate Member of the Department of Sociology at the University of Oxford. Gabriella completed her PhD as a Marie Curie Fellow at the London School of Economics and later held a British Academy postdoctoral fellowship at the University of Oxford, Department of Sociology and Nuffield College. She is currently researching diaspora and identity politics, the repatriation of cultural heritage, nationalism and national populism.

Christina Fuhr is Research Fellow at the Woolf Institute and St Edmund's College in Cambridge, UK. As part of her work at the institute, she researches the impact of austerity on foodbanks and homeless shelters in the UK and Germany.

Sarah Greenwood is the London foodbank network manager for The Trussell Trust. She is responsible for managing a network of 38 foodbanks working from 104 centres across Greater London.

Michelle Howlin is Chief Executive of Waltham Forest Community Credit Union. Michelle holds an MSc in local economic development from the London School of Economics and has led the credit unions' 5,000 members, nine staff and 43 volunteers since August 2012.

Paul A Jones runs the Research Unit for Financial Inclusion in the Faculty of Education, Health and Community at Liverpool John Moores University.

Jon Lawrence is Reader in Modern British History at the University of Cambridge and Fellow of Emmanuel College. He is currently writing a history of everyday life in postwar England using the surviving field notes of major social science studies.

Thomas Jeffrey Miley is Lecturer of Political Sociology in the Department of Sociology at Cambridge. He received his BA from UCLA (1995) and his PhD from Yale University (2004). He has lectured at Yale University, Wesleyan University and Saint Louis University (Madrid), and he has been a Garcia-Pelayo Research Fellow at the Centre for Political and Constitutional Studies in Madrid. His research interests include comparative nationalisms, language politics, the politics of migration, religion and politics, regime types and democratic theory.

John Morris is the centre manager of the Cambridge Money Advice Centre, a debt advice charity that supports people living with unmanaged debt. He has a scientific and pastoral background with experience of giving information, advice and advocacy to people with long-term health conditions.

Chris Price is the Director of Pecan, a charity based in Peckham, south-east London. Pecan works primarily with surrounding communities in Southwark as well as people from across London.

These include ex-offenders and their families, refugees and asylum seekers, young people and long-term unemployed people. Prior to this he was Director of Development at Welcare, a South London charity working with children and families. Outside of work he is a Methodist local preacher and Cub Scout leader.

Stefan Selke is Professor of Sociology at Furtwangen University, Germany. His work focuses on social change. He led a major research project monitoring foodbank use across Germany, and is also involved in social activism and advocacy.

Martin Stone is a social housing consultant. He specialises in issues relating to the causes and consequences of homelessness. Since 2008 he has led the Muswell Hill Churches Soup Kitchen for homeless people. Here, he developed innovative methods to communicate with people self-harming, those using drugs and alcohol, and those suffering from mental illness. His work has been published in Reflective Practice by *Gillie Bolton* (Sage Publications, 2014) and gained media attention with the BBC and the New York Times.

Sabine Werth is a social worker who founded Germany's first food rescue organisation, the Berliner Tafel,which developed into a nationwide network of foodbanks. At present, she is Chairwoman of the Berliner Tafel.

ONE

Introduction: social activism, belonging and citizenship in a period of crisis

Shana Cohen and Jan-Jonathan Bock

The repeated political and economic crises in Europe over the past few years – whether related to years of austerity imposed by national governments, the inflow of refugees, or the UK vote on membership of the European Union (EU) – have arguably intensified existing disaffection with political elites and confusion over the political and social meaning of citizenship. Is citizenship related to place of birth, to individual political behaviour, to shared values and personal or collective contributions to social solidarity, or a combination of all of these? How should public institutions and political rhetoric cultivate notions and practices of citizenship? More practically, how can politicians and policymakers promote a concept of citizenship and a related set of actions, such as civic engagement or political participation, when they are perceived as so distant from the majority of the population?

This volume brings together academics and practitioners in the UK and Germany who associate citizenship with the structural organisation and experience of social solidarity and likewise, going beyond distinctions often made in policy between individual behaviour and collective action. They are responding in their work to trends that have developed over past decades, namely the decline of trust in public institutions, rising economic insecurity and diminishing state intervention, to alleviate the effects of this insecurity. The most noticeable and negative consequences of the latter have been dramatic changes in welfare policies that limit eligibility and force more self-reliance, even among vulnerable populations facing complex and difficult circumstances, often involving health problems (Connor, 2010; Bonoli and Natali, 2012; Wiggan, 2012). The aim of the volume is to demonstrate how, in this era of economic and social pressure, academics analysing the potential transformation of society and individual identity, and social activists engaged directly with the destructive impact of welfare policy, are evoking a constructive alternative to more public expressions of disenchantment and disaffection. The choice of Germany and the UK is to illustrate the effects of the timing of austerity measures, or earlier in Germany, differences in welfare policies and political systems – namely regionalism in Germany and centralisation in the UK, and the role of civic and faith-based charities in addressing the demand and need generated by the decline in public benefits.

Citizenship and the gap between political elites and the public have been the subject of increasing academic interest and concern, not only due to declining voter participation rates but also to the rise of populist movements, whether on the political left or (mostly) right. In many cases, this left–right distinction is increasingly difficult to make. A survey conducted for the UK-based Hansard Society on trust in politicians found that respondents considered the accountability they faced in their work to be very different from 'the unaccountability of elected representatives'. Respondents perceived a 'basic lack of performance delivery mechanisms available to citizens to hold them [politicians] in check' (Hansard Society, 2010, p 11). Similarly, a report from the British Regulatory Policy Institute entitled *Trust in the System* argued that '[p]arties must become more responsive to the public as a whole and less self-absorbed' (2009, p 5). Commenting on the British referendum on European Union membership, the American philosopher Michael Sandel explained the frustration generated by the gap between political elites and the public:

> There is a widespread frustration with politics, with politicians and with established political parties. This is for a couple of reasons; one of them is that citizens are rightly frustrated with the empty terms of public discourse in most democracies. Politics for the most part fails to address the big questions that matter most and that citizens care about: what makes for a just society, questions about the common good, questions about the role of markets, and about what it means to be a citizen. A second source of the frustration is the sense that people feel less and less in control of the forces that govern their lives. And the project of democratic self-government seems to be slipping from our grasp. (Cited in Cowley, 2016)

In the atmosphere of frustration described by Sandel, whether in the UK, Germany or elsewhere in Europe, performing the job of representation becomes commendable, and the conveyed sense of duty a sentiment to be respected and noted rather than expected. After the murder of the British MP Jo Cox in June 2016, days before the referendum on membership of the EU, one of her constituents remarked that 'for the first time in many, many years, we actually had an MP that was interested in Birstall [her constituency], and interested in us, and interested in the people and the businesses here' (cited in Hume and Sterling, 2016). However, the failures of contemporary representative politics have not precluded instances of striving for a common good by individual citizens, particularly at a grassroots level. In other words, engagement with the 'big questions' posed by Sandel still exists, even if not to the needed depth in political debate. The purpose of this volume is to offer examples of this engagement. The book also provides a platform for discussing how grassroots activism can edify abstract notions of a 'just society', the meaning of citizenship, and abstract questions relevant to the sustainability and, if necessary, transformation of democratic political systems.

Austerity, political crisis and social activism in the UK and Germany

One of a series of critical self-reflective statements from international agencies, the article 'Neoliberalism oversold?' (Ostry et al, 2016), written by economists from the International Monetary Fund, questions the social costs of pursuing this particular economic ideology. Stating that 'the evidence of the economic damage from inequality suggests that policymakers should be more open to redistribution than they are' (2016, p 41), the authors suggest that 'fiscal consolidation strategies—when they are needed—could be designed to minimize the adverse impact on low-income groups' (2016, p 41). Significantly, they conclude that '[a]usterity policies not only generate substantial welfare costs due to supply-side channels, they also hurt demand—and thus worsen employment and unemployment' (2016, p 41).

Yet, the consequences of austerity have gone beyond short- or even medium-term material impact. They have revealed the long-term incapacity of the state to confront urgent problems, such as the influx of refugees into Germany, deter the rise of mass anxiety over diminishing life opportunities, and, inversely, inspire optimism through leadership. This incapacity can be attributed to the decline of representative politics, which reflect in turn the widening gap between political and economic elites on the one hand, and the majority of the population on the other. The result of the gap has been what scholars such as Peter Mair (2006) and Wendy Brown (2015) have called democracy without a demos, without popular participation, and even without interest in politics, though perhaps still in democracy as a political system (Crouch, 2004; Cook et al, 2016). Mair also writes that despite 'quite consistent evidence of popular indifference to conventional politics and, more arguably, to democracy', there has been 'a distinct renewal of interest in democracy (if not necessarily in politics as such)' (2006, p 28). He then asks how these contrasting trends can be reconciled.

This book reflects an interest in democracy and, more pointedly, in how to express and practice citizenship, particularly in relation to helping others and generating a physical and social space for individual belonging. The contributions to the volume were written five to six years after the imposition of austerity policies in the UK, and more than a decade after their implementation in Germany. The German chapters were written during a period of political unease because of the Eurozone crisis, the influx of refugees and questions about integration into German society. A few of the British chapters were written after the EU referendum. The referendum in the UK revealed the political potency of economic disenfranchisement, anxiety about immigration and its impact on quality of life, alienation from elites, and the absence of any significant or substantial policy framework to promote social solidarity. Feelings simmering for years, even decades, now had a moment of expression. As a taxi driver in Manchester told Shana Cohen in 2010, or before austerity and long before the referendum: "My wife, who has been sick, has struggled for years to get benefits. If she had a dot on her forehead [if she was of Asian origin], it would have been easier." The imposition of austerity measures could only exacerbate the perception of competition for scarce resources, whether among different ethnic groups or otherwise, and of political disinterest in the wellbeing of much of the population.

According to the Oxford English Dictionary, the term austerity refers to 'difficult economic conditions created by government measures to reduce public expenditure' (The Oxford English Dictionary, 2016). Jamie Peck (2012) explains how austerity, and specifically cuts to public benefits, has become a tenet of neoliberalism: 'according to the neoliberal script, public austerity is a necessary response to market conditions, and the state has responded by inaugurating new rounds of fiscal retrenchment, often targeted on city governments and on the most vulnerable, both socially and spatially' (2012, p 626). In Germany, this retrenchment started in 2003 under the then Chancellor Gerhard Schröder, who announced a set of labour market and welfare reforms through a general strategy called Agenda 2010, intended to reduce unemployment and induce economic growth. At that point,

Germany had high unemployment and relatively high levels of public debt, repercussions from the country's reunification in 1990 and a lack of adjustment during the 16-year reign of Schröder's predecessor, Helmut Kohl.

Described by some as 'the sick man of Europe' at the turn of the century, Germany's government pursued the same 'Third Way' model (Giddens, 1998) of the then British Prime Minister, Tony Blair: give more power to the market and reduce the scope of the state, purportedly to boost innovation, employment and self-reliance. To achieve this, labour rules were rendered more flexible, subcontracting with few obligations towards employees became easier, social security was cut back, and those on unemployment benefits had to accept job offers or face sanctions. Schröder presented the Agenda 2010 strategy as an attempt to free the creative forces of the market, on the one hand, and to encourage citizens and involve them in addressing the circumstances that lead to unemployment and inactivity, on the other. Just as Blair, Schröder – nominally a social democrat from the SPD party – faced resistance in his own party and from his coalition partner, the Greens, as well as from academics and trade union members.[1] Schröder, however, pressed ahead.[2]

The overall goal was to decrease non-wage labour costs and make German companies more competitive globally, at the cost of increasing insecurity among workers. The key slogan of the new strategy was *fördern und fordern* – or to support those who were keen to help themselves, while simultaneously demanding self-activation and commitment. The reforms encouraged the growth of flexible, temporary and part-time work, while also limiting the job security of part-time employees, who could now be fired more easily. It also introduced a kind of part-time mini-job paying 450 euros a month tax-free. The reform package reduced unemployment assistance to basic existence levels after 12 months of joblessness, replacing a policy that had sought to reflect individual living standards by pegging state assistance to previous salaries and contributions. The Left party, which came into existence in response to the reform, denounced Schröder for creating 'poverty by law' (Kipping, 2006).

Welfare recipients were pressured to take low-paid and precarious jobs despite the insecurity and, as has happened in the UK, became trapped in a pattern of moving in and out of benefits, including the periods of limbo after a job has ended and before benefits have started again. Again, as in the UK, the consequence of deregulation has been a dramatic rise in job insecurity and low-paid positions, with some workers holding multiple jobs. In 2010, over 23% of employment situations in Germany were low-paid (Bosch, 2012, p 8). However, it should be noted that Germany's federalist and subsidiarity traditions have provided some counterweight to welfare reform, unlike the dramatic impact cuts in benefits have had on the UK's centralised system (Leisering, 2005, p 1).

The reforms under the British coalition government, elected in 2010, and the subsequent Conservative government, elected in 2015, have gone further than those in Germany, using austerity in effect to reshape the social role of the state. Cameron's widely criticised notion of a 'Big Society' (Cabinet Office, 2010) reflected the shared party consensus between at least New Labour and the Conservatives that voluntary sector and grassroots actors should assume more responsibility for local social problems, and that individuals should assume more responsibility for their own behaviour if they wished to access public benefits. In both countries, the state can facilitate action at a local and individual level, whether through grants or punitive measures, but not increase its own intervention. As Mayer (2013) writes of welfare reform in Germany, 'the state is supposed to promote and enable the activities of its citizens rather than merely hand out benefits and thereby enforce the "passivity of citizens"' (Mayer, 2013).

Indeed, national and local organisations in the two countries have responded to economic pressure, particularly the rise of poverty and corresponding trends of unemployment, insecure employment and increasingly punitive welfare systems. The Trussell Trust and Tafel national networks of foodbanks discussed in this volume are examples of such organisations. Though Germany possesses one of the strongest economies in Europe, according to the Paritätische Gesamtverband's widely discussed report, as of 2016, approximately 12.5 million people, out of a total population of over 80 million, were classified as poor, that is, as earning less than 60% of the median household income (Paritätische Gesamtverband, 2016). This figure was the highest since German reunification in 1990. As in the UK, the working poor constituted a growing percentage of this trend, or over three million, due at least in part to the erosion of labour protections (Somaskanda, 2015).

In the UK, the rise in poverty, particularly among families where one or more parents work, since the beginning of austerity measures in 2008 has been striking. As of 2013, there were more individuals in working families living in poverty, 6.7 million, than in workless and retired families combined, or 6.3 million (Morris, 2013). A 2016 Joseph Rowntree Foundation study found that 1.25 million people, including 312,000 children, were destitute 'at some point in 2015'

(Case, 2016). A third of this population possesses a complex need, and the causes of destitution included illness, unemployment and sanctions, or withdrawal of benefits, due to, for instance, having missed Jobcentre appointments (Rickman and McKernan, 2016).

Among others, faith-based organisations have tried to compensate for the diminished safety net and public sector support. For instance, the Church of England's organisation to combat poverty, the Church Urban Fund, provides small levels of funding through the Together Grants (Church Urban Fund, 2016b) and Near Neighbours (Church Urban Fund, 2016a) (funded in turn by the Department for Communities and Local Government). Increasingly, grant recipients reflect soaring social need at a local level.[3] The Archbishop of Canterbury has lent vocal support to credit unions, which he considers an important ethical alternative to the private banking sector (see Chapter Six); local churches in the working-class London Borough of Peckham founded a service to help people seeking employment, including those who have served prison sentences (Chapter Seven); the Christian faith has inspired The Trussell Trust's foodbank network, as its leader, Sarah Greenwood, explains (Chapter Nine); and even Cambridge's Money Advice Centre is inspired by the Christian idea of charity (Chapter Five). The mobilisation of a Christian ethics of care and sacrifice is a central feature in most practitioners' accounts. At the same time, other faith groups have either established or expanded initiatives, for instance, the local Muslim foodbank Sufra NW in London, and national volunteering initiatives, such as Mitzvah Day (Jewish), Sewa Day (Hindu) and Sadaqa Day (Muslim).

In addition to investing in social services, the Church of England and the Catholic Church have issued highly critical political statements concerning welfare reform. The bishops in the House of Lords have acted to block welfare reforms deemed unfair to the poor. The Cardinal (then Archbishop) Vincent Nichols, leader of the Catholic Church in England and Wales, decried in 2014 the demise of the safety net and the punitive behaviour of public agencies, like Job Centres, which can withdraw unemployment benefits. He described the 'basic safety net' as no longer existing, provoking a 'real, real dramatic crisis' (BBC News, 2014). After Nichols' statement, 27 Anglican Bishops and 16 other faith leaders wrote a letter at the beginning of Lent in 2014 to the *Daily Mirror*, a Labour-supporting British newspaper, criticising the prevalence of foodbanks and growing malnutrition, and calling on the then Prime Minister David Cameron to recognise his 'acute moral imperative to act'. The letter states that 'as a society, face up to the fact that over half of people using foodbanks have been put in that situation by cutbacks to and failures in the benefit system, whether it be payment delays or punitive sanctions' (Beattie, 2014).[4] In Germany, the Protestant and Catholic Churches have shaped the importance of the Diakonie (Protestant) and Caritas (Catholic) charity organisations, which assume welfare functions and para-state responsibilities across the country. Unlike much of the faith-based social programmes in the UK, as non-profit organisations, Diakonie and Caritas are funded almost entirely by the state. Besides the two church-based institutions, there are four more officially recognised organisations providing welfare and other charitable services on behalf of the German state: the Arbeiterwohlfahrt (workers' welfare); the Paritätische Gesamtverband (humanitarian orientation); the German Red Cross; and the Jewish welfare organisation, Zentralwohlfahrtsstelle der Juden in Deutschland. The six constitute the Federal Association of Independent Welfare Organisations (BAGFW).

The BAGFW organisations receive over 90% of their revenue from state sources, and their representatives wield important lobbying power regarding issues of welfare and social assistance in Germany (Bundesarbeitsgemeinschaft der Freien Wohlfahrtspflege e.V., 2016, pp 14-15). In 2012, the six organisations employed over 1.6 million people, supported by up to three million volunteers (Bundesarbeitsgemeinschaft der Freien Wohlfahrtspflege e.V., 2012, p 10). Without their work and expertise, Germany's welfare state would struggle to function: the BAGFW organisations manage hospitals and emergency services, care homes, youth homes, child daycare facilities, support centres and workshops for disabled people, hospices, blood donation services, migrant support projects, advice courses for expectant mothers, unemployment support, multi-generation homes, shelters for domestic abuse victims, for migrants, and for homeless people, job qualification courses, and much more. In 2015, the six organisations took the lead in providing shelter, accommodation and legal assistance for asylum seekers, who were entering the country in unprecedented numbers, accompanied by volunteer training sessions and counselling for overworked helpers. The country's capacity to absorb over one million people depended also in large part on the six welfare organisations, their structures, expertise and personnel. The BAGFW's strong regional presence and positive reputation across German society allow the six organisations to maintain relatively high levels of social assistance even in the face of national government cuts. They also have important political advocacy roles. Beyond practice, though, in both countries, faith-based organisations (FBOs) increasingly represent a different mode of social contact from the managerial model of government, in that FBOs advance principles of social solidarity and individual dignity.

Citizenship and belonging in an era of economic and political crisis

Austerity policies are symptomatic of the larger retreat of states from ensuring the link between individual security and social and political belonging (Povinelli, 2011; Butler and Athanasiou, 2013; Bhattacharyya, 2015). Without this positive link, any threat to security, such as an influx of refugees from the Middle East, reinforces the negative equation with political and social insignificance.

In a 2016 interview with Jan Bock, Heiko Maas – the German Minister of Justice, from the Social Democratic Party, vocal in his condemnation of emergent far-right movements – commented that the notion of political belonging is "about guaranteeing a minimum level of security and certainty in one's personal living environment, social environment, economic environment. That's an intrinsic human need – but increasingly difficult to address." He remarked that, as security has become more elusive, "the sense of a political home is becoming more volatile, too. There is a sense of longing for belonging in the sense that one's homeland is a place in which people experience security and certainty." As noted earlier, Sandel indicates that the failure of successive governments, regardless of ruling political party, has been not only to provide the necessary material support to meet basic needs and ensure opportunities exist for work and income but also to understand the importance of a narrative of belonging.

Though critical of government policy, the practitioners writing here have differed in their responses from groups who, according to Heiko Maas, have reacted to economic insecurity by seeking "distance from their society". For him, "that's the first step by which certain groups and people become estranged from society. They take up extremist positions instead, political or religious." In contrast, our practitioner contributors, whether involved in foodbanks or other services, such as advocacy and advice, address directly the challenge of renewing and sustaining a society, as well as both the immediate and sustained experience of belonging. Practitioner and academic chapters demonstrate how social cooperation and respect for individual dignity can inform concepts and policies that link the enhancement of individual wellbeing to practices of social solidarity, and thus of local forms of belonging, across socioeconomic, religious and ethnic differences.

The multidisciplinary and interprofessional nature of the volume, and its practical and academic focus on the changing orientation of citizenship in an era of duress, differs from that of the majority of books about austerity. These have largely concentrated on critiquing the ideology of austerity (Blyth, 2013), the future of democracy under austerity (Stiglitz, 2013; Streeck, 2013), class transformation (Standing, 2011), the dominance of neoliberalism (Crouch, 2011) and its hegemony in political and individual consciousness (Lazzarato and Jordan, 2014), and political alienation, protest and new forms of civic identity (Chomsky, 2012; Benski et al, 2013; Della Porta, 2014; Haiven and Khasnabish, 2014; Burawoy, 2015).

The volume originated in a workshop on community activism and economic policy in Berlin and London, held in Cambridge in November 2014. The workshop was part of a three-year comparative study of how community activists seek to develop trust among local residents in the context of austerity and prevalent disaffection with politics. The aim of combining practitioner and academic analyses is to examine how they correspond at a juncture of political alienation and rising assumption of community responsibility for social problems, the orientation they believe policy should adopt, and the vision that, together, they evoke of our social future. By bringing together practitioners and academics, the volume mirrors the intent of other interprofessional publications like the journal *Global Policy*, but rather than concentrate on global problems, the chapters narrate a very local vision of helping others against the backdrop of increasingly pressured, sometimes volatile, economic and political contexts.

The academic policy and political critiques in Parts I and III, as well as the practice-based chapters in Part II, implicitly claim that the distance the state has taken from creating socioeconomic opportunity and ensuring basic needs, particularly through transforming welfare and allowing for the rise of flexible labour arrangements, undermines trust in political elites and diminishes the association of the state with social responsibility. Yet, it is the conception of responsibility, and of how the state can contribute to sustaining a society, that is so lacking in European political discourse. The practice-based chapters offer case studies of addressing immediate crisis, most importantly, hunger, and longer-term problems, such as debt. They also demonstrate the importance of faith as a motivating factor for individuals and an influence on the valuation of solidarity and individual dignity, as well as the practical role of faith-based organisations in meeting basic needs (O'Toole and Braginskaia, 2016).

More broadly, practitioners show how the logic and desired impact of charitable services often differ deliberately from government welfare programmes, in that they emphasise the importance of collectivity and recognition of individual dignity and rights to instigating individual change. In fact, their efforts suggest that assuming social responsibility is a necessary duty of citizenship and social solidarity itself is a right, not just a choice, evoking new ways of conceptualising and implementing through policy the connection between the individual, state and society. Concepts such as 'community' do not signify a utilitarian method for the state to reinforce individual responsibility (Mayer, 2013), and the necessity of self-organisation at a local level, both of which complement neoliberal economic policy, but rather something more profound and reflective of changes needed in the function of the state. The demand of activists is for the state to recognise the importance of social relations across class, religion, ethnicity, gender and even nationality to constructive social change, and thus to intervene in their development. The academic chapters explore modes of critiquing the consequences of contemporary economic and social policy, and concomitant practices of individualism, community and society. They contend that values and social belonging cannot be separated out from individual decision making and behaviour. However, policy has failed to recognise this relationship, devising instead programmes that focus on categorising and responding to individual actions.

Balibar (2013) highlights the contradictions between the idea of individual citizenship and a vibrant democracy. He notes the inherent conflict of asking for allegiance by different individuals to a common polity. In response, Balibar calls for relating the sustainability of democracy to the consistent destruction and renewal of notions of citizenship, based, in turn, on the transformation of political and public institutions. Citizens necessarily belong to, and perpetuate, a community in which individual rights frame social relations. These rights are not fixed in time, but rather are achieved, fought for, lost and won, over periods of conflict and transformation. Balibar's is a kind of insurrectional citizenship that both challenges the decline or emptiness of existing rights regulated by a distant state and brings about new rights corresponding with a different organisation and power of institutions.

This volume suggests that analysing the practice of social good and acknowledging its role in individual identity and community formation can inform the development of alternative public expectations of state authority and responsibility and, likewise, of a new meaning and obligation of citizenship. The influence of activism over conceptions of citizenship and the state's intervention may potentially be greater than in other areas because of the lack of private sector interest in welfare. As Patrick Diamond notes in Chapter Two, the demise of the post-war welfare state has not led to increasing private sector involvement, which has been the case in other sectors like prisons and education, because of perceived risk.

More profoundly, the stress on the importance of social relations and cooperation in overcoming social problems among all of the contributing practitioners testifies to the necessity of integrating a social vision into policy and the function and representation of public institutions (Unger, 2014). Jon Lawrence, in Chapter Fourteen, states that 'the challenge for politicians is to develop a vision of the future that recognises that individualism and community need not be polar opposites; a vision capable of reconciling this urge to be both free and connected'. In her chapter on the German Tafel organisation, which distributes food to other charities and churches, Sabine Werth (Chapter Eight) offers an example of the practical achievement of this task and the urgency of connecting the individual and community in addressing problems such as poverty. She differentiates her organisation from 'soup kitchens' aimed solely at feeding individuals, rather than providing opportunities for social interaction: 'For me, soup kitchens have always been the epitome of societal impoverishment. People eat their meals silently, and, when finished, solitarily return to their homes or the streets. From the very beginning, [we] believed that the establishment of a sense of sense of community was essential – from the time waiting in the queue until after the meal.' (p 134).

She cites as evidence the fact that many beneficiaries arrive before their allotted time to receive food because they 'enjoy speaking with one another during the waiting period'. When volunteers provide coffee and cake during the waiting period, Werth says, they help prevent 'a sense of shame or stigmatisation among clients. Instead, they create a sense of neighbourliness. Friendships have blossomed, and sometimes even relationships.' (p 134). Referring to a foodbank in London run by the comparable national organisation, The Trussell Trust, Sarah Greenwood (Chapter Nine) quotes a foodbank manager: 'Often foodbank clients tell us the emotional support is almost as good as the food.' She quotes another manager: 'Increasingly, people have no community to link to. It is a real show of fragmentation in our society. People don't even have social contacts.' (p 149). In both Germany and the UK, then, the materiality of providing food, or even addressing a basic need like hunger, represents only one component of the activity itself, which is to promote a sense of social belonging, local community and the possibility of social solidarity.

For Christopher Baker (Chapter Fifteen), the motivation to form relationships and build community evokes the potential of a new *Zeitgeist* 'based on the desire for reconnectivity after 40 years of neoliberalised imaginaries and assumptions of monadic disconnectivity' (p 272). The desire for reconnectivity responds to the depreciation of optimism and progress as political and policy ambitions. Sabine Werth admits in Chapter Eight that 'even as the founder, I have always been clear about this: I would rather not live with the need for Tafels.' Her prediction, however, is that 'the social circumstances that bring people to use Tafels will not change any time soon'.

Despite the ongoing and seemingly insurmountable challenge of social problems, such as hunger and malnourishment, exacerbated by austerity measures and poverty, for Baker, it is important to develop a values-based approach to theorising citizenship. The beliefs that motivate individuals to act and identify and guide them as citizens can provide the basis for an alternative form of civic engagement to the neutralised, generic notion of citizenry that no longer inspires action. This approach means not assuming that policies such as basic income will instigate new practices of solidarity, because individuals now possess more free time. Van Parijs (2000) writes that basic income 'would promote real freedom for all by providing the material resources that people need to pursue their aims'. Yet, as the contributions to this volume indicate, policy to provide access to material resources does not necessarily yield an experience of social belonging. For this, policy would need to acknowledge the significance of social relations and a framework for social solidarity based on social responsibility and individual civic engagement.

It is important, if not critical, to note that the expression of a set of values does not mean that they always translate into practice, whether in everyday interaction or long-term strategies for organisational survival. In her analysis of the German Tafel foodbank, Christina Fuhr (Chapter Eleven) argues that volunteers and guests seldom bridge an existing social gap. Martin Stone (Chapter Ten), the leader of a London-based soup kitchen, explains that the rushed delivery of standardised meals in food charities does not induce trustworthiness conducive to solidarity. The strong stigma attached to indebtedness has also deterred clients at the Cambridge Money Advice Centre from creating lasting relationships with their highly motivated volunteer advisers. The challenges faced by charities raise a fundamental question: are these emergent kinds of active citizenship achieving the sense of belonging actors aspire to? Or does the constant pressure to fill the gap created by public sector cuts mean they will always, ultimately, be constrained by the everyday impact of an ideology of self-responsibility and penalisation for needing help?

Furthermore, the pressure from diminishing resources to become more professionalised has sometimes affected the capacity of charities to continue to work with vulnerable, marginalised groups that require intensive service. In their chapter on micro credit unions, Michelle Howlin and Paul A Jones (Chapter Six) show how expanding credit schemes during a time of growing demand, combined with the desire to guarantee low interest rates, requires greater financial sustainability. This move, paradoxically, means that credit applications from 'high-risk individuals' may have to be rejected. The market logic reshapes charitable objectives. Contributions to this volume, such as Amardeep Bansil's chapter on the advice sector (Chapter Four), illustrate that charities' aspirations to produce solidarity and community can be undermined or tested by the reorganisation demanded by funding cuts, although, as Bansil shows, pressures can also push organisations to become more efficient and focused. However, the importance of generating an experience of social belonging and individual dignity to service delivery still evokes an alternative to the anger often expressed in nationalist and extremist politics – a conception and practice of locally relevant citizenship based on inclusion and respect. In short, rather than focusing on what is going wrong in democracies, namely inequality and political disaffection, the volume highlights social behaviour and values that may, in turn, indicate a way forward for political debate and policy (Green, 2016; Williams, 2016).

The organisation of the book

The book builds a narrative of how policy has failed to account for social belonging and, likewise, provide a framework for social solidarity in welfare reform though in practice the experience of belonging seems critical for instigating changes in individual behaviour and self-confidence. Part I, on the social consequences of welfare policy, examines policy attempts to address related aspects of poverty and consolidate a social role for the state through specified responsibilities, whether through providing health services, unemployment insurance, or other benefits. The contributors, Patrick Diamond and Gabriella Elgenius, analyse the flaws of welfare policies and their decline under neoliberalism and specifically austerity in the UK.

Part II, concerning the practice of social good, is comprised of practitioner case studies. The section shows how grassroots activism translates abstract notions of a 'just society' fashioned by policymakers.

It thereby documents how the lived economic and social consequences of welfare policies are addressed by social initiatives in Germany and the UK. It also offers an arguably different perspective to both the pacified citizenry and the demise of any hope for collective control over and benefit from resources. Certainly, each of the authors, writing from personal experience, expresses profound disappointment at the failure of the state to care for the most vulnerable and marginalised populations. For example, Amardeep Bansil describes the case of a woman, Ingrid, who came to the Citizens Advice Bureau for which he works. She lives in council housing, speaks basic English, and suffers from anxiety, depression, severe headaches and unexplained visual-field loss. She has no family or friends to rely on for support, cannot work, and so is reliant on Employment and Support Allowance, Housing Benefit and Council Tax Reduction. After the introduction of the 'bedroom tax', or a tax on unoccupied bedrooms in social housing, she was told that her two-bedroom flat was under-occupied. She was also deemed fit to work, which caused her to lose her remaining benefits. The response of organisations such as Citizens Advice is to scrutinise comprehensively the issues facing individuals, and to advocate where they can to restore benefits and/or help to locate other sources of income and support. The point is that they are not 'passive' when faced with the destructive consequences of welfare policy, but rather constantly and emphatically seek to demonstrate their agency in contradistinction to the punitive and seemingly uncaring state.

Part III, on social change and neoliberalism, returns to the presentation of academic research. First, Christina Fuhr looks at the practice of social initiatives in Germany and the UK and contests the extent to which such initiatives provide places of social belonging through the demonstration of social solidarity. The other chapters, by Stefan Selke and Thomas Jeffrey Miley, focus on criticising political unwillingness to combat the causes and effects of inequality, leaving social questions increasingly to private actors. In Chapter Twelve, Selke shows how the neoliberal privatisation of social care establishes an 'economy of poverty', turning hardship into a profitable business. He argues that the Tafel foodbanks employ the rhetoric of morality – they claim to save food, distribute resources and create a support infrastructure for people in need. However, in order to be successful, the charity has to cooperate with political and economic actors, such as, for example, the car manufacturers that sponsor Tafel vans, or politicians who accept patronage for the organisation. The Tafel contributes, Selke states, to a system that institutionalises and normalises inequality and poverty, and reinforces an ideological position that places responsibility on private agencies for addressing injustice and hardship.

In Chapter Thirteen, Miley (p 221) outlines a broader criticism of the dominant political systems over the past century, which he describes as having provided 'institutional guarantees for the perpetuation of hierarchical, authoritarian social relations'. He writes that the 'social-democratic compromise, it is too often forgotten, was but a compromise, never a panacea'. The social rights generated in this compromise came 'through the expansion of vast bureaucratic state hierarchies'. The result was a 'paternalistic state, rendering its services to a pacified citizenry. A state that could intervene to ameliorate the effects of capitalist social-property relations, but at the expense of burying forever the now-forgotten dream of workers' control over the means and ways of subsistence and production.' The strategy of intervention is vanishing, along with the pacification of citizenry, perhaps negating the possibility of any declaration of 'dead and buried'.

Part IV, on situating solidarity in perspective, continues to provide a critical platform to discuss the meaning of citizenship. Jon Lawrence and Christopher Baker question assumptions about social life and agency, and the implications of these assumptions for citizenship. Lawrence critiques the seeming distinction between individualism and community, and Baker, following theoretical challenges to the assumption of unencumbered citizenship posited by Rawls and his followers, argues for integrating emotions and values into a conception of embodied, encumbered citizenship. In Chapter Fourteen, Lawrence asks why we are so 'wedded to the idea of social fragmentation and the collapse of society' (p 241), and suggests that rather than assuming a historical advance of individualism, it is more fruitful to avoid the dichotomy of the concepts of individualism and community. He shows that most people in their daily lives draw on both of them creatively.

In Chapter Fifteen, building on the challenge to focusing on rights in a liberal democracy versus the agency of citizenship, Baker follows Chantal Mouffe's notion that 'citizenship is a process of becoming – of acquiring a clear sense of identity as a citizen' (p 260). Exploring how church-based activists look to process as much as ends, Baker argues that their desire to instigate spiritual transformation and their value-based motivation add depth to Mouffe's conception, which still makes assumptions about the neutrality of critical concepts of liberty and equality. Instead, as Baker and the other contributors indicate, the concepts that have historically defined the meaning and practice of democracy are susceptible to transformation. Change can be positive if there is more awareness of the social context and the significance of collectivity as a means of improving individual circumstances and sense of worth.

Finally the Conclusion analyses how two forms of citizenship are emerging in the current era of economic and political uncertainty and duress. There is an 'angry citizen', protesting against migration, the EU and political elites, and a 'social citizen', protesting as well, but through social action and local civic engagement. This chapter suggests how the latter, quieter form of citizenship should become part of further research and a political agenda that adopts the principles of collective action. Rather than segregate sectors, a move that perpetuates divisions in social responsibility and social problems, policy would bring together relevant actors, whether in government, charities, or the private sector, to enforce solidarity as a norm and to devise a collective material response.

Notes

[1] Shortly after his address to the German parliament, in which he outlined his plans in March 2003, over 400 German scientists signed an open letter to castigate the proposals; they accused Schröder of punishing and blaming those who found themselves in unemployment, and of hollowing out Germany's welfare state, which had been an important cornerstone in attempts to overcome the appeal of National Socialism after 1945. The academics warned that Germany's post-war social consensus, based on redistribution and social justice, was under threat.

[2] Consequently, a significant part of the SPD split to found a new movement, called the Election Alternative for Work and Social Justice (WASG), led by the former finance minister in Schröder's cabinet, Oscar Lafontaine. In 2007, the WASG merged with Germany's Party of Democratic Socialism (PDS) and founded The Left (Die Linke), which became the third-largest parliamentary party after the 2013 elections.

[3] This was my observation from conducting evaluations for both programmes over a four-year period.

[4] In practice, though in some ways reliant politically on Conservative Party support, bishops in the House of Lords have sometimes been more vocal than the Labour Party in their opposition to welfare reforms, tabling significant amendments to proposed legislation (Grice, 2013). One notable example is the Bishop of Ripon and Leeds' amendment to 2012 legislation excluding child benefit from a proposed household benefit cap (to £26,000). The amendment passed by 252-237.

References

Balibar, E. (2013) 'On the politics of human rights', *Constellations*, 20, 18-26.

BBC News (2014) 'Catholic archbishop attacks welfare reform', *BBC News*, [Online] Available at: www.bbc.co.uk/news/uk-26200157 [Accessed 28 August 2016].

Beattie, J. (2014) '27 bishops slam David Cameron's welfare reforms as creating a national crisis in unprecedented attack', *Daily Mirror*, [Online] Available at: www.mirror.co.uk/news/uk-news/27-bishops-slam-david-camerons-3164033 [Accessed 28 August 2016].

Benski, T., Langman, L., Perugorría, I. and Tejerina, B. (2013) 'From the streets and squares to social movement studies: What have we learned?' *Current Sociology*, 61, 541-61.

Bhattacharyya, G. (2015) *Crisis, Austerity, and Everyday Life: Living in a Time of Diminishing Expectations*, New York, NY: Palgrave Macmillan.

Blyth, M. (2013) *Austerity: The History of a Dangerous Idea*, Oxford: Oxford University Press.

Bonoli, G. and Natali, D. N. (eds) (2012) *The Politics of the New Welfare State*, Oxford: Oxford University Press.

Bosch, G. (2012) 'Prekäre Beschäftigung und Neuordnung am Arbeitsmarkt', *IAQ Standpunkt*, [Online] Available at: www.iaq.uni-due.de/iaq-standpunkte/2012/sp2012-02.pdf [Accessed 28 August 2016].

Brown, W. (2015) *Undoing the Demos: Neoliberalism's Stealth Revolution*, Berkeley, CA: Zone Books/Near Futures.

Bundesarbeitsgemeinschaft Der Freien Wohlfahrtspflege E.V. (2012) *Einrichtungen und Dienste der Freien Wohlfahrtspflege: Gesamtstatistik 2012*, Berlin: BAGFW.

Bundesarbeitsgemeinschaft Der Freien Wohlfahrtspflege E.V. (2016) *Jahresbericht 2015*, Berlin: BAGFW.

Burawoy, M. (2015) *Public Sociology: Öffentliche Soziologie gegen Marktfundamentalismus und globale Ungleichheit*, Landsberg: Beltz.

Butler, J. and Athanasiou, A. (2013) *Dispossession: The Performative in the Political*, Cambridge: Polity.

Cabinet Office (2010) *Building the Big Society*, London: Cabinet Office.

Case, R. (2016) *1.25 million people are destitute in the UK*, Joseph Rowntree Foundation, [Online] Available at: www.jrf.org.uk/press/destitute-uk [Accessed 28 August 2016].

Chomsky, N. (2012) *Making the Future: Occupations, Interventions, Empire and Resistance*, London: Penguin.

Church Urban Fund (2016a) *Near Neighbours*, Church Urban Fund, [Online] Available at: www.cuf.org.uk/near-neighbours [Accessed 28 August 2016].

Church Urban Fund (2016b) *Together Grants*, Church Urban Fund, [Online] Available at: www.cuf.org.uk/together-grants [Accessed 28 August 2016].

Connor, S. (2010) 'Promoting "Employability": The Changing Subject of Welfare Reform in the UK', *Critical Discourse Analysis*, 7, 41–45.

Cook, J., Long, N. J. and Moore, H. L. (2016) *The State We're In: Reflecting on Democracy's Troubles*, New York, NY: Berghahn.

Cowley, J. (2016) 'Michael Sandel: "The energy of the Brexiteers and Trump is born of the failure of elites"', *New Statesman*, [Online] Available at: www.newstatesman.com/politics/uk/2016/06/michael-sandel-energy-brexiteers-and-trump-born-failure-elites [Accessed 28 August 2016].

Crouch, C. (2004) *Post-Democracy*, Cambridge: Polity.

Crouch, C. (2011) *The Strange Non-Death of Neo-Liberalism*, Cambridge: Polity.

Della Porta, D. (2014) *Social Movements in Times of Austerity: Bringing Capitalism back into Protest Analysis*, London: Polity.

Giddens, A. (1998) *The Third Way: The Renewal of Social Democracy*, Cambridge: Polity.

Green, D. (2016) *How Change Happens*, Oxford: Oxford University Press.

Grice, A. (2013) 'Exclusive: Archbishop of Canterbury, Justin Welby, urged to scrap most bishops' seats in House of Lords', *The Independent*, [Online] Available at: www.independent.co.uk/news/uk/politics/exclusive-archbishop-of-canterbury-justin-welby-urged-to-scrap-most-bishops-seats-in-house-of-lords-8610096.html [Accessed 28 August 2016].

Haiven, M. and Khasnabish, A. (2014) *The Radical Imagination: Social Movement Research in the Age of Austerity*, London: Zed Books.

Hansard Society (2010) *Audit of Political Engagement 7: The 2010 Report with a focus on MPs and Parliament*, London: Hansard Society.

Hume, T. and Sterling, J. (2016) 'Killing of British politician Jo Cox stuns nation', *CNN*, [Online] Available at: http://edition.cnn.com/2016/06/16/europe/british-mp-jo-cox-attacked/ [Accessed 28 August 2016].

Kipping, K. (2006) '345 Euro sind schon Armut per Gesetz, weitere Kürzungen führen zur Verelendung', *Pressemitteilun Die Linke Bundestagsfraktion*, [Online] Available at: www.linksfraktion.de/pressemitteilungen/345-euro-sind-schon-armut-per-gesetz-weitere-kuerzungen-fuehren-verelendung/ [Accessed 13 March 2016].

Lazzarato, M. and Jordan, J. D. (2014) *Signs and Machines: Capitalism and the Production of Subjectivity*, Cambridge, MA: Semiotext(e)/The MIT Press.

Leisering, L. (2005) 'The Welfare State in Postwar Germany', in B. Vivekanandan and N. Kurian (eds) *Welfare States and the Future*, Basingstoke and New York, NY: Palgrave Macmillan: 113-130.

Mair, P. (2006) 'Ruling the Void? The Hollowing of Western Democracy', *New Left Review*, 42.

Mayer, M. (2013) 'The Ambiguity of Participating the Social City', *Journalment*, [Online] Available at: http://journalment.org/article/ambiguity-participating-social-city [Accessed 15 June 2016].

Morris, C. (2013) *Eight Key Joseph Rowntree Foundation Research Findings from 2013*, Joseph Rowntree Foundation, [Online] Available at: www.jrf.org.uk/blog/eight-key-joseph-rowntree-foundation-research-findings-2013 [Accessed 28 August 2016].

O'Toole, T. and Braginskaia, K. (2016) *Public Faith and Finance: Faith responses to the financial crisis*, Bristol: University of Bristol.

Ostry, J. D., Loungani, P. and Furceri, D. (2016) 'Neoliberalism: Oversold?' *Finance & Development*, 53, 2, 38-41.

The Oxford English Dictionary (2016) *Austerity*, Oxford Dictionaries. [Online] Available at: www.oxforddictionaries.com/definition/english/austerity [Accessed 28 August 2016].

Paritätische Gesamtverband (2016) *Armutsatlas [Poverty Atlas]*, Berlin: Paritätische Gesamtverband.

Peck, J. (2012) *Austerity Urbanism: The Neoliberal Crisis of American Cities*, New York, NY: Rosa Luxemburg Stiftung.

Povinelli, E. A. (2011) *Economies of Abandonment: Social Belonging and Endurance in Late Liberalism*, Durham, NC: Duke University Press.

Regulatory Policy Institute (2009) *Trust in the System: Restoring trust in our system of government and regulation*, Oxford: Regulatory Policy Institute.

Rickman, D. and Mckernan, B. (2016) 'Sixteen of the Most Senseless Benefit Sanction Decisions known to Man', *The Independent*, [Online] Available at: http://indy100.independent.co.uk/article/sixteen-of-the-most-senseless-benefit-sanction-decisions-known-to-man--x1dmkd2_Me [Accessed 28 August 2016].

Somaskanda, S. (2015) 'Rich Germany Has a Poverty Problem: Inequality and underemployment are on the rise in Europe's economic powerhouse', *Foreign Policy*, [Online] Available at: http://foreignpolicy.com/2015/05/05/rich-germany-has-a-poverty-problem-inequality-europe/ [Accessed 28 August 2016].

Standing, G. (2011) *The Precariat: The New Dangerous Class*, London: Bloomsbury Academic.

Stiglitz, J. E. (2013) *The Price of Inequality*, London: Allen Lane.

Streeck, W. (2013) *Gekaufte Zeit: Die vertagte Krise des demokratischen Kapitalismus*, Berlin: Suhrkamp.

Unger, R. M. (2014) *The Religion of the Future*, Cambridge, MA: Harvard Univerity Press.

Van Parijs, P. (2000) 'A Basic Income for All', *Boston Review*, [Online] Available at: http://new.bostonreview.net/BR25.5/vanparijs.html [Accessed 28 August 2016].

Wiggan, J. (2012) 'Telling stories of 21st century welfare: The UK Coalition government and the neo-liberal discourse of worklessness and dependency', *Critical Social Policy*, 32, 383-405.

Williams, F. (2016) 'Critical Thinking in Social Policy: Challenges of Past, Present, and Future', *Social Policy and Administration*, 50, 628-647.

Part I
The social consequences
of welfare policy

TWO

Fulfilling basic human needs: the welfare state after Beveridge

Patrick Diamond

This chapter draws on contemporary political history and social policy to examine how the welfare state has developed in the United Kingdom since 1945. Alterations in the structure of Britain's economy and society after the Second World War have made it harder for the traditional welfare state to respond adequately to a profusion of basic human needs. The rise of new issues and challenges has been notable, including changes in the demographic structure of society combined with the burdens imposed by the growth of a post-industrial economy and the loss of skilled manufacturing employment. The chapter assesses the implications of these structural changes in welfare and social policy among the advanced capitalist countries, focusing principally on the United Kingdom. It then considers the case for an alternative model of 'relational' welfare employing new tools and strategies to address changing human needs and hardships.

The starting-point for any historical analysis is inevitably Beveridge's landmark 1942 report, *Social Insurance and Allied Services*. This statement is widely regarded as the foundation of the modern welfare state in Britain, building on the reforms of the 1906-14 Liberal government. As Beveridge's biographer Jose Harris points out, Beveridge's study was based on existing practice reflecting the development of social policy since Lloyd George, who tentatively introduced a national system of social insurance. Beveridge's report was concerned with how to address material needs by tackling the five manifest evils of want (material poverty), disease (ill health), ignorance (lack of education), squalor (poor housing and environmental conditions) and idleness (long-term unemployment). The social progress that resulted from the implementation of Beveridge's recommendations in post-war Britain was palpable. Material deprivation and extreme poverty in old age markedly declined. There were significant improvements in the physical environment resulting from slum clearance and an expansion of social housing. The reforms had a major influence on other states, including Germany, where Beveridge was engaged to provide advice on schemes of post-war reconstruction (Harris, 1977).

Nonetheless, by the 1960s, dissatisfaction with Beveridge's settlement began to grow (Deacon, 1996). What unified many of the critiques was the apparent failure of the welfare state to address essential human needs. First, relative poverty did not disappear but re-emerged as a new social problem, partly as a consequence of rising inflation that eroded the value of state benefits. Governments in the 1960s and 1970s sought to address this situation by indexing benefits and prices while increasing the generosity of social security, but poverty and inequality continued to rise. Second, in the 1970s, a feminist critique of the welfare state developed, attacking orthodox social policy for reinforcing inequalities between women and men, while failing to address the implications of radical changes in family life. The dominance of the male breadwinner model in the system of contributory social insurance largely ignored the needs of women. Third, a critique of welfare bureaucracy emerged in the 1980s and 1990s that was influential on the Right as well as among elements of the Left. The New Right exploited growing dissatisfaction with the welfare state as public attitudes became more hostile and punitive. Governments responded by reining in entitlements and cutting back benefits, especially for those of working age. This trend has continued to the present day, more recently driven by heightened concerns about the entitlement of immigrants to welfare services.

Moreover, Beveridge's vision came under direct challenge as new issues and problems emerged that could not be adequately dealt with through the current policy framework, itself the product of debates about social reconstruction during the Second World War. The first issue was that inequality and polarisation have been more significant than anything Beveridge envisaged in the 1940s. The scale of inequality has been driven by structural changes in the economy and labour market, alongside discretionary policy decisions by governments. The post-war aspiration of greater social mobility and fluidity in the class structure, the basis of the new social democratic 'consensus', has been completely undermined. Class background has remained a powerful determinant of life-chances in Britain. Beveridge focused on the abolition of extreme poverty, which had become more prominent in the interwar period, but did not anticipate the growth of inequality in the income and wealth distribution driven by Britain's liberal political economy in the late 20th century.

The second issue is increasing costs: the welfare state appears better suited to tackling 'symptoms' rather than the underlying structural causes of social problems. Novel issues have emerged not anticipated in the 1940s and 1950s relating to lifestyle and long-term health conditions together with changing demography and the ageing society. Beveridge assumed that the average worker would live on average five years into retirement – rather than 25. Social change in Britain created new pressures from the transformation in the structure of family life to the emergence of an ethnically diverse society creating new inequalities. Beveridge was convinced that unemployment was a cyclical problem; he did not foresee the rise of long-term rates of worklessness. He took for granted the persistence of stable family structures built around a predominantly male breadwinner model.

Finally, new intellectual paradigms within the social sciences have made alternative forms of treatment and provision possible, particularly relating to the psychological causes of deprivation and distress. Beveridge's vision was mainly focused on addressing material deprivation; 'non-material' human needs scarcely featured in his thinking about social policy. Since the 1990s, there has been a growing interest among economists and social scientists in the factors that influence human wellbeing, life satisfaction and happiness. These experts argue that wellbeing has increasingly diverged from economic growth and that material progress should no longer be the central goal of modern societies (Lane, 2001). Since the early 20th century, it has been assumed that the capitalist economy would generate the surplus necessary for investment in the welfare state. An economic system that no longer accorded priority to growth in Gross Domestic Product would have significant implications for the future shape of the welfare state.

In the light of the debate about the future of capitalist growth, it is necessary to consider how the welfare and social security system of the future can more efficiently address a diverse range of human needs, as elaborated in the work of Amartya Sen and Martha Nussbaum. Doyal and Gough (1991) define needs as 'what, if not met, can cause serious harm or socially recognisable suffering'. Four distinctive types of need can be identified: physical needs, including shelter and food; skills and capabilities, notably access to human capital; care and advice, especially family and peer support; and psychic needs: understanding, love, and happiness (YF, 2006). There have been numerous attempts to map human needs in Britain from Frederick Engels' studies of the British working class to Charles Booth's maps of London poverty in the late 19th century (Mulgan, 2016). More recently, social scientists from Peter Townsend to Danny Dorling have attempted to map poverty and deprivation in British society.

The chapter is structured in the following way. The first section considers Beveridge's founding vision of the welfare state and its view of how to address human needs most effectively. The second section examines why the optimism of those who founded the post-war welfare state was confounded alongside the nature of the critiques that have emerged since the 1960s. Section three addresses why social change created 'new' human needs that were not visible to the welfare state's creators. Finally, the fourth part of the chapter analyses a new framework for how the welfare state might more effectively respond to human needs centred on the concept of relational welfare. A series of overarching conclusions are then drawn.

The welfare state under Beveridge

The first Beveridge report was published in 1942, prosaically entitled *Social Insurance and Allied Services*. It sold thousands of copies; Beveridge exclaimed: 'It's been a revelation to me how concerned people are with conditions after the war' (cited in Kynaston, 2007, p 41). Welfare states across the industrialising countries were the product of several political forces: first, citizens' need to be protected from risks that they did not want to face alone; second, the response of political elites to the evidence that too much poverty and deprivation had an adverse impact on the productive potential of the workforce; and third, the development of Weberian bureaucracies that made it possible to deliver welfare services at scale through national systems (Harris, 1977; Mulgan, 2016). As Mulgan (2016) emphasises, the welfare state's purpose was to socialise risk and to protect individuals and families from the uncertainties of life instead of relying on informal networks of voluntary organisations, charities and churches. This would reduce insecurity and ensure a more efficient workforce, vital to the aims of political stability and nation building. The welfare state was the key institution through which the working class in Britain was successfully accommodated within the prevailing political order, avoiding the violent upheaval and conflict that characterised many other European societies. Alongside these functionalist explanations, the British welfare state expressed an ethic of decency and social solidarity.

The Beveridge report made some important arguments that continue to frame social policy debates 70 years later. The first was to acknowledge the scope and scale of social welfare provision already in place in Britain, much of it operated by voluntary and charitable providers, while decrying the 'complex of disconnected administrative organs' through which services were delivered (Beveridge, 1942, p 6). The patchwork of provision would be remedied by Beveridge's recommendation to put in place a national system of social insurance; a comprehensive National Health Service available to all on the basis of need; family allowances with extra support for additional children across the country; and macroeconomic policies to maintain full employment through planning and demand management (Harris, 1977). The onus was on universalism, which meant the abolition of the long-despised means tests that had primarily characterised interwar social provision (Kynaston, 2007).

The second overarching argument of Beveridge was that the welfare state would not function effectively if it was centred on a passive *transactional* relationship between the citizen and government. Instead, there had to be cooperation between the state and the individual. The security afforded by collective social provision was only possible in return for service and contribution by individual citizens, anticipating the debate about rights and responsibilities in the 1990s (Beveridge, 1942, pp 6-7). Like his Liberal contemporary, John Maynard Keynes, Beveridge sought to maintain the boundary between the state and the market and to identify strict criteria for government intervention in markets that threatened to curtail human liberty (Harris, 1977).

Despite their association with the post-war consensus in Britain, Beveridge's reforms created a major rift within the wartime coalition. Conservative MPs, including Winston Churchill, as well as Whitehall officials were nervous about the sheer ambition and scale of Beveridge's report (Kynaston, 2007, p 25). The Labour Party, in contrast, was strongly committed to Beveridge's proposals. In 1943, 97 Labour parliamentarians defied the government whip to vote for immediate implementation of Beveridge's reforms (Thorpe, 2015). As David Kynaston recounts, Churchill eventually accepted the proposals but remained suspicious of Beveridge's intentions. The Conservatives were already anticipating the leviathan state of collectivism that was to grow under the Attlee governments in the late 1940s.

Ironically, Beveridge did not like the term 'welfare state', preferring to couch his reforms as advancing the social services state (Harris, 1977). Moreover, by 1948 Beveridge was already questioning the character of the post-war welfare system. During the Second World War, he had been relatively sympathetic to collectivism and 'state socialism', given the evident success of the wartime planned economy. By the end of the war, however, doubts emerged as Beveridge feared individual liberty and voluntarism were being weakened (Harris, 1977, pp 453-4). A subsequent paper by Beveridge (1948), *Voluntary Action: A Report on Methods of Social Advance*, emphasised the importance of the voluntary sector, especially the dense network of Friendly Societies. It acknowledged that citizens had non-material needs and that a good society was more likely to emerge by reinforcing the moral character of individuals rather than relying solely on interventions by state institutions (Harris, 1977). Beveridge was concerned in the report to ensure 'room, opportunity and encouragement for voluntary action in seeking new ways of social advance ... services of a kind that often money cannot buy' (cited in Cottam, 2008, p 3). Beveridge's 1948 report was criticised for failing to consider other forms of mutual aid and self-help, such as cooperatives and trade unions (Cole, 1949). Harris (1996) notes the tensions and disagreements surrounding the report's publication. The committee of experts assembled by Beveridge could not agree on whether the voluntary sector had a continuing role to play in welfare provision, or whether this function had effectively been taken over by the state. Moreover, Beveridge's worldview was already colliding with the realities of social change in post-war Britain. The ethic of altruism, self-help and public service that appeared robust in the aftermath of the Second World War was being gradually worn away in the 1950s by the rise of working-class consumerism and popular leisure (Addison, 2010). The welfare state fostered greater economic security, choice and individualism, perversely threatening the communitarian sentiments on which the welfare state had been founded in the early 20th century (Harris, 1996). This weakening of communal attachments reopened the long-term question of the moral viability and political legitimacy of the welfare state in the 1980s and 1990s.

Post-war critiques of the welfare state

Beveridge's reforms were the centrepiece of the post-war social settlement. Despite economic difficulties that grew more acute in the late 1940s, it appeared that Britain was on the road to irreversible social progress. All of the major parties accepted the case for active government intervention to protect citizens from the adversities generated by the capitalist economy. Nonetheless, by the 1960s, many of the expectations raised by the Beveridge report had not been met. The problem of relative poverty had far from disappeared after 1945, despite the reformist intentions of the Attlee governments. One of Beveridge's principal assumptions in the 1942 report was that national insurance contributions should be levied at a flat rate, rather than being 'earnings-related', as was the case in most other industrialised countries (Kynaston, 2007). This premise was increasingly problematic in an affluent society with rising inflation. Wages grew, but the value of state benefits inevitably declined. As a consequence, relative deprivation and poverty increased, especially among children and pensioners (Townsend, 1979). The 1964 Wilson government sought to introduce earnings-related unemployment and sickness benefits, while Barbara Castle implemented an earnings-related pension scheme in 1975 when she was Secretary of State for Health and Social Services. Both initiatives were promptly abolished by the Thatcher governments, which sought to rein in government spending and cut back the welfare state.

Second, Beveridge assumed that in the aftermath of the Second World War, women workers mobilised as part of the war effort would return to domesticity and childrearing. As a consequence, the system of national insurance was built predominantly around the husband's earnings (Kynaston, 2007). However, women's participation in the labour force grew significantly after 1945. By 1955, 45.9% of women of working age were active in the labour market; this had increased to 55.1% in 1975 and 66.6% by 1995 (Walsh and Wrigley, 2001). Beveridge's reforms thus did not anticipate the rise of the dual-earner household; nor did they consider what should happen to those spending time outside the labour market as carers who then became economically independent, especially divorced women.

Third, Beveridge insisted in the 1940s that the welfare state would not function effectively if it was regarded as a 'soft touch'. Rights to universal benefits and services had to be matched by the obligation to find paid employment. He argued that 'an assistance scheme which makes those assisted unamenable to economic rewards and punishments while treating them as free citizens is inconsistent with the principles of a free community' (cited in Kynaston, 2007, p 26). But the growth of long-term unemployment since the 1970s as a consequence of deindustrialisation and the decline of manufacturing have created renewed policy challenges. The evidence indicates that the demise of British manufacturing and manual work leads not only to growing levels of joblessness but also to family breakdown and the weakening of social cohesion (Power, 2012). To reduce worklessness, welfare recipients have been forced to accept jobs below their labour market potential. The growth of low-skilled labour has depleted the stock of human capital while attenuating the problem of in-work poverty: governments have to create complex systems of public subsidy, including tax credits, in order to make work pay. By 2010, the UK had one of the highest rates of worklessness in the European Union: nearly one in four working-age adults did not work (10.8 million people). Indeed, 4.8 million people lived in households where no-one was working (DWP, 2010). The growth of low pay and labour market insecurity are problems that Beveridge scarcely foresaw in the 1940s.

Welfare policy and social change

The legacy of the Beveridge settlement has been an emphasis on financial efficiency and cost management in the welfare state, alongside a consequent neglect of neighbourhood institutions, communities and culture (Cottam, 2011; Power, 2012). Not only have new policy challenges undermined the efficacy of the Beveridge settlement, but there is a growing divergence between the services that are provided by the welfare state, and the changing character of human needs. Inevitably, Beveridge did not foresee the emergence of new issues such as social isolation, which was partly a consequence of earlier reforms that improved general health trends and increased longevity (Addison, 2010; Cottam, 2011). The disappearance of traditional community structures alongside the observed decline of the extended family has increased the risk of social exclusion among vulnerable groups such as the elderly. Loneliness in the UK remains a bigger cause of premature death than smoking but welfare states are barely equipped to address social isolation (Mulgan, 2016). Cottam (2008) has demonstrated that the post-war centralised mass bureaucratic welfare system was poor at supporting groups in need, especially families under stress.

The inadequacy of existing welfare structures is evident in relation to inequality and polarisation. Beveridge envisaged an inclusive social security system in a society where material deprivation was widely prevalent. His vision did not foresee heightened class stratification and the emergence of social strata increasingly cut off from mainstream society. The so-called 'underclass' debate, which first emerged in the late 1960s in the United States (Murray, 2015), remains controversial and its relevance to Britain is questioned (Mulgan, 2016). The underclass debate is linked to the growth of worklessness and social exclusion in traditional white working-class communities, entrenching pockets of spatial disadvantage in northern England, central Scotland and South Wales. It is argued that job shedding and automation are eroding the supply of low-skilled and intermediate employment; individuals who lose their jobs are increasingly at risk as their skills rapidly become obsolete (Mulgan, 2016). Traditional welfare bureaucracies have struggled to cope with these challenges.

Second, the increasing costs of the welfare state have weakened its political legitimacy. The rise in costs was in part the consequence of the reactive nature of the welfare system, which rarely acknowledged the importance of anticipating and preventing problems from occurring at the outset. There was also a low rate of investment in public institutions that could tackle issues more effectively at source, as families became increasingly locked into a 'cycle of need' (Cottam, 2008; Power, 2012). The lack of investment relates to the debate about the role of civil society and the voluntary sector addressed by Beveridge in his 1948 report. If ideas such as the 'Big Society', David Cameron's flagship social policy reform, are to have a positive impact on the most disadvantaged citizens and places, an active but 'light-handed' state is necessary to ensure resources are in place while overseeing the framework of provision (Power, 2012). At the time of writing (spring 2016), the Conservative government has come under attack following major cuts in voluntary sector budgets, new regulations that seek to prevent charities from criticising government policy and receiving state support, and deep cuts in the welfare budget (Power, 2012). Overall, too little attention had been paid historically to how civil society and government should work together.

Third, traditional welfare bureaucracies have struggled to cope with new pressures and demands: changes in family life, demography and the status of women redefine what is required from the welfare state. The emergence of long-term health conditions such as diabetes and their correlation with lower participation in the labour market requires a markedly different response from the welfare system. Dispensing cash benefits and services is an inadequate response where the aim is to improve life-chances, including participation in the community. In the UK, one in six adults suffers from a neurotic disorder such as long-term depression or anxiety. The increasing incidence of mental illness is said to reflect the growth of social isolation, as individuals are more likely to live alone. Moreover, health outcomes in the UK such as recovery rates from heart disease and cancer depend on where you live (Power, 2012; Mulgan, 2016). Where old age lasts longer, the emphasis shifts from pension provision to the availability of social care for groups suffering from dementia or physical ill health (Deacon, 1996; Mulgan, 2016). Furthermore, different minority ethnic groups experience markedly different outcomes on the main social and economic indicators: for example, Pakistani and Bangladeshi households are most likely to be living in poverty (YF, 2006). This confirms that a 'one-size-fits-all' approach to welfare provision is increasingly obsolete.

Finally, developments in technology, and in the medical and social sciences, affect what the welfare state is able to provide. New techniques and treatments, from neuroscience to cognitive behavioural therapy and psychoanalysis, have likewise created new demands for welfare provision (Cottam, 2008). 'Predicative algorithms' make it possible to more accurately predict which groups might be vulnerable to poor outcomes. Technology allows the state to empower user groups through mechanisms such as direct payments and individual learning accounts; digital technologies allow greater user feedback and create more opportunities for peer support (Mason, 2015). These digitally based developments have occurred as interest has grown in the 'non-material' dimensions of human need and wellbeing in contemporary societies. Finally, new structures of investment are emerging to tackle systemic social problems, particularly 'social impact bonds', which raise new sources of funding instead of relying on traditional government spending (Mulgan, 2016).

A relational welfare state

The demise of the welfare state has been predicted for several decades in the face of structural pressures such as globalisation, and the erosion of the powers and capacities of government. Yet it is striking that welfare states have broadly survived, having been characterised by remarkable underlying resilience. One reason is that private insurance markets do not function effectively in the welfare field: markets rely on the risk aversion of purchasers and the likelihood of very small numbers of claims (Mulgan, 2016); as a consequence, insurance providers have traditionally been reluctant to get involved in the welfare system.

The lack of any public appetite for a shift to market-based welfare models adds to the urgency of revisiting current social security arrangements in a climate where poverty has been rising and there have been dramatic cuts to public institutions and welfare benefit regimes. Cottam (2008, 2011) outlines five overarching principles that can underpin a new *relational* welfare settlement in the UK:

• first, a shift 'from need to capability' that focuses on what people can do rather than what they cannot do. This emphasis on capabilities is rooted in the work of the development economist Amartya Sen. The principal purpose of the welfare system is not to distribute cash benefits and services, but to improve the resilience of individuals, families and communities, focusing on the supply of assets, skills, networks and non-cognitive capabilities. Commitment devices such as home–school contracts and employment plans for welfare claimants have a role to play while helping individuals to fulfil their civic obligations (Power, 2012; Mulgan, 2016);

- second, the importance of ensuring that systems are universal and inclusive. For example, all governments since the 1990s have sought to invest in programmes designed to intervene in so-called troubled families, but all families are in need of support at particular points in the lifecycle, for example, through pre-school childcare. Protecting the individual from risks also means strengthening the social contract that underpins the welfare system (Mulgan, 2016). There is debate under way about whether medical treatment ought to be conditional on a healthy diet and whether parents who fail to supervise their children appropriately should face sanctions in relation to the welfare support they receive from the state;
- third, deploying a range of resources rather than just money: time, assets, social capital and so on. As Beveridge foresaw in the late 1940s, welfare states have become too focused on distributing government money and imposing professional interventions on individuals. The state needs to draw on wider networks of community assets and resources, capturing the gains of collaboration and the 'sharing economy' (Power, 2012; Mason, 2015; Mulgan, 2016). Social needs can often be met by drawing on the existing resources of communities, alongside the skills and capabilities of individuals within them;
- fourth, creating bottom-up systems where power is devolved and decentralised to users and communities. Devolution to city regions and counties may in the long term promote greater innovation in social policy through decentralisation. One effect of greater devolution may be the introduction of innovative policies such as basic income. For example, the city of Utrecht in the Netherlands is enacting a pioneering basic income scheme. Decentralisation can help to foster a stronger culture of trialling and testing new programmes and interventions in the welfare state. Welfare systems need to embrace experimentalism, making systematic use of trials, including randomised control trials, combined with rigorous evaluation of evidence (Mulgan, 2016);
- fifth, delivering social policies through networks in civil society in order to promote interaction and peer group involvement, not just prescribing benefits and services to individuals. One example of harnessing civil society networks is the creation of local currencies that enable poorer groups to purchase essential items such as food and fuel at lower cost than in private markets.

The task ahead is to translate these high-level governing principles into the practical implementation of social policy and welfare programmes across the diverse nations and regions of the United Kingdom, drawing on best practice from the European Union and beyond. This approach requires an open culture of 'disciplined pluralism' where there is scope for radical experimentation and innovation within national frameworks of standards and rules (Kay, 2003).

Conclusion

The issues addressed in this chapter have arisen throughout the history of post-war Britain, but have become even more urgent since the financial crisis of 2008. The crisis did not create the new pressures on the welfare state, but it has accentuated a number of pre-existing trends. The 2008 global financial crisis was a reminder that capitalism, for all its dynamism and innovation, in not always well equipped to meet basic human needs. Increasing levels of consumer debt have been the direct consequence of the contraction in real wages and the inadequacy of household incomes. But more fundamentally, rising economic growth and material progress have not necessarily led to more stable and contented societies.

The crisis has resulted in a wave of 'austerity' policies over the past eight years that have weakened the universality and inclusivity of the welfare state in most advanced economies. The financial crash was viewed as an opportunity to rebalance the economy and society in order to better address human needs. However, unlike the 1930s depression, which led to the enactment of radical social reforms in the post-war settlement, it appears that the opportunity for major alterations in the policy landscape has thus far been missed; in fact, there has been a reversion to pre-crisis policy models, alongside major cuts in the fabric of the welfare system. Without fundamental changes in policy regimes, the structural conditions that led to the crisis in the industrialised economies are more likely to reoccur; even worse, fundamental human needs are in danger of continuing to be ignored.

References

Addison, P. (2010) *No Turning Back: The Peacetime Revolutions of Post-War Britain*, Oxford: Oxford University Press.

Beveridge, W. (1942) *Social Insurance and Allied Services*, London: HMSO.

Beveridge, W. (1948) *Voluntary Action: A Report on Methods of Social Advance*, London: George Allen and Unwin.

Cole, G. D. H. (1949) 'Reviewed Work: Voluntary Action: On Methods of Social Advance', *The Economic Journal*, 59, 399-401.

Cottam, H. (2008) *Beveridge 4.0*, London: Participle.

Cottam, H. (2011) 'Relational Welfare', *Soundings*, 48, 134–44.

Deacon, A. (1996) 'The Dilemmas of Welfare', in S. J. D. Green and R. C. Whiting (eds) *The Boundaries of the State in Modern Britain*, Cambridge: Cambridge University Press: 67–83.

Doyal, L. and Gough, I. (1991), *A Theory of Human Needs*, Basingstoke: Macmillan.

DWP (2010) *State of the Nation Report: Poverty, Worklessness, and Welfare Dependency in the UK*, London: HM Government.

Harris, J. (1977) *William Beveridge: A Biography*, Oxford: Oxford University Press.

Harris, J. (1996) 'Political Thought and the State', in S. J. D. Green and R. C. Whiting (eds) *The Boundaries of the State in Modern Britain*, Cambridge: Cambridge University Press: 15–28.

Kay, J. (2003) *The Truth About Markets*, London: Allen Lane.

Kynaston, D. (2007) *Austerity Britain 1945-51*, London: Bloomsbury.

Lane, R. E. (2001) *The Loss of Happiness in Market Democracies*, New Haven, CT: Yale University Press.

Mason, P. (2015) *Post-Capitalism: A Guide to our Future*, London: Allen Lane.

Mulgan, G. (2016) 'New Social Contracts', *NESTA Blog*, 13 January, [Online] Available at: www.nesta.org.uk/sites/default/files/new_social_contracts.pdf.

Murray, C. (2015) *Losing Ground: American Social Policy 1950 to 1980*, New York, NY: Basic Books.

Power, A. (2012) '"The Big Society" and Concentrated Neighbourhood Problems', *Report for the British Academy Series on New Paradigms in Public Policy*, London: British Academy.

Thorpe, A. (2015) *A History of the Labour Party*, Basingstoke: Palgrave MacMillan.

Townsend, P. (1979) *Poverty in the United Kingdom: A Survey of Household Resources and Standards of Living*, Harmondsworth: Penguin Books.

Walsh, A. and Wrigley, C. (2001) 'Womanpower: The Transformation of the Labour Force in the US and the UK since 1945', *Recent Findings in Economic and Social History*, Nottingham: University of Nottingham.

YF (2006) 'Mapping Britain's Unmet Needs', *A Report Prepared for the Commission on Unclaimed Assets*, London: Young Foundation.

THREE

Social division and resentment in the aftermath of the economic slump

Gabriella Elgenius

This chapter analyses the social impact of hard-time experiences of the economic downturn in 2008 that engulfed the rich world in a similar fashion to the Great Depression of the 1930s. The standard definition of recessions – two successive quarters of negative growth – fails to capture the harsh realities of those affected and ignores the social repercussions associated with austere times. The arguments put forward are the following: the recent recession (increasingly referred to as the Great Recession) has, as the worst economic slump since the Second World War, adequately been labelled the 'nastiest recession' to date, as it has hit groups already fighting socioeconomic vulnerability disproportionately (Tunstall and Fenton, 2009; Clark and Elgenius, 2014; Clark and Heath, 2014). Moreover, our findings of hard-time experiences account for patterns of hardship – due to cuts in welfare provisions and squeeze in income – alongside an unequalising trend for (always widely dispersed) wealth to increase relative to Gross Domestic Product (GDP) over time. Thus, hard-time experiences have persisted despite signs of a recovering economy since 2014, and the rhetoric of 'being in it together' and the associated One Nation politics appears incorrect at best. The shared experiences or shared burdens implied with the One Nation concept stray far from our material. In a similar fashion, references to a 'Big Society' or to 'communities' and 'hard-hit communities' must be used with caution for reasons that will be explained. Our empirical findings highlight that social relations are undermined by austerity, as division, resentment and (some dimensions of) isolation follow the aftermath of the recession. The most salient patterns of our material show resentment between those in work, resenting the benefits of those without work, and those without work on benefits resenting other sub-groups on different benefits.

Project background and methodology

This work builds on the social capital discourse in relation to the economic crisis and its social implications in the UK and the US, and is a product of the research collaboration Social Change: A Harvard–Manchester Initiative based at the Institute of Social Change at Manchester, directed by Robert Putnam and Ed Fieldhouse. This text draws on the British findings and the part of the programme coordinated by Anthony Heath. Tom Clark (*The Guardian*) together with Anthony Heath, produced the volume *Hard Times: The Divisive Toll of the Economic Slump* (2014)[1] analysing the divisive social consequences of hard times (on civic life, ethnic relations, family life, apathy and political attitudes). The author of this chapter, Gabriella Elgenius, undertook the qualitative work for this volume. The other participants, Paul Hepburn, James Laurence, Yaojun Li, Chaeyoon Lim, Siobhan McAndrew, Lindsey Macmillan, Robert Ford and Maria Grasso, contributed with expertise in their various fields. This *Hard Times* project was named after Charles Dickens's novel *Hard Times – For These Times* (1854), which appraised the social and economic pressures of the times.

The collection of qualitative data, on which this chapter is based, allowed for purposive sampling to understand individual experiences of socioeconomic vulnerability. In-depth and semi-structured interviews were conducted in order to obtain first-hand experiences that illuminate the quantitative findings. The qualitative material was integrated into the volume *Hard Times* and was analysed in a feature in *The Guardian*, 'Benefits crackdown leads to divide and rule within poor communities: the coalition's skivers v strivers message is inflaming resentments between those affected by the economic slump' (Clark and Elgenius, 2014). This chapter is therefore closely connected to these two publications. The findings elaborated upon here relate to some patterns associated with hardship faced by vulnerable groups in the aftermath of the recession. The interview period stretches over 2012-13, and interviews were conducted in England and Scotland, in person or via telephone. The demography of the sample intended to cover different forms of socioeconomic vulnerability. Complementary purposive sampling techniques – maximum variation sample – were required at various stages of the interview process to gain insight into various forms of socioeconomic vulnerability. Thus, interviews were conducted with people with disabilities, ethnic minorities, unskilled people without secondary education, single mothers, the unemployed and young people. Critical sampling was used to include the experiences of those in employment, low-income working households or families just managing, the squeezed middle, or the too rich too poor, who find themselves in a situation where bills and absolute needs do not match. This group included professionals and university-educated individuals. Families with low to middle incomes are found at the bottom half of the income distribution but above the bottom 10 per cent.

Focusing on hard-time experiences of groups facing socioeconomic vulnerability requires particular sensitivity to voluntary participation, informed consent, anonymity and non-disclosure. The goals and limitations of our research were shared with the participants, some of whom were recruited via research networks, Jobcentres, support networks, and organisations including Citizens Advice, the Resolution Foundation and Save the Children. Interviewees were assured of their right to withdraw from the interview at any time and guaranteed confidentiality with regard to their statements. We acknowledge the many interviewees who generously contributed to this research by exploring sensitive issues within the framework of this project.

The nasty recession: a tornado, not a storm

Groups already fighting socioeconomic vulnerability, mentioned earlier, took the hardest hit during the recent recession. The economic crisis has been described as a 'financial storm', but its ferocious impact on society was more like that of a tornado – hitting some while leaving others more or less untouched. As highlighted by Clark and Heath (2014):

> [t]here is, then, nothing new in the idea that hard times hit unevenly – biting in different ways in different towns, and even in different homes. This time, however, the great gulf in conditions that opened up between different parts of the population *before* the slump has, as we shall see, warped every element of the social response. (p 28, emphasis in original)

The aftermath of the recession may therefore well be described as one of 'disproportionate suffering being meted out to the poor' – and as a feature of unequal societies facing disproportionate levels of unemployment, job insecurity and poverty. The recession hit relatively small sections of the population already struggling from socioeconomic vulnerability, quite contrary to the political rhetoric of 'being in it together' or that of 'One Nation'. Thus, the Institute for Fiscal Studies (IFS), in reviewing living standards, inequality and poverty, concluded that the 'effect of the Great Recession has not been evenly felt across different kinds of households' (Belfield et al, 2014, p 56).

The *dip* of the economic slump is modest in the context of decisively marked and raised levels of affluence since the beginning of the 20th century. The disproportionate experiences of hardship stand in sharp contrast to this relatively small dip and against the backdrop of wealth increase and raising affluence that, theoretically speaking, could be shared to a higher degree. More specifically, the period between 1929 representing pre-Depression peak rates (in 2008 prices below) and 2007 (when the GDP national income per head was at its peak) constitutes a period during which British incomes increased by 470% (Clark and Heath, 2014, p 20, GDP 1900-2010). These large overall increases in British incomes were concentrated at the top end.

Instances of absolute poverty rose across the UK in the aftermath of the recession, measuring household income before and after housing costs having been deducted, and in consideration of the variation in housing cost trends across income groups. (On average, housing costs for low-income households, largely rented, have risen relative to high-income ones that are often owned outright or paid with mortgages, rates for which have declined.) According to the IFS, when measuring income before housing costs in 2011-12 as many as 10.8 million individuals (16.85% of the population) fell under the poverty line (equal to 60% of 2010-11 median income in real terms). The same figure was 16.8% of the population for 2012-13. Calculated *after* housing costs, the individuals affected in 2011-12 increased to 14 million (22.4%). In the years to follow, 23.2% of the population fell under the poverty line in 2012-13 and 21.6% in 2013-14 (Belfield et al, 2014, pp 32-5, 55-7; 2015). According to the Trussell Trust, foodbank numbers 'soared' and 'millions of Britons' could not afford to eat, and the activities of its foodbanks increased steadily during 2007–08 and 2009–10. The use of foodbanks is demonstrated by the drastic increase in three-day emergency food supplies given to households in crisis, the numbers rose from 61,468 (2010–11) to 346,992 (2012–13) to 913,138 (2013–14) and 1,109,309 (2015–16) (Moreton, 2015; Garratt et al, 2016; Owen, 2016; TT, 2016).

Concerns about food deprivation are found in our material as interviewees talk about 'cutting back on food'. Weekly expenditure is described in detail by many: "I've been asked a thousand times 'how can you survive on £10 a week?' Well, a lot of rice, a lot of pulses, a lot of pasta and some egg." When asked about the future, this interviewee reasoned: "I probably, if my life continues like this, I don't know, I'll probably get some disease in five or six years, if I'm like this, because of ... malnutrition ... I'm either going to be here or I'm not ..." (unemployed, male, 47).

Parents described how they made sure that their children had something to eat before they did. One mother on Jobseeker's Allowance (JSA) volunteered:

> "My partner, he sometimes lives on a box of cereal for maybe three days, and then I will [have] one meal a day, it's just my son, he's three and he eats loads, and I just need to make sure that he has food there at dinner time." (Unemployed, female, 20)

Interviewees disclosed that they have 'gone down a dress size' (unemployed, female, 60) or several sizes during the course of events that turned into periods of homelessness: "I went from a size 12 to a size 6 in two months. I was not eating or sleeping well" (unemployed, female, 20).

The difficulties of paying for necessities are brought up by all of our interviewees: "I get £68 a week and that has to cover rent, your energy bills, utility bills, television licence, the payday loans. So I don't have anything really much for food but my brothers been helpful," a female unemployed interviewee (60) explained. She also spoke about dreading the supermarket:

> "When you go out shopping for food and people are filling up their trollies and you think oh I used to be able to do that and you think I mustn't get [caught at] the till because if I haven't got enough money that would be terrible. So I always make sure that I have added it all properly in my head and that I've got enough money with me to pay."

When asked whether she had anyone to talk to about her situation, she responded:

> "I couldn't tell anybody. Other than my family and close people, I wouldn't want anybody else to know my situation, because it would seem embarrassing. I think so. Yeah, you just have to put a bit of a face on, you know, and make out everything is okay. I've sold some things on eBay. Some items that I didn't want, so some money there. But that all goes, just swallowed up in different bills and things you are paying ... I'm looking round at things all the time in case I've got something to sell. It's a bit difficult. I just never ever thought that I would be in this situation."

This interviewee had stopped working to care for her ageing mother, and after the mother passed away found it impossible to return to employment. She concluded: "My brother sends me a bag from Tesco, I would be so ashamed to go to a foodbank."

Continuing the theme on spending on food, and leaving aside the mention of payday loans and the shame associated with poverty, the accounts here are consistent with the analysis of the Institute for Fiscal Studies (Belfield et al, 2014). Official expenditure data used to calculate inflation shows that spending on food to eat *at home* has been substantially squeezed as part of a downward trend in spending, which looks relatively sharper among poorer social groups. Among our interviewees, those at the less deprived end of the scale, such as one professional, employed, 39-year-old single mother, would typically mention arrangements of shopping in pairs to take advantage of offers such as two-for-one or of sharing less expensive family packs.

Falls in real earnings hit working households hard. In comparison, benefit entitlements initially remained more stable at the outset of the recession in 2008, when compared with the then inflated incomes. The subsequent reduction of benefit entitlements, coinciding particularly with the new government in 2010, produced a sharp rise of absolute poverty as mentioned earlier. The squeeze of incomes was the sharpest since the 1860s, but the inflation rate held different implications for different groups. Thus the *inflation rate* as one rate hitting all equally is also a gross misrepresentation of actual cost of living (see Clark and Heath, 2014). The families in our sample felt the rise in unavoidable costs for items such as food, rent and heating, and did not, for instance, benefit from the fall in mortgage interest payments. The low- to middle-income families in 2014 were as many as six million working households, or around ten million adults (Belfield et al, 2014). Within this group, 80% earned less than £21,000 sterling (the median gross wage), even though 83% of all households had at least one member in full-time work. These families remained outside the system of means-tested benefits, and were highly vulnerable to changes in circumstances despite being in full-time work (Finch, 2016). Moreover, in terms of economic recovery, 'increasing real earnings will boost incomes towards the top of the distribution, while on-going cuts to benefits and tax credits reduce incomes towards the bottom' (Belfield et al, 2015, p 56).

Ongoing cuts to benefits and tax credits hit people with disabilities especially hard. A United Nations-led inquiry by the Convention on the Rights of Persons with Disabilities concluded that people with disabilities were 'disproportionately and adversely' affected by austerity policies (and the cumulative impact of spending cuts including other social care budgets) undertaken by the UK government to reduce public spending between 2010 and 2016 (Committee on the Rights of Persons with Disabilities, 2016). The inquiry stated that the hardship, induced by the disproportionate cuts for people with disabilities, amounted to systematic violations (Butler, 2016; Committee on the Rights of Persons with Disabilities, 2016). Clark and Elgenius (2014) noted that people with disabilities suffered from being pitted against working families or strivers and feared being labelled lazy skivers or scroungers. The Committee on the Rights of Persons with Disabilities reported further that disabled people continue to suffer stigmatisation as burdens for taxpayers and have experienced increasing hostility and attacks to their personal integrity (Committee on the Rights of Persons with Disabilities, 2016; see also Butler, 2016).

Interviewees with disabilities in our study were well aware of the harsh realities of cuts and threats of further cuts to already strained budgets. One disabled couple, a 60-year-old former aircraft fitter with advanced cancer and his wife, 53, a former teacher, spoke about the horror of 'brown envelope days':

Wife: "Some days, when you're not feeling very well, and there's a lot going on with you, and you get another letter through the letter box, and they're going to be looking at this or that, and think, I just don't know why I am bothering."

Husband: "It's horrible when you hear the postman come up the path, you don't even see what comes through the letter box."

Wife: "If it's a brown envelope ..."

Husband: "Because if it's a brown envelope ..."

Wife: "That means the government letter ..."

Husband: "It's no life really, is it?"

Wife: "No."

The fear of brown envelopes is a fear of the government's austerity policies and cuts to Housing Benefit, Disability Living Allowance (DLA) and Employment and Support Allowance.

Social division and isolation: lingering social repercussions

The recession exposed societal problems of isolation, resentment and division, but the social repercussions lingered even with signs of economic recovery. The social damage caused by hardship was analysed by the classic studies of the Great Depression of the 1930 that explored unemployment, poverty and material hardship (see Bakke, 1933; Jahoda et al, 1974). The study, by Jahoda et al (1974), of the small industrial village of Marienthal, located on the Fischa-Dagnitz River in the Steinfeld district of Austria, explored ways in which prolonged periods of unemployment lead to social apathy and less utilisation of remaining opportunities. The village had depended on the one mill that closed after the Great Crash of 1929, turning Marienthal into a centre of unemployment, where industrial production decreased by nearly 40% in the 1930s. The authors describe a weary community as 'the slump had long since seeped from silent factories to somewhere under the skin' (Jahoda et al, 1974). This study of the Great Depression offered no optimism about community cohesion, community spirit or social engagement in the face of austerity. On the contrary, the findings saw pervasive unemployment depriving the population socially, too, and social relations deteriorating alongside economic deprivation. The scholars noted that the Marienthal community was increasingly deprived of its 'collective energy' and suffered a 'complete civic collapse' under enduring hardship (Laurence, 2015), with membership of voluntary organisations and associations suffering despite lowered fees for the unemployed (Jahoda et al, 1974, p 40). Post-war studies of poverty, such as Harrington's work *The Other America: Poverty in the United States* (1997), later challenged the discourse of unqualified prosperity in post-war America, pointing towards the extent of poverty but also its paralysing impact of hopelessness, psychological deprivation, isolation and division as the main concomitants of poverty.

The recent recession – with squeezed incomes and reduced benefits – also affected social relations. Arguably, Britain suffered a social recession alongside the economic downturn, with a decline of both formal volunteering (in organisations and associations) and informal volunteering (helping family, friends or neighbours) since 2008. Generally speaking, average figures do not adequately measure hard-time experiences or repercussions for volunteering, since the majority do not experience the full impact. Thus, the decline in informal volunteering was especially sharp for regions with higher levels of unemployment during the recession and for socioeconomically disadvantaged groups. Laurence and Lim (2015) explain the decline as embedded in the organisational infrastructure of norms of trust and reciprocity. Engagement in associations and organisations (see Putnam, 2000) is one way to measure collective energy and connectedness. Social capital and social resources are generated by connectedness offered through social organisation, networks and trust, and facilitate cooperation. Social resources such as these tend to be in deficit among disadvantaged groups (Laurence and Lim, 2015).

The British evidence on associational life of community organisations is 'grim', according to Clark and Heath (2014): both the number of volunteers and the level of their commitment declined with the economy. The percentage of those engaged in formal volunteering declined from around 44% offering some help to organisations before the recession in 2005 to 42% in 2008 and to 37% in 2010. Moreover, the average time spent helping others fell from around three hours 10 minutes to two hours 10 minutes per month. The levels of informal volunteering declined even more and as much as 12% per cent during the same period (Laurence, 2015; Laurence and Lim, 2015). These decline levels are, if anything, even greater when considering the average number of hours volunteered, and constitute a dramatic change as they cover the whole population, including people who have never volunteered. The sharp decline in informal volunteering (as a result of lack of trust, motivation and/or financial resources needed to take part) points to vulnerable households becoming less involved in communal activities and possibly towards becoming more isolated.

The definition and significance of social capital constitutes a complex task and its assessment depends on different scholarly traditions. The measure for isolation is also complex as it is related to 'low indicators on all measures of social capital' (Richards and Heath, 2015). Richards and Heath (2015) suggest that 5-7% of the UK population live in isolation in terms of *not* having 'someone to discuss personal matters with', a pattern that is more marked among unemployed people or those with low educational attainment. Many of our interviewees, some of whom belong to these groups, stated that they had 'no one to talk to' or turn to in case something happened. One male interviewee, for example, said: "Since my youth work days, I've liked bringing people together, I liked doing diverse things, I liked working outside the box." The same interviewee, however, states that now, since the recession, "I don't get involved; I don't even put myself out there." Withdrawing from his family is part of this: "I try to distance myself when there is a family function because I cannot carry my weight like I used to." He explains how he cannot bear the relatives seeing that he is no longer able to turn up "with a big pot of seasoned meat" and says: "There is a distance that worries me if anything should happen. That's the worst thing. I know where my family is, it is just the distance. It [my situation] is not tearing us apart it's just *keeping us apart*" (unemployed, male, 47, emphasis added).

Many related stories illustrate how interviewees reflect on their shrinking social network with few or no friends. Interviewees would mention that they used to volunteer 'a couple of times a week', but fewer formal activities and less formal engagement have seemingly followed the recession. Interviewees were asked about close friends or people they could turn to in their hour of need. A lack of someone to talk to was a noticeable effect of hard times in our sample: "At the moment, I am on my own, kind of thing ... I used to volunteer over the years including for Citizens Advice Bureau: I have not done anything for about two years ... it drives me mental, stir crazy" (disabled, female, 55). Interviewees described being alone as a result of lack of funds to take part in social activities, go to public places, keep in touch or contribute to gatherings, and they talked about feeling ashamed of and being exhausted by their situation.

For the purpose of this chapter, one salient pattern in the qualitative material is discussed below as the discourse of resentment between those in work – resenting the benefits of those without work – and those without work on benefits resenting other groups on different benefits. The narrative of resentment as a dimension of socioeconomic vulnerability was found throughout the interviews with hard-hit families. Arguably, the divisive public discourse on scrounging, coupled with having no one to ask for help in an hour of need or not being able to afford necessities, contributes to undermining communities rather than strengthening them. As one disabled 55-year-old female interviewee with brittle-bone disease explained: "People are turning against their neighbours and their friends. But I think it's been done so that people don't actually stand up." This statement encapsulates the sense that in prolonged periods of austerity vulnerable groups find themselves further isolated by accusations of being work-shy or skiving on benefits (Clark and Elgenius, 2014).

An analysis of the British Social Attitudes survey by Park et al (2014) found a declining trend in support for welfare and redistribution since the mid-1980s, a trend that declined further as Britain's economy entered the recession (Baumberg, 2014). The proportion agreeing that the government should spend more on benefits fell from 55% in 1987 to 36% in 2004. When the economy started to contract, so did support for redistribution, with 27% in favour of redistributive welfare (2009). A few years later, 74% agreed that the 'government pays out too much in benefits' (YouGov, 2012), while 60% per cent of British households on less than £10,000 per annum agreed that 'there are many fraudulent benefit claimants' (Kellner, 2012). Further, 60% on less than £10,000 per annum and 73% on £10,000-19,999 agreed that at least a significant minority or around half of claimants lie about their circumstances in order to obtain higher welfare benefits (for example by pretending to be unemployed, ill or disabled) or by deliberately refusing to take work when suitable jobs are available (YouGov, 2012). Our qualitative data also reveal a complex picture emerging with regards to deservedness. Interviewees would, as a rule, state that scrounging on benefits was a widespread problem, but virtually all argued that this affected people on different benefits from their own.

In line with our arguments about political fragmentation *among* recessionary victims, the resentment felt by struggling working families towards the unemployed on JSA and related benefits was to be expected. Such resentment was narrated with discourses of working families who deserve help as per their hard work, as opposed to the non-working families. One of our professional employed mothers, for instance, noted that her family – as a working family – were 'just managing' and highlighted their 'very tiring battle' trying to pay their bills. She argued: "[We're] being made to feel as though, as a working family, we're not valued as much as someone out of work." With reference to the latter, such experiences were juxtaposed against the perceived realities of 'non-working families', 'sleeping off life on benefits', 'their weekly trips' and "young girls who've got I forget how many children" (employed, female, 37). In a similar fashion, we found complaints from small families about unfair benefits given to large families and parents "on benefits [who] have got four or five kids" or "laptops and the latest iPhones" (employed, female, 39). In contrast, big families mentioned that small families benefitted from the maternity grant for their first child. Moreover, struggling families and those living in partnership questioned couples being paid "£30 less" for "living together" (unemployed, female, 26).

The stress and pressure associated with looking for work was, in turn, highlighted among the unemployed, who argued for the dedication of fellow jobseekers: "I see people going to the work club and they are just writing, writing, writing [applications and letters]." Unemployed interviewees would bring up tax credits that aim to help low-waged families and conclude: "You get more help now if you are in work" (unemployed, female, 60). Interviewees receiving JSA also pointed to those on DLA or to those who received health-related payments as being better off, and as the only people doing well at the moment:

> "I have a couple of mates that are claiming disability that are not disabled, those are the only people I know that are doing well. Apart from that, no.... One has got a bad back

and one is saying he's going a bit loopy ... I know they are not – they are out there drinking all the time. Yeah, there is nothing wrong with either of them." (Unemployed, male, 42)

Another unemployed 47-year-old man contributed:

"A young man I used to work with gets Employment and Support Allowance, and so he doesn't really have to go to work.... He's clearing £400 a month without doing anything ... I'm clearing £240 a month, and I'm running backwards and forwards ... in the Work Programme twice a week."

These interviewees seem to be unaware of the cuts to DLA.

Similarly, those interviewees relying on DLA would in turn urge the government to incentivise the "lazy ones" by telling "these people on Jobseeker's ... there's work there, you do it or you lose your money" (unemployed, male, 60). The sanctions applied to those claiming JSA have not registered with them. The interviewees with disabilities were clearly very concerned about the exclusive term 'working families' and felt stigmatised for being unable to work. For example, one 53-year-old female, disabled by an amputation of her leg, argued: "I don't like this title that Cameron keeps saying, the hardworking families. Well, we were the hardworking families until the illness took [our] jobs.... I feel like I'm getting stabbed in the back." Other disabled interviewees described how they had been treated with contempt, rather than compassion, and the 'brown envelope days', mentioned earlier, tell us how commands and demands for proof are experienced as threatening: "We just feel like beggars, sitting there with our hands out." An existence overshadowed by 'brown envelopes' speaks of official intrusion, personal capability assessments, ongoing struggle with debts and the bedroom tax (or penalty for under-occupancy), and has led to missed meals, fears of eviction and strained relationships. Thus, welfare provisions, originally arranged to help those in need are increasingly interpreted as 'an instrument of punishment' (Clark and Heath, 2014, p ix). Hard-time experiences breed resentment and the animosity is seemingly often directed at people – by objective measures – more or less in the same boat.

Crucially, few raged against the bankers, and such concerns were only occasionally articulated: "Where is all this money, all this electronic money that's gone missing? How has it gone missing?

Who is accountable for it?" (unemployed, male, 47). Instead, constant resentment was fuelled by the belief that other poor people were somehow getting a better deal and were better off. For many of the interviewees, amid mentions of 'layabouts', merely asking for their thoughts on social security invited a defensive response. However, the system or the people responsible for the scrounger label were rarely challenged, leaving Britain's poor further vulnerable to division. A couple of interviewees, all exceptionally well educated, challenged the scrounger discourse. A university student from an impoverished background argued: "I think that it is rubbish about them [benefits] being too generous." Another indebted professional (employed, male, 50), also with a university degree and supporting a family of five, dismissed concerns about scrounging: "Rich people don't pay any tax at all, and what they should pay is ridiculously low anyway ... [so] ... who's the scrounger?"

Division within the One Nation

The One Nation politics, based on the general improvement of conditions for all, needs to be scrutinised against the backdrop of the hard-time experiences of the few. First, the One Nation discourse appears, in view of our findings, as rhetorical at best. The *failure to act* on a One Nation basis demonstrates a lack of consideration for 'all'. Second, the One Nation politics evokes a fundamentally nationalist rhetoric of the nation as homogenous and as one, which creates further resentment and the pointing of fingers within diverse societies. With reference to the latter, the electoral campaign and subsequent win for the so called Brexiteers in favour of leaving the European Union (EU) in 2016 contained similar discourses of scroungers, and skivers versus strivers, as those expressed about and within struggling groups. The One Nation constitute no less than a deceptive portrayal of a society in crisis.

The One Nation rhetoric was once evoked by the Conservative Prime Minister Benjamin Disraeli in the 1860s and 1870s, and has since been rekindled, and redefined, by a number of political leaders, perhaps most effectively during wars in the face of well-defined enemies. The One Nation has since been recycled by parties on both sides of left and right, following a tradition of claiming to 'govern for everyone' (Seawright, 2010; Wintour, 2012; White, 2015; Umunna, 2016). Ed Miliband, leader of the Labour party in 2012, invited members of his party to become 'a One Nation party', 'a One Nation government' to build 'a One Nation Britain', as he evoked Disraeli's vision of 'a Britain where *patriotism, loyalty, dedication to the common cause* courses through the veins of all and nobody feels left out' (Miliband, 2012, emphasis added). David Cameron, on his re-election as Prime Minister in 2015 (and following the independence referendum in Scotland in 2014), took on the One Nation with additional meaning, as he promised to 'bring our country together, our United Kingdom together ... I want my party, and I hope a government I would like to lead, to reclaim a mantle that we should never have lost – the mantle of One Nation, one United Kingdom' (cited in White, 2015; Parker and Vina, 2016).

The analogy of the One Nation Britain has recalled dimensions of a shared destiny and shared prosperity in classical nationalist terms and cannot be separated from the rhetoric of 'all in it together' or the dedication to a common cause. Its rhetoric reinforces the nation as one, equal, and classless, as a community of shared experiences, and ignores evidence to the contrary, with implications for those, who, by objective standards, are left out without access to such a community. A single, part-time employed mother (38), who described herself as British Black Caribbean, articulated this as follows: "They talk about one nation but it is not like that... They lie. One nation? We are not *one* nation."

Promoting society as one of shared burdens stands in stark contrast with reality and seemingly contributes to resentment. Public discourses of the 'common cause' in austere times have, to various degrees and from different perspectives, linked austerity to the development of community spirit. The public discourse even suggested that: 'Every cloud has a silver lining and in these dark economic times, it seems it is the UK's volunteer movement that may be set to flourish' (Jackson, 2009; BBC, 2009). Taking this even further, 'thanks to the recession, we're no longer obliged to keep up with the Joneses. Instead, we're rediscovering the joys of old-fashioned neighbourliness' (Fellowes, 2009, in *The Telegraph*). The allegedly thriving formal voluntary sector was discussed in other newspapers, too, including the *Observer*, *Guardian* and *Mirror*. The experiences of hard times, as recounted in this study, were in no single instance described as a struggle of keeping up with the Joneses.

Claims that Britons have demonstrated a 'Blitz-style spirit to deal with the hardship' may acknowledge the severity of hardship, but have simultaneously insisted it brought out 'the best in people', who 'rally round to help each other' (Beattie, 2008, citing Liam Byrne in the *Mirror*). Arguably, this is not coherent with our findings. As Carr (2016) puts it:

> As in the 1930s, we live in times of governmental appeasement tempered by the language of war. However, in the age of Cameron rather than Chamberlain the broad political concern before us is economic, not military. Spreadsheets and graphs, rather than maps and flight patterns, dominate the agenda. (p 1)

The return of war-inspired national rhetoric with regards to the recession was perhaps to be expected, but public discourses did not consider the various dimensions of hard times and misrepresented the experiences of them. Notably, the so-called old-fashioned neighbourliness, collective mindedness, or community spirit may well have been formed and fostered through enforced national bonds during the Second World War. For instance, remarking on the corrosive effect on inequality, Judt (2010) wrote in *Ill Fares the Land* about austerity of the wartime period as contributing to fostering neighbourliness. However, the mobilisation took place in a different socioeconomic context and in the face of a well-defined and external enemy. (In the UK, domestic disunity may also have been challenged through strikes and demonstrations for peace. Nairn (1977) argues, for example, with reference to the First World War, that it virtually saved England from civil war.)

The mantle of the One Nation and its stated aim to improve conditions for all appears especially deceitful in its failure to act on a One Nation basis, but also with wider implications for discourses of national belonging increasingly evoking 'oneness' of the nation. As a political strategy, it is supported by essentialist understandings of a nation state that is homogeneous, joining the *one* people with the *one* state. Homogenous nations are impossible to find empirically, but clearly exist as an aspiration, which accounts for discourses on migrants supposedly challenging the alleged oneness, undeserving of membership. As Calhoun (2007) argues, nations matter through their rhetoric and understanding of national solidarity through the lens of nationalist claims (on, for example, membership). The essence of such claims can be described as an ideology of the 'first person plural' (Billig, 1995, p 70) nations are constructed through a process that relies on a coherent master narrative (of we) and does not accommodate contradictions of excluded or vulnerable groups (Bhabha, 1993). As Anderson (1991) once put it, the nation is therefore imagined as a horizontal, equal brotherhood. Nations, imagined by their design and rhetoric as homogeneous and equal – despite all evidence to the contrary – promote the dominant majority culture (Guibernau, 1996), masking their exclusive and unequal nature (Elgenius, 2011, 2016, 2017) and thereby justify 'the existence' of states and governments in the present (see Tilly, 1975; Seton-Watson, 1977; Colley, 1992; Breuilly, 1993; Hroch, 1996). In other words, both the inequality and heterogeneity of nations stand in sharp contrast to the discourse of nations, based on social solidarity, similar experiences and the same identity.

Thus, the discourses of scroungers and skivers have been articulated against 'all' in other contexts, too, and as a 'territorially bounded view of the world which supports the superiority of the entitlements of the native population' (Andreouli and Stockdale, 2009, p 164). National identity as *one identity* does little else but enforce hegemonic narration of the past, present and future, which, by default, are challenged by rival narrations, identities and members (Elgenius, 2011). Clearly, promoted notions of 'continuous occupancy' within a given territory seldom survive critical reflection and neglect competing strands of identities and the stratified sociopolitical and socioeconomic realities (Heath et al, 2007, 2009; Elgenius, 2016, 2017).

There is more to say about the essentialism of nationalist politics in relation to hard-time experiences, especially in the context of Brexit and the Leave campaign, based on the rhetoric of othering and 'deservedness' of citizenship (rights and duties). In public discourse, British citizens were turned into 'migrants' through a process that stripped them of their rights within an economic system induced by the racialisation of socioeconomic inequalities (Bhambra, 2016b). In such a context, the discourse of 'the left behind', the less educated, the poor and the disenfranchised contributed to the racialisation of the working class as the 'white British working class', and as those who had been forgotten or tricked out of their rights. Simultaneously, ethnic groups were blamed for inequalities increasingly shared by the working classes regardless of skin colour. The analysis here must therefore include the '*left out* as well as those who perceive themselves as *left behind*' (Bhambra, 2016a, emphasis in original). Race and ethnicity are crucial dimensions of the politics for all, recently a vessel for resentment and othering invoked by national populism, camouflaging stratified structures on the grounds of class, ethnicity and race. 'Ethnic penalties' paid on the grounds of ethnicity and race with regard to access to and opportunities in the labour market demonstrate similar ethnic hierarchies in western economies (Heath and Cheung, 2007). In the UK, the number of minorities obtaining qualifications has not been matched by the job market with the number of second-generation Black British, British Pakistani and Bangladeshi people experiencing continuing discrimination. With regard to the latter, individuals of Pakistani and Bangladeshi background are three times as likely to live in poverty than those identifying as White British (Li and Heath, 2015).

The nationalist, One Nation rhetoric, in its various guises and applications, is deceptive in its stated intentions of 'governing for all', 'promoting strong and active communities', and 'building a Big Society'. The Big Society ideology, proposing a merger of free market and voluntarism, was associated with the 2010 Conservative election manifesto and the intended devolved responsibility to local communities and volunteers. However, its stated intentions of promoting active communities 'encouraging voluntarism' and devolving responsibility to local communities and volunteers (rather than promoting a big welfare state) are at odds with the realities of declining formal and informal volunteering and diminishing statutory and third sector services (DCLG, 2006; Conservative Party, 2008, 2010; House of Commons Public Administration Select Committee, 2010; Alcock, 2011; Goodley et al, 2014; White, 2015). It may therefore not come as a surprise that over the past 30 years, the figures on *'almost never' trusting* the governments of *any* party 'to place the needs of the nation above the interests of their own political party' increased from 11% in 1986 to 32% in 2013 (Park et al, 2014).

Conclusion

The standard British (and EU) way of defining a recession along the lines of two successive quarters of negative growth fails to capture the destructive social impact associated with hard-time experiences, austerity and increasing costs of living. In reality, vulnerable groups paid a high price for the economic slump. The impact of ensuing austerity measures is thus contrary to the claims of all in it together or still in it together, as discussed in this chapter. Associated implications of social inequality are beyond the scope of the chapter, but it is arguably crucial to address factors other than ability and effort that affect social mobility.

The recession and its aftermath have exposed a divided society with hard-hit groups within. Hard-time experiences undermine social networks and social relations in more ways than one, and to a degree that the traditional notion of a national community must be questioned. This chapter has explored the social resentment associated with hard-time experiences and finds that people often direct feeling of animosity towards those who – by objective measures – are in the same boat as themselves. The experiences of those affected point towards social networks being damaged by hard times and austerity politics, as different socioeconomic groups are hit with different levels of intensity during and after recession by rises in unavoidable costs and differential inflation rates. It is within such contexts that the political rhetoric of the One Nation or Big Society is deceptive and at odds with the stated intentions of promoting strong and active communities. The political rhetoric and policies associated with the economic downturn stand in sharp contrast to the experiences of hardship and socioeconomic deprivation and highlight a failure to act on the basis of One Nation and promote a Big Society. Such hard-time experiences have undermined – rather than strengthened – social relations and communal activities.

Note

[1]   I gratefully acknowledge the contributions by Anthony Heath and Tom Clark to this study.

References

Alcock, P. (2011) *Big society or civil society? A new policy environment for the third sector*, Centre for Third Sector Research. Funded by the Economic and Social Research Council and The Cabinet Office, University of Birmingham and Southampton: Office for Civil Society.

Anderson, B. (1991) *Imagined Communities: Reflections on the Origin and Spread of Nationalism*, New York, NY: Verso.

Andreouli, E. and Stockdale, J. E. (2009) 'Earned Citizenship: Assumptions and Implications', *Journal of Immigration Asylum and Nationality Law*, 23, 164-80.

Bakke, W. E. (1933) *The Unemployed Man: A Social Study*, London: Nisbet.

Baumberg, B. (2014) 'Benefits and the cost of living: Pressures on the cost of living and attitudes to benefit claiming', in A. Park, C. Bryson and J. Curtice (eds) *British Social Attitudes 31, NatCen Social Research*, London: Sage Publications: 95-122.

BBC (2009) 'Osborne gambles with cut plans', *BBC News*, [Online] Available at: http://news.bbc.co.uk/2/hi/8292680.stm [Accessed 18 November 2016].

Beattie, J. (2008) 'Recession is bringing out 'Blitz spirit' claims minister', *Mirror*, [Online] Available at: www.mirror.co.uk/news/uk-news/recession-is-bringing-out-blitz-spirit-368102 [Accessed 18 November 2016].

Belfield, C., Cribb, J., Hood, A. and Joyce, R. (2014) *Living standards, Poverty and Inequality in the UK: 2014*, Joseph Rowntree Foundation and the Economic and Social Research Council, Institute for Fiscal Studies, [Online] Available at: www.ifs.org.uk/uploads/publications/comms/R107.pdf [Accessed 11 November 2016].

Belfield, C., Cribb, J., Hood, A. and Joyce, R. (2015) *Living standards, Poverty and Inequality in the UK: 2015. Joseph Rowntree Foundation and the Economic and Social Research Council*, Institute for Fiscal Studies, [Online] Available at: www.ifs.org.uk/uploads/publications/comms/R107.pdf [Accessed 11 November 2016].

Bhabha, H. (ed) (1993) *Nation and Narration*, London: Routledge.

Bhambra, G. (2016a) 'Class Analysis in the Age of Trump (and Brexit): The Pernicious New Politics of Identity', *The Sociological Review Blog*, [Online] Available at: www.thesociologicalreview.com/blog/class-analysis-in-the-age-of-trump-and-brexit-the-pernicious-new-politics-of-identity.html [Accessed 18 November 2016].

Bhambra, G. (2016b) 'Viewpoint: Brexit, Class and British 'National' Identity', Discover Society, [Online] Available at: http://discoversociety.org/2016/07/05/viewpoint-brexit-class-and-british-national-identity/ [Accessed 18 November 2016].

Billig, M. (1995) *Banal Nationalism*, London: Sage Publications.

Breuilly, J. (1993) *Nationalism and the State*, Manchester: Manchester University Press.

Butler, P. (2016) 'UK austerity policies "amount to violations of disabled people's rights. UN says measures aimed at reducing public spending since 2010 have affected disabled people disproportionately"', *The Guardian*, [Online] Available at: www.theguardian.com/business/2016/nov/07/uk-austerity-policies-amount-to-violations-of-disabled-peoples-rights [Accessed 07 November 2016].

Calhoun, C. (2007) *Nations Matter: Culture, History and the Cosmopolitan Dream*, London: Routledge.

Carr, R. (2016) *One Nation Britain: History, the Progressive Tradition, and Practical Ideas for Today's Politicians*, London: Routledge.

Clark, T. and Elgenius, G. (2014) 'Benefits crackdown leads to divide and rule within poor communities: The coalition's skivers v strivers message is inflaming resentments between those affected by the economic slump', *The Guardian*, [Online] Available at: www.theguardian.com/society/2014/apr/30/benefits-crackdown-divide-and-rule-poor-communities-coalition [Accessed 18 November 2016].

Clark, T. and Heath, A. F. (2014) *Hard Times: The Divisive Toll of the Economic Slump*, New Haven, CT: Yale University Press.

Colley, L. (1992) *Britons: A Forged Nation 1707–1837*, New Haven, CT: Yale University Press.

Committee On The Rights Of Persons With Disabilities (2016) *Inquiry concerning the United Kingdom of Great Britain and Northern Ireland carried out by the Committee under article 6 of the Optional Protocol to the Convention. 6 October 2016. CRPD/C/15/R.2/Rev.1*, Convention on the Rights of Persons with Disabilities. [Online] Available at: www.ohchr.org/EN/HRBodies/CRPD/Pages/InquiryProcedure. aspx' [Accessed 18 November 2016].

Conservative Party (2008) *Conservatives green paper on civil society, A Stronger Society: Voluntary Action in the 21st Century. Responsibility Agenda Policy*, Green Paper No.5, London: Conservative Party Headquarters.

Conservative Party (2010) *Big Society*, Gov.uk, [Online] Available at: www.gov.uk/government/uploads/system/uploads/attachment_ data/file/78979/building-big-society_0.pdf [Accessed 18 November 2016].

DCLG (Department For Communities And Local Government) (2006) *Strong and prosperous communities. The Local Government White Paper. Presented to Parliament by The Secretary of State for Communities and Local Government by Command of Her Majesty October 2006. Volume 1*, Department for Communities and Local Government, [Online] Available at: www.communities.gov.uk [Accessed 18 November 2016].

Dickens, C. (1854) *Hard Times. For these times*, London: Bradbury and Evans.

Elgenius, G. (2011) *Symbols of Nations and Nationalism: Celebrating Nationhood*, Basingstoke: Palgrave Macmillan.

Elgenius, G. (2016) 'The Principles and Products of the Identity Market: identity, inequality and rivalry', in G. Olofsson and S. Hort (eds) *Class, Sex and Revolutions. Göran Therborn – a critical appraisal*, Stockholm: Arkiv Förlag: 337-353.

Elgenius, G. (2017) 'Ethnic Bonding and Homing Desires: The Polish Diaspora and Civil Society Making', in K. Jacobsson and E. Korolczuk (eds) *Civil Society Revisited: Lessons from Poland*, Oxford: Berghahn Books: 257–285.

Fellowes, J. (2009) 'Everybody needs good neighbours', *The Telegraph*, [Online] Available at: www.telegraph.co.uk/news/5195355/ Everybody-needs-good-neighbours.html [Accessed 18 November 2016].

Finch, D. (2016) *Hanging on: The stresses and strains of Britain's 'just managing' families*, Resolution Foundation Report, [Online] Available at: www.resolutionfoundation.org/app/uploads/2016/09/Hanging-On.pdf [Accessed 18 November 2016].

Garratt, E., Spencer, A. and Ogden, C. (2016) *#stillhungry: Who is hungry, for how long, and why?* London: Research Report by West Cheshire Food bank, The University of Oxford, The University of Chester, The Trussell Trust, Cheshire West Citizens Advice Bureau, DIAL West Cheshire (DIAL House), Chester Aid to The Homeless and The Debt Advice Network.

Goodley, D., Lawthom, R. and Runswick-Cole, K. (2014) 'Dis/ability and austerity: beyond work and slow death', *Disability & Society*, 29, 980-984.

Guibernau, M. (1996) *Nationalisms: The Nation-State and Nationalism in the Twentieth Century*, Cambridge: Polity.

Harrington, M. (1997) *The Other America: Poverty in the United States. Originally published in 1962 by Macmillan Publishers*, New York, NY: A Touchstone Book by Simon and Schuster.

Heath, A. and Cheung, S. Y. (eds) (2007) *Unequal Chances: Ethnic Minorities in Western Labour Markets*, Oxford: Oxford University Press for the British Academy.

Heath, A., Curtice, J. and Elgenius, G. (2009) 'Individualization and the Decline of Class Identity', in M. Wetherell (ed) *Identity in the 21st century: New Trends in Changing Times*, Basingstoke: Palgrave Macmillan: 21-40.

Heath, A., Martin, J. and Elgenius, G. (2007) 'Who Do We Think We Are? The Decline Of Traditional Social Identities', in A. Park, J. Curtice, K. Thomson, M. Phillips and M. Johnson (eds) *British Social Attitudes: the 23rd Report – Perspectives on a Changing Society*, London: Sage for the National Centre for Social Research: 1-34.

House Of Commons Public Administration Select Committee (2010) *The Big Society Seventeenth Report of Session 2010-12*, London: Administration Select Committee, Parliament Publications.

Hroch, M. (ed) (1996) *From National Movement to the Fully-Formed Nation: The Nation-Building Process in Europe*, Oxford: Oxford University Press.

Jackson, M. (2009) 'Volunteering "flourishing" in recession', *BBC News*, [Online] Available at: http://news.bbc.co.uk/1/hi/uk/8008428.stm [Accessed 18 November 2016].

Jahoda, M., Lazarsfeld, P. F. and Zeisel, H. (1974) *Marienthal: The Sociography of an Unemployed Community*, [First published 1933], London: Tavistock Publishers.

Judt, T. (2010) *Ill Fares the Land: A treatise on our present discontents*, London: Penguin.

Kellner, P. (2012) 'A quiet revolution', *Prospect Magazine*, [Online] Available at: www.prospectmagazine.co.uk/magazine/a-quiet-revolution-britain-turns-against-welfare#.U1pEefaVTe5 [Accessed 18 November 2016].

Laurence, J. (2015) *The UK experienced a sharp drop in volunteering behaviour following the Great Recession*, The London School of Economics British Politics and Policy, [Online] Available at: http://blogs.lse.ac.uk/politicsandpolicy/drop-in-volunteering-post-recession/ [Accessed 18 November 2016].

Laurence, J. and Lim, C. (2015) 'Doing good when times are bad: volunteering behaviour in economic hard times', *The British Journal of Sociology*, 66, 319–344.

Li, Y. and Heath, A. (2015) *CSI 10: Are we becoming more or less ethnically-divided?* Briefing note, Oxford Centre for Social Investigation, Nuffield College, University of Oxford, [Online] Available at: http://csi.nuff.ox.ac.uk/wp-content/uploads/2015/03/CSI_10_Ethnic_Inequalities.pdf [Accessed 18 November 2016].

Miliband, E. (2012) *Speech at the Labour Conference*, Labourlist, [Online] Available at: http://labourlist.org/2012/10/ed-milibands-conference-speech-the-transcript/ [Accessed 18 November 2016].

Moreton, C. (2015) 'Food banks in the UK: Volunteers face a growing battle as benefits crisis bites. Food banks barely existed when David Cameron came to power in 2010, but now there are 425 across the country', *The Independent*, [Online] Available at: www.independent.co.uk/news/uk/home-news/food-banks-in-the-uk-volunteers-face-a-growing-battle-as-benefits-crisis-bites-a6762011.html [Accessed 18 November 2016].

Nairn, T. (1977) *The Break-up of Britain: Crisis and Neo-Nationalism*, London: New Left Review Editions.

Owen, J. (2016) 'Britons driven to food banks by poverty seen as 'collateral damage' by DWP, says Trussell Trust', *The Independent*, [Online] Available at: www.independent.co.uk/news/uk/home-news/britons-driven-to-food-banks-by-poverty-seen-as-collateral-damage-by-dwp-says-trussell-trust-a6794101.html [Accessed 18 November 2016].

Park, A., Bryson, C. and Curtice, J. (2014) *British Social Attitudes 31, NatCen Social Research*, London: Sage Publications.

Parker, G. and Vina, G. (2016) 'Cameron seeks to regroup Tories with 'one nation' Queen's Speech', *London: Financial Times*, [Online] Available at: www.ft.com/content/25df2b9e-1c4b-11e6-a7bc-ee846770ec15 [Accessed 18 November 2016].

Putnam, R. D. (2000) *Bowling Alone: The Collapse and Revival of American Community*, New York, NY: Simon and Schuster.

Richards, L. (2015) *CSI Report 8: Are we becoming lonelier and less civic in Britain?* Briefing note, Oxford Centre for Social Investigation, Nuffield College, University of Oxford, [Online] Available at: http://csi.nuff.ox.ac.uk/wp-content/uploads/2015/03/CSI_8_Social_Capital.pdf [Accessed 18 November 2016].

Richards, L. and Heath, A. (2015) *CSI 15: The uneven distribution and decline of social capital in Britain*, Briefing note, Oxford Centre for Social Investigation, Nuffield College, University of Oxford, [Online] Available at: http://csi.nuff.ox.ac.uk/wp-content/uploads/2015/11/CSI_15_The_uneven_distribution.pdf [Accessed 18 November 2016].

Seawright, D. (2010) *The British Conservative Party and One Nation Politics*, New York, NY and London: Continuum.

Seton-Watson, H. (1977) *Nations and States*, London: Methuen.

Tilly, C. (ed) (1975) *The Formation of National States in Western Europe*, London: Princeton University Press.

TT (The Trussell Trust) (2016) 'End of Year Stats: Trussell Trust foodbank use remains at record high with over one million three-day emergency food supplies given to people in crisis in 2015/16', *The Trussell Trust Blog*, [Online] Available at: www.trusselltrust.org/news-and-blog/latest-stats/end-year-stats/ [Accessed 18 November 2016].

Tunstall, R. and Fenton, A. (2009) *Communities in recession: the impact on deprived neighbourhoods*, London: Joseph Rowntree Foundation.

Umunna, C. (2016) 'Every party lays claim to the One Nation mantle, but it's an aspiration not a reality', *The Independent*, [Online] Available at: www.independent.co.uk/voices/every-party-lays-claim-to-the-one-nation-mantle-but-its-an-aspiration-not-a-reality-a6943321.html [Accessed 18 November 2016].

White, M. (2015) 'Cameron vows to rule UK as 'one nation' but Scottish question looms', *The Guardian*, [Online] Available at: www.theguardian.com/politics/2015/may/08/david-cameron-uk-one-nation-scotland-election [Accessed 18 November 2016].

Wintour, P. (2012) 'Ed Miliband moves to claim Disraeli's 'one nation' mantle', *The Guardian*, [Online] Available at: www.theguardian.com/politics/2012/oct/02/ed-miliband-one-nation-speech1 [Accessed 18 November 2016].

YOUGOV (2012) *Prospect Survey Results Welfare Reform. 23 February 2012*, YouGov, [Online] Available at: https://d25d2506sfb94s. cloudfront.net/cumulus_uploads/document/x3d4a39z0a/YG-Archives-Prospect-Results-welfareReform-120130.pdf [Accessed 11 November 2016].

Part II
The practice of social good

FOUR

Austerity and social welfare in the UK: a perspective from the advice sector

Amardeep Bansil

The advice sector has always had a pivotal role in assisting the destitute and most vulnerable in society. With austerity, its pivotal role has increased in importance, particularly in the United Kingdom (UK). The roots of austerity can be traced to the financial crisis of 2008 (Oxfam, 2013), which required the UK government to bail out British banks to prevent a collapse of the banking system; this led to an economic recession considered to be one of the worst in British history.

The cost of the bail-out is considered to be in the region of £141 billion, with estimated liabilities amounting to over £1 trillion (NAO, 2013). The Labour government introduced counteractive measures in the form of a fiscal stimulus programme (BBC, 2008) (including a temporary reduction in VAT and bringing forward investment spending) in an attempt to revive and stabilise the economy, which temporarily staved off the full impact of austerity.

Following the general election in 2010, the newly formed Conservative–Liberal Democrat coalition government promptly withdrew the stimulus programme and implemented severe spending cuts, mainly in the form of cuts to social security and public services, which the government felt were necessary to reduce the budget deficit and promote economic growth (HM Treasury, 2010).

This is the point at which the advice sector felt the full blast of austerity. There was a heightened demand for free advice that was difficult to meet due to the reduction in funding and resulting effect on service delivery. This necessitated large organisations within the sector to consider more creative and effective ways of enabling members of the public to access services, information and advice to help them with their problems.

Citizens Advice has always been a key player within the advice sector and is the UK's largest provider of free advice for members of the public. It is a network of 316 independent charities (referred to as Citizens Advice Bureaux, or CABs)[1] throughout the UK that gives free, confidential, impartial and non-judgemental information and advice to assist people with the problems they face. The twin aims of the Citizens Advice service are to provide the advice people need for the problems they face and *to improve the policies and principles that affect people's lives.*

This chapter examines the implementation of austerity measures and their impact on the advice sector and on vulnerable groups in the London Borough of Havering and the Royal Borough of Greenwich. I held roles as a volunteer, paid staff member and trustee at Havering CAB from April 2009 to November 2011, and I have been a paid staff member at Greenwich CAB since November 2011.

There are pockets of deprivation concentrated within two areas of Havering that fall into the category of the 10% most deprived areas in England, and 11 small areas in Havering falling into the category of the 20% most deprived areas in England (London Borough of Havering, 2013). Greenwich has the fifth highest unemployment rate of any London borough at 8.1%, and 48% of 19-year-olds in the borough have no qualifications, the highest rate in London (London's Poverty Profile, 2016).

In this chapter I argue that the austerity measures, particularly the welfare benefit reforms and legal aid cuts, have had a detrimental effect on vulnerable groups, including disabled people. The evidence presented in the chapter suggests that there is a direct correlation between legislative reforms and flawed decision-making processes by government departments (including the Department of Work and Pensions) necessitating a growing reliance on the advice sector.

The financial crisis and its impact on the advice sector

In 2009, the country was in the first stages of the economic recession and local and national institutions were attempting to take pre-emptive measures to reduce its impact. Citizens Advice had a comprehensive training programme that covered 11 enquiry areas; however, in anticipation of the increased demand for services, it developed an accelerated training programme for debt and welfare benefits, delivered by individual bureaux within the network, including Havering CAB.

Prior to the onset of austerity, Havering CAB had been focusing on expanding its operations and range of services. This was mainly due to the fact that funding for various projects was readily available and funders were more generous with grants that were able to cover the full costs of the proposed work. In addition, the grants would be awarded for multi-year work to enable full project development and impact measurement. A majority of the grants did not have onerous reporting conditions attached to them, enabling the bureau to focus on effective delivery.

Furthermore, funding could readily be obtained for innovative and collaborative work that was instrumental in facilitating greater synergy between stakeholders, leading to stronger relationships. One example of this is when Havering CAB worked closely with the council to develop its public contact centres and library outreach activities to improve access to a range of services for members of the public throughout the borough. Through this initiative, vulnerable and isolated groups were able to receive advice and support from the council and independent organisations, including Havering CAB, at a location convenient to them.

The increased funding streams allowed organisations within the advice sector to operate at optimum capacity and have sufficient resources to provide an effective service. There was also adequate provision for training that greatly assisted in staff development.

As the initial impact of the economic recession hit in 2009, there was still sufficient funding available for projects to address the effect, from both local and national sources. In Havering, the council readily funded additional advice sessions throughout the borough to meet the projected demand. Havering CAB was also taking appropriate steps to strengthen itself by holding more volunteer recruitment drives to support its core services.

Nationally, the government accepted the severity of the situation and provided funding for projects such as the Mortgage Rescue Scheme, which was set up to help vulnerable households who were at risk of having their homes repossessed as a result of increased unemployment brought on by the recession (Department for Communities and Local Government, 2008). Havering CAB was involved in this scheme and worked closely with the council to develop and deliver the project.

The full impact of austerity became apparent within the advice sector following the 2010 general election. The newly formed Conservative–Liberal Democrat coalition government wasted no time in implementing cuts to public spending.

Each independent Citizens Advice Bureau secures its core funding from the local authority in which it is situated, most commonly in the form of annual or multi-year grants. The amount of funding differs drastically across local authorities (depending on their budgets) and CABs have to adapt their level of service based on this. The core funding is important as it is the only consistent form of income available to CABs and is critical in meeting staff and operational costs.

Spending cuts to public services affected both central and local government funding, which had a knock-on effect on the advice sector; funding became more competitive with multi-year grants being replaced by service-level agreements, contracts and loans for charities.

The spending cuts required councils across the country to undergo major restructures and to prioritise funding to ensure continuity of their own essential services. Organisations within the advice sector were placed at the end of the line for funding, with most funding either reduced or withdrawn completely. Havering CAB was no exception; it fell victim to the cuts imposed by the council and had no choice but to re-evaluate its service strategy. To make it worse, the council expected Havering CAB to provide the same level of service as before, albeit with less money to deliver those services.

As part of the new service strategy, Havering CAB had to consider whether to continue operating advice sessions at all locations within the borough with limited resources or to focus on providing advice at key areas without compromising the quality of advice. After careful consideration and in-depth discussions with volunteers and paid staff members the decision was made to implement the latter option. To put things into perspective, services at Havering CAB reduced from 13 open-door advice sessions per week in 2009 to just seven in 2015 as a result of the reduction in funding.

The changes to the local funding structure also affected the continuation of existing projects funded through alternative sources to the council. Stakeholders were reluctant to continue to extend funding without confirmation of financial stability, which led to restructures and the loss of experienced personnel when these projects came to an end.

Furthermore, funders were no longer covering the full cost of projects, with organisations being invited to bid for smaller grants for projects covering shorter periods. These short-term projects were not always viable as there simply would not be enough time to implement and deliver the projects effectively. As a result, most organisations had to resort to finding multiple funding streams for worthwhile projects, which had more onerous reporting and monitoring conditions attached to them.

Havering CAB had always operated on limited resources and relied heavily on volunteers, who are considered an integral resource. The loss of personnel following the austerity measures placed a significant strain on internal support mechanisms. Advisers were expected to continue to see multiple clients on a daily basis, providing the same thorough and holistic service, which was stressful and demanding; it was typical for staff to perform multiple roles and remain after contracted hours (without any extra pay) to ensure that acceptable standards were met. The increased pressure on the service also affected the ability to recruit and retain volunteers.

Citizens Advice and each bureau within its network are individually governed by a board of trustees, which assumes overall responsibility for the organisation. Traditionally, boards have met on a quarterly basis to discuss aspects of governance. Trustees could easily be recruited, as this time commitment was manageable.

The continual changes produced by the cuts necessitated a departure from the conventional approach of meeting a handful of times a year to more regular meetings and greater expectation for trustees to be more involved. This in turn made it more difficult to recruit and retain trustees, as prospective trustees were unable to commit sufficient time to the bureau.

Boards had to begin operating in a much more strategic manner to avoid bureaux potentially closing down in the near future. Trustee leads were established to improve policies and practices and to strengthen the management function. In addition, subcommittees were formed to consider commercially sustainable options, such as setting up social enterprise schemes and potentially merging with local advice agencies as a way of ensuring survival.

Overall, in my opinion, although the austerity measures have been brutal, they have changed the way boards operate for the better, as there is now an emphasis on taking proactive and realistic long-term measures to ensure the continued existence of their organisation.

Impact of austerity on vulnerable groups

The economic recession and subsequent spending cuts placed millions of households in financial hardship and poverty, and those already facing poverty saw their situation worsen. In 2013, 7.8% of the UK population was considered to be in persistent income poverty (defined as being in poverty both in the current year and at least two out of the three preceding years), equivalent to around 4.6 million people (ONS, 2014). This section explores two important austerity measures, namely legal aid and welfare reforms, and their impact on impoverished and vulnerable groups.

Legal aid

Legal aid is designed to help those with a low income obtain expert advice and representation, and it aims to avoid potential miscarriages of justice. It is administered by the Legal Aid Agency, which funds solicitors' firms and advice agencies to advise people on their legal problems. This type of funding was an essential funding stream for some advice agencies and greatly improved the quality of advice being offered to the public.

Havering CAB received legal aid funding for welfare benefit, which permitted it to employ an expert to provide legal advice (and representation) to those clients who qualified for assistance. The typical client base included a substantial number of disabled clients whose medical conditions understandably meant that they had to rely on the welfare benefit system for support. The role of the expert was integral in championing their rights and providing vital support when unreasonable decisions relating to their eligibility for welfare benefits were made against them.

Notwithstanding the above, the expert provided support to advisers, which in turn assisted with their development. This enhanced the service provision as clients who did not qualify for legal aid could still be given expert advice and be supported by generalist advisers. With an improved understanding of complex benefit areas, the bureau actively participated in policy initiatives to ensure that benefit authorities could routinely be kept under check when clients' rights were being infringed. This facilitated greater synergy between involved parties to ensure effective mechanisms were in place to resolve problems without unnecessary delay.

Under pressure to cut budgets, the government introduced changes to the provision of legal aid for a number of civil cases (Legal Aid, Sentencing and Punishment of Offenders Act 2012), including welfare benefits. It argued that people were often in a position to resolve cases of their own accord without needing to resort to expert help, and that court and tribunal processes could be avoided in this way.

The government criticised the legal aid system as being an 'extraordinary, generous system' but through the cuts failed to take appropriate measures to protect vulnerable groups. The reforms removed whole categories of law for the scope of legal aid and implemented restrictive criteria for those categories that remained.

Considerable changes to eligibility were made to family, immigration, housing, debt and employment cases. Support for welfare benefit cases was almost completely withdrawn and only existed for appeals to the upper tribunal or high court. Discretionary funding, known as exceptional case funding, is still in place, although it is notoriously difficult to secure due to its stringent eligibility criteria and lengthy application process.

The changes dealt a serious blow to Havering CAB's finances, which affected service delivery. The welfare benefit expert post was made redundant and those clients who previously qualified for assistance now had to be seen through the normal channels by generalist advisers who were nevertheless expected to provide similar levels of expert advice.

Moreover, the changes to legal aid for other enquiry areas, such as employment, housing and family law, led to a considerable increase in demand in services that is still prominent today. At Greenwich CAB, clients frequently request assistance with complex legal enquiries and are often directed to the service by solicitors' firms or specialist advice agencies that are unable to assist them under the new legal aid structure.

In particular, there has been a surge in demand for assistance with civil cases involving family law, including separation, divorce and child contact. Litigants in person find it difficult to comprehend the complex court processes involved and often require assistance.

This clearly contradicts the government's argument that people are capable of resolving their disputes without expert help. The government has also failed to adequately invest in information sources for potential litigants, placing this burden on the advice sector instead.

Citizens Advice provides each of its member organisations access to its information system (known as Advisernet), which contains general information on an extensive range of enquiries. It also provides detailed reference books for some of the enquiry areas, for instance, employment and welfare benefits.

Nevertheless, members are not well equipped to replace expert advice on the strength of information systems alone, which are in essence very general. This is illustrated by the following case study:

> John recently separated from his wife and they both agreed that their son, Jack, would remain with her. They verbally agreed on contact visits; however, following an altercation John's wife is refusing him any access to their child. He has tried to resolve matters with his wife but she is uncooperative. He has been advised to apply to court for child contact but needs help doing so.

An adviser would be in a position to provide general advice on John's situation, but would lack the knowledge and training to help him complete the appropriate court forms or to represent him in court.

In this situation, the adviser would have no choice but to refer John to a solicitor, whose services he may not be in a position to afford.

The changes in legal aid have placed destitute and vulnerable people at a clear disadvantage and have led to an increase in miscarriages of justice (Rowe, 2015). We find that people are deterred from taking legal action to protect their rights either because they are too intimidated to do so or because they simply cannot get the support they need due to the overstretched resources of the advice sector. The government's notion of creating a litigant in person scenario is utterly preposterous, as the existing legal framework for most civil cases remains complex, even for experienced advisers.

Welfare Reform Act 2012

The Welfare Reform Act 2012 (HM Government, 2012) was enacted on 8 March 2012 and forms part of the Conservative–Liberal Democrat government's policy to reduce welfare dependency and to support working families. The changes brought about by the Act have considerably changed the landscape of welfare benefits and include the following notable reforms that will be explored in more detail within this section.

- Under-occupancy charge: perhaps one of the most controversial reforms of the Act was the change to Housing Benefit brought about by imposing an under-occupancy charge on social housing tenants, which penalised tenants for having a spare bedroom. The official rationale of the reform was twofold: first, to encourage social housing tenants living in properties too big for their needs to move into smaller ones so the housing stock could be better utilised, and second, to reduce the overall Housing Benefit bill (Wilson, 2013).
- Personal Independence Payment: this replaced Disability Living Allowance, the previous disability benefit for working-age claimants. Eligibility is measured against a set of daily living and mobility descriptors, with claimants having to score a minimum of eight points in order to qualify for the standard rate or 12 points for the enhanced rate of either component. The government's claims that it is a fairer disability benefit with straightforward application criteria have been strongly contested since its implementation.
- Mandatory reconsiderations: prior to the Act, a benefit claimant could appeal an adverse decision directly to a tribunal without requesting the relevant benefits authority (Department for Work and Pensions, HM Revenue & Customs, local councils and so

on) to reconsider the decision. The Act introduced the notion of mandatory reconsiderations, which now requires all benefit claimants to challenge adverse decisions with the administering benefits authority before appealing to the tribunal.

The following section focuses on the impact of these reforms on vulnerable and disabled groups and the role of the advice sector through a case study that represents a common pattern seen by advisers at Greenwich CAB.

Ingrid is single and lives on her own in her two-bedroom flat, which was provided to her by the council. She suffers from anxiety and depression and has unexplained visual-field loss, which has rendered her partially sighted. She also experiences severe headaches on a daily basis, which are under investigation. She has been living in London for a number of years and has a basic grasp of English. She has no family or friends in London.

The onset of Ingrid's medical conditions required her to stop working and she had no choice but to claim an earnings replacement benefit known as Employment and Support Allowance (ESA). She also had to claim Housing Benefit for assistance with her rental payments and Council Tax Reduction to cover her council tax.

Ingrid was initially informed that not all of her housing costs could be covered as she was under-occupying her property by one room, and a charge was duly applied to her Housing Benefit award. She was expected to meet the difference from her income, which solely consisted of her ESA payments.

As part of her ESA claim, Ingrid had to attend a medical assessment in order to determine whether she qualified for the benefit. Soon after this assessment she was informed that she had failed to satisfy the relevant criteria and was capable of work. This decision automatically caused her other benefits to be suspended, which in turn caused her to accrue rent and council tax arrears.

Ingrid approached the bureau for assistance at this stage, as she was simply overwhelmed with having no income to survive on due to the lack of benefit payments. Ingrid was simply not in a position to meet her needs. She was unable to pay for basic amenities like gas and electricity and could not afford even to buy food; she had had to be issued with food vouchers frequently to ensure that she had some sustenance.

It was important for an adviser to take a holistic approach in Ingrid's case as multiple enquiry areas, namely welfare benefits, debt and housing, would need to be dealt with simultaneously in order to address her situation. This approach would also help identify any potential entitlements and support mechanisms Ingrid could benefit from.

Furthermore, Ingrid's case justifiably warrants a more hands-on approach because of her personal circumstances. Advisers are often trained to empower clients where possible, especially if they are capable of handling aspects of their enquiry competently and on their own, but this was not the case with Ingrid, who required support to manage her affairs due to the nature of her medical conditions.

The following aspects of Ingrid's case were evaluated as part of the holistic approach:

Mandatory reconsiderations

ESA has been specifically designed for people who are not capable of working due to the severity of their medical condition. In order to qualify, a claimant must score 15 points from a set of physical and mental health descriptors. If they are deemed capable of work, they have the right to appeal. Prior to the introduction of mandatory reconsiderations, a claimant could appeal directly to a tribunal and would be paid an assessment rate until the appeal was concluded, which was vital in ensuring that they had some level of income to survive on.

ESA has always been the subject of controversy, particularly with the way in which medical assessments are conducted. The Department for Work and Pensions (DWP) outsources this function to external healthcare organisations. Claimants like Ingrid usually have to travel to an assessment centre and are then examined by a healthcare professional in line with the ESA descriptors. We have found that these organisations are notorious for frequently making wrong decisions by conducting assessments that do not accurately reflect the severity of the claimant's medical conditions. Such assessments are regularly challenged and successfully appealed at tribunal level.

Mandatory reconsideration represents a particularly harsh reform, especially for those challenging an ESA decision, as a claimant is unable to receive any assessment rate payments during the reconsideration stage unless the original decision is changed. If unchanged, claimants have the right to appeal to the tribunal and their payments are only reinstated when the DWP is aware that an appeal has been lodged. The whole process could last for two months and a claimant could be without any money during this period.

Ingrid was in this position, and was assisted by Greenwich CAB in requesting a mandatory reconsideration. In the interim, her options were limited – she could either claim another earning replacement benefit, specifically Jobseeker's Allowance (JSA) or apply for short-term support from the council's Emergency Support Scheme. Both these options were problematic ones, as Ingrid would have had to prove that she was available for work in order to claim JSA – which she was unable to do as she was signed off sick by her doctor – and support under the council scheme was purely discretionary.

Under-occupancy charge

Ingrid was directly affected by the under-occupancy charge because she had a spare bedroom, and although there are exemptions to the charge for certain groups (foster carers, members of the armed forces and so on), Ingrid did not fall into any of these categories. She was against moving to a smaller property as her existing one was suitable for her needs and situated within walking distance of her GP, whom she visited frequently. She was familiar with her local surroundings and had accessible transport links around her. As she was partially sighted these factors were extremely important to her physical and mental wellbeing and it was unreasonable to penalise her for staying in her property. This clearly demonstrates that the rationale behind the reform is dubious and that it failed to consider important aspects that affect vulnerable and disabled groups.

Ingrid's housing need represented another vital social need. From our observations, Greenwich council faced a conundrum as it acknowledged the plight of vulnerable and disabled groups but had to adhere to the law. This particular reform led to a surge in applications for discretionary housing payments that, if approved, would cover the shortfall brought about by the under-occupancy charge.

Discretionary housing payments ultimately come out of the council's budget and Greenwich council set up a dedicated team to identify and assist groups affected by the welfare reforms. This further contradicts the official rationale behind the policy and raises the question as to whether there are genuine savings to be made to the overall Housing Benefit bill. Money spent on these initiatives could be utilised to develop better local services for vulnerable groups or fund the advice sector, rather than support redundant government policies.

Personal Independent Payments

In Ingrid's case the bureau anticipated that because of her medical conditions there was a strong chance that she would qualify for Personal Independent Payments (PIPs) and it helped her to make the application. The application process was relatively straightforward – Ingrid had to make an initial claim over the phone and later received a detailed questionnaire to complete where she had to outline the effect her medical conditions had on her.

The bureau helped Ingrid to complete the form and shortly after she was invited to a medical assessment for the final part of the claim. We had reservations about this particular part of the process as it involved the same organisations used to conduct the medical assessments for ESA. Predictably, Ingrid's claim was refused and she had to be assisted yet again in challenging another wrong benefit decision.

Maladministration on top

In addition to dealing with the constantly changing benefits landscape, claimants and advisers have to put up with the high levels of maladministration prevalent in all benefit authorities. There was no exception in Ingrid's case. Her welfare benefits, debt and housing issues were all interrelated and some of the issues could have been resolved with better internal communications between benefit authorities.

Ingrid was constantly receiving letters threatening action for both her rent and council tax arrears. As she is partially sighted, she found it difficult to read the correspondence and soon began to fear any correspondence she received. Ingrid's Housing Benefit and Council Tax Reduction were administered by the council – the same organisation chasing her for her rent and council tax payments – yet there was a serious lack of internal communication between departments.

Ingrid was not aware that her Housing Benefit and Council Tax Reduction should continue as long as she reports her change of circumstances to the council. Prior to the introduction of mandatory reconsiderations, ESA claimants would have continued receiving these benefits whilst their appeal was pending without necessarily having to update the council.

Since their introduction, these payments are automatically suspended when the ESA payments stop and payment is only resumed once the claimant informs the council of their change of circumstances; Ingrid was not aware of this until she sought advice from the bureau. There is a concern that decision letters produced by the benefit authorities are not in a format that is easy to read and that they fail clearly to explain the impact of the decision on any other benefits claimants may be receiving.

Ingrid's ESA and PIP appeals were successful, which considerably improved her financial situation. She no longer received threatening letters regarding rent and council tax arrears as the departments concerned had been made aware of her vulnerable status. The increase in Ingrid's income also meant that she herself could cover any shortfall in her rent in the event of her discretionary housing payments ceasing.

Cases like Ingrid's are seen on an almost daily basis and are never quite straightforward. There is a desperate need for better support mechanisms for vulnerable groups at a local level and improved internal processes within benefit authorities to avoid protracted resolution times.

Conclusion

Since the financial crisis of 2008 the Conservative–Liberal Democrat government and the subsequent Conservative government have constantly been implementing various legislative reforms and spending cuts to reduce the budget deficit. Whether these have been effective is questionable; public debt has risen from 56.6% of Gross Domestic Product (GDP) in 2009 to 90% of GDP in 2013, amounting to around £1.39 trillion (ONS, 2013). The austerity measures have hit the poorest people the hardest and also represent a form of attrition, both to the advice sector and in relation to disability rights.

The evidence presented in this chapter exposes the vulnerabilities of the advice sector brought on by the austerity measures, particularly in relation to funding. Furthermore, the government's attempts to reduce welfare dependency through the reforms contained within Welfare Reform Act 2012 clearly failed to consider how they would affect disabled people who are the hardest hit by the reforms.

What needs to change? The government needs to take drastic measures to safeguard the interests of destitute and vulnerable people, beginning with overhauling the welfare reforms explored in this chapter. The rationale behind mandatory reconsiderations was to improve the decision-making processes by the Department of Work and Pensions; in practice, they appear to be used more as a deterrent and are unfair (Bloomer, 2014).

It is common industry knowledge that mandatory reconsiderations are rarely effective and almost always proceed to appeal. Worryingly, recent statistics from the Ministry of Justice indicate that there is a steady increase in the success rates of appeals at tribunal level – across all benefits – indicating that the reform has not had the desired effect of improving the quality of decision making.

Furthermore, there are concerns that PIPs are not as fair or as straightforward as the government purported them to be. PIP appeals administered by the Tribunal Service in Sutton (where a majority of Greenwich residents' cases are heard) have risen from 1,287 in April to June 2014 to 14,751 in October to December 2015, with a 61% success rate (Ministry of Justice, 2015). This represents an alarming increase and is unlikely to change unless government policy changes.

In April 2013, 3,665 households in Greenwich were identified as being affected by the under-occupancy charge. To date, 878 council tenants have accrued rent arrears due to the reforms and only 374 have managed to move to smaller accommodation. At the end of December 2015, 2,295 households remained affected by the reforms, including vulnerable and disabled households.[2] People in these categories will continue to require ongoing support and it is unreasonable to continue to subject them to these reforms.

Fortunately, many councils across the UK are carefully considering the impact of the welfare reforms on their residents and are taking proactive measures to minimise their impact. Greenwich council has an anti-poverty strategy that highlights the council's commitment to minimising the negative impact of welfare reforms on families and continuing to promote access to education, training and work opportunities as a way out of poverty (Royal Borough of Greenwich, 2008).

On an operational level, it is vital that advice sector trustees undertake a progressive and adaptive approach and deviate from conventional methods of governance. It would be helpful for boards to actively recruit and retain trustees with previous experience in the advice sector to ensure that the right decisions are being made.

Charities need to champion the fact that they are exactly that – a charity – and take more creative steps to market their work through social media or similar means. They also need to push their boundaries and consider ways of generating income through their own resources with a view to becoming commercially sustainable in the long run.

Almost all organisations within the advice sector have led relentless campaigns that have critically evaluated the spending cuts and their impact on vulnerable groups and are continuing to do so. Citizens

Advice has led successful campaigns to prevent further cuts to legal aid and is considering more creative and practical ways for members of the public to access information and advice.

In conclusion, if things continue the way they have been for the past few years, a number of charities in the advice sector will close or have no choice but to merge with other organisations. There is a limit as to how far a service can contract and still be viable as an entity in its own right. Undeniably, there is a clear value placed on the importance of advice agencies, but without any adequate, consistent core funding the existence of such organisations cannot be sustainable.

Note

[1] Citizens Advice has recently been rebranded and local offices are now known as 'network offices' instead of 'bureaux'.

[2] Royal Borough of Greenwich Welfare Reform Update – December 2015.

References

BBC (2008) 'Pre Budget Report November 2008', *BBC News*, [Online] Available at: http://news.bbc.co.uk/1/shared/bsp/hi/pdfs/24_11_08_pbr_completereport.pdf [Accessed 05 April 2016].

Bloomer, N. (2014) 'Thousands left in limbo in benefit appeals system grinding to a halt', *The Guardian*, [Online] Available at: www.theguardian.com/society/2014/jun/18/thousands-limbo-disability-benefit-appeals-grind-to-halt [Accessed 05 April 2016].

Department for Communities and Local Government (2008) *About the Mortgage Rescue Scheme: Government Mortgage to Rent*, HM Government, [Online] Available at: www.gov.uk/government/uploads/system/uploads/attachment_data/file/15121/1495994.pdf [Accessed 05 April 2016].

HM Treasury (2010) *Spending Review 2010*, HM Treasury, [Online] Available at: www.gov.uk/government/uploads/system/uploads/attachment_data/file/203826/Spending_review_2010.pdf [Accessed 05 April 2016].

HM Government Legislation (2012) *Welfare Reform Act 2012* [Online] Available at: www.legislation.gov.uk/ukpga/2012/5/pdfs/ukpga_20120005_en.pdf [Accessed 05 April 2016].

London Borough of Havering (2013) *Demographic, Diversity and Socioeconomic Profile of Havering's Population*, London Borough of Havering, [Online] Available at: www.havering.gov.uk/Documents/Equality-and-Diversity/Appendix%202_Demographic,%20Diversity%20and%20Socio-economic%20Profile%20of%20Havering's%20Population%20Jan-13.pdf [Accessed 05 April 2016].

London's Poverty Profile (2016) *Greenwich*, The London's Poverty Profile, [Online] Available at: www.londonspovertyprofile.org.uk/indicators/boroughs/greenwich/ [Accessed 05 April 2016].

Ministry of Justice (2016) *Tribunals and Gender Recognition Certificate Statistics Quarterly*, Ministry of Justice, [Online] Available at: www.gov.uk/government/uploads/system/uploads/attachment_data/file/528233/tribunals-commentary.pdf [Accessed 05 April 2016].

NAO (2013) *HM Treasury Resource Accounts 2012-13: The Comptroller and Auditor General's Report to the House of Commons*, National Audit Office, [Online] Available at: www.nao.org.uk/wp-content/uploads/2013/07/HMT-Accounts-2012-13.pdf [Accessed 05 April 2016].

ONS (2013) *Government Deficit and Debt Under the Maastricht Treaty, Calendar Year 2012*, Office for National Statistics, [Online] Available at: www.ons.gov.uk/economy/governmentpublicsectorandtaxes/publicsectorfinance/bulletins/eugovernmentdeficitanddebtreturn/2013-10-02 [Accessed 05 April 2016].

ONS (2014) *Persistent Poverty in the UK and EU: 2014*, Office for National Statistics, [Online] Available at: www.ons.gov.uk/peoplepopulationandcommunity/personalandhouseholdfinances/incomeandwealth/articles/persistentpovertyintheukandeu/2014 [Accessed 17 August 2016].

Oxfam (2013) *The True Cost of Austerity and Inequality. UK Case Study*, Oxfam International, [Online] Available at: www.oxfam.org/sites/www.oxfam.org/files/cs-true-cost-austerity-inequality-uk-120913-en.pdf [Accessed 05 April 2016].

Rowe, R. (2015) 'Legal Aid Reforms "Risk Serious Miscarriages of Justice"', *BBC News*, [Online] Available at: www.bbc.co.uk/news/uk-32072457 [Accessed 05 April 2016].

Royal Borough of Greenwich (2008) *Royal Borough of Greenwich Homelessness Review and Homelessness Strategy 2014-19*, Royal Borough of Greenwich, [Online] Available at: www.royalgreenwich.gov.uk/info/200117/homeless/1539/homelessness_strategy [Accessed 05 April 2016].

Wilson, W. (2013) *Under-Occupation of Social Housing: Housing Benefit Entitlement*, London: House of Commons Library, [Online] Available at: http://researchbriefings.parliament.uk/ResearchBriefing/Summary/SN06272 [Accessed 05 April 2016].

FIVE

Breaking the hold of debt: Cambridge Money Advice Centre

John Morris

Situated 80 km north of London, Cambridge is a world-famous university city, and very much a beacon of prosperity and enterprise in the Home Counties that surround the capital. The well-established university and teaching hospital, together with the recent growth of biomedical, science and business parks, creates the illusion of a city with exclusively affluent, middle-class residents. But among its population of 124,000 (in 47,000 households, UK 2011 census figures) there exists a significant number of people who live in relative poverty, typically in social housing on post-war estates to the north and east of the historic city centre. Cambridge City Council has stated that, while the average annual household earnings in Cambridge were £37,344 in 2012, a fifth of households in the city has annual earnings of £19,169 or less, and one in 10 households earns £16,518 or less each year (Cambridge City Council, 2014). It was the acknowledgement that Cambridge is a two-tier society – where the 'have-nots' live on minimum wage employment or state benefits and are vulnerable to falling into debt – that stirred the compassion of the founding members of the Cambridge Money Advice Centre (MAC). In 2005, drawing volunteers from several Cambridge churches, MAC began offering free debt advice to anyone who felt they could not manage their debts. In subsequent years, we have built up a wealth of experience of working with all sections of the city and surrounding towns and villages. This period of time has seen economic prosperity and high public spending, followed by a financial crisis, which spawned a decade of deepening austerity that is nevertheless showing signs of slow economic recovery.

The Money Charity estimates that, excluding mortgages, the average debt per UK household is currently £7,118 (The Money Charity, 2017). Other estimates that make media headlines are as high as £9,000 (Rickard Straus, 2015). Of more importance is the level of 'unmanaged debt'. The Money Advice Service (MAS) defines this as finding bills and credit commitments a heavy burden, or having fallen behind or missed payments in at least three of the preceding six months. MAS estimates that an alarming one in six adults in the UK is over-indebted. Its research further shows that in the UK you are more likely to be in debt if you are young (particularly aged 25-34), your income is low (particularly below £10,000 per year), you have children, are a single parent or rent your home. Levels of indebtedness in Cambridge (13.6%) and London (17.4%) are close to the UK average of 16.1%. Of that 16.1%, only 17% seek debt advice (Money Advice Service, 2016).

MAC only interacts with a very small proportion of the estimated 2,000-3,000 Cambridge adults in debt who seek help for money-related problems. Between July 2005 and June 2016, MAC has formally advised a total of 256 clients, either individual adults or couples, and also referred a similar number to other, more relevant sources of support. On rare occasions, a client's problems may be resolved in a single two-hour meeting. More commonly, however, work with a client requires three to six meetings, over a period of time ranging from six months to two years. Sometimes, the advice period can be considerably longer, for example if we need to supervise a client's long-term repayment plan. I suggest that the gap between the number of people in Cambridge who would benefit from the advice we can offer, and the actual number accepting debt advice, results from a sense of shame – a societal stigma associated with being in debt. Over recent years, levels of indebtedness of our clients have risen in line with national trends. Between 2005 and 2016, the average household debt of our clients increased from around £10,000 to an average of around £13,000 (Money Advice Service, 2016).

I assumed my role as the centre manager in July 2014, and this chapter explains how the financial crisis and austerity measures, exacerbated by structural changes in credit availability, caused this significant increase. With a growing emphasis on the importance of individual achievement, the stigma attached to financial collapse has also become a greater burden for people facing ever-greater hardship. Austerity has not just affected the bank accounts of Britons, but also levels of self-esteem and the possibility of community life. One particularly detrimental consequence of this emphasis on the achieving individual, and the ensuing humiliation of purported failure, is the difficulty we face in establishing new and enduring social relations through charitable work – even for a charity based on the Christian faith, such as MAC. Shame and guilt are common feelings reported by our clients, and they adversely affect the character of the new relationships we aspire to achieve through our intervention.

Personal reasons for debt

As required by English charity law, MAC is governed by a board of volunteer trustees who employ me as centre manager to oversee the day-to-day operations of the charity and recruit and resource a team of eight volunteer debt advisers. In the UK, anyone giving debt advice must be authorised and regulated by the Financial Conduct Authority (FCA). The FCA requires agencies to adhere to a strict code of conduct, and MAC's parent organisation, Community Money Advice, ensures MAC delivers a high-quality service. By comparison with charities that offer a largely self-help service or refer potentially long-term clients to national debt advice services, the MAC debt adviser's work is considerably more demanding. MAC prides itself on supporting clients throughout their journey to becoming debt-free. As a result, the duration and intensity of client contact is variable and unpredictable. By contrast, most face-to-face work undertaken by volunteers in other welfare services brings immediate and obvious results: the client is helped with practical needs around their home, goes away with a box of food from a foodbank, or is accommodated in a shelter for the homeless.

Our clients get into debt for a number of reasons. The first major reason to consider is lifestyle. For many, living beyond one's means has become the norm. A society based on consumption – which prizes fashionable clothes, high-specification television sets, and subscription TV and smartphone services – has relegated saving for purchases to a quaint ambition, often associated with the everyday life of previous generations who lived through two world wars, inter-war depression, and post-war austerity. 'Living for the moment' requires one to survive from pay cheque to pay cheque, or from benefits payment to benefits payment. Borrowing is used to finance a household need that had not been saved for, or a lifestyle that would be considered beyond the household's reasonable expectations. The politically right-wing sections of the British print media rail against such behaviour when it is financed by benefits or loans that are never repaid. The bitter irony is that the same media positively portray celebrity lifestyles marked by excessive spending, and carry advertising that proclaims that self-worth is only achieved through self-indulgence with luxury items.

Debtors' sheer sense of humiliation and the fear of being judged, including by those in their immediate social environment, often prevents them accessing any form of debt advice. The following example illustrates the kind of lifestyle that leads to spiralling debt:

Barbara had a mild learning disability and lived in isolation from family and society. She developed a shopping addiction, compulsively purchasing clothing and household items by mail order. Such catalogues offered her – someone on low income – a way of accessing credit to make routine purchases. Catalogue payment schemes boasted of very modest weekly repayments, but the overall cost of credit was typically double the cost of the original item, which itself may not have been offered at the most competitive price. With Barbara's first catalogue came an introduction to another catalogue, with a promotional voucher to lure her into more purchases, and hence more debt. A third catalogue, which probably came from the same parent company as the previous two, soon followed. By the time Barbara was referred to us, she had amassed 10 catalogue debts, totalling £12,000. Furthermore, she had four store and credit card debts, with outstanding balances of around £1,000 each. As a compulsive purchaser, Barbara considered such purchases essential parts of living a normal life. She only recognised the outstanding balances as true debt when the total repayments became overwhelmingly unaffordable. Missed payments resulted in interest charges and fees, as the overall debt seemed to be spiralling ever upwards.

A second reason causing unaffordable debt is a lack of money skills. Some of the clients who have been with us the longest simply lack the financial literacy and budgeting skills to manage their day-to-day spending in such a way that permits them to set aside money to pay bills. To them, 'credit' is not just the visible and familiar concept of borrowing from a lender, but it also comes in a form of services that are provided before payment: bills for council tax and utilities relate to services seemingly supplied without choice, and require payments on timescales that are out of sync with the frequency of customers' income receipts. Contracts for TV and internet services, or smartphones, constitute another form of hidden credit, and are offered liberally to our clients. Even from the first month of the typical two-year contract, these can prove unaffordable. This situation is only exacerbated by the challenge to manage monthly payments when income from wages or benefits are paid at different frequencies. Poor parental role modelling or low educational achievement are often the root cause of money mismanagement, as the following example demonstrates:

David had three children and lived entirely on benefits income. He received £170 every week in Child Tax Credit, £250 per fortnight in unemployment benefits, £550 on a four-weekly cycle for disability allowance and child benefits, and £200 each calendar month in child maintenance payments. His regular outgoings, including debt repayments, were all paid monthly, with the exception of weekly rent payments. His cognitive disability made it extremely difficult to manage his household annual budget of £25,000; he had no surplus of income over expenditure to contribute to savings. The purchase of food, clothing, and gas and electricity meter credits was a very haphazard affair, as he was unable to build up any significant interim funds with which to plan a month's spending on such essentials. He often had to rely on emergency food parcels from his local foodbank.

A third reason for getting into high levels of debt is a sudden fall in income. Unforeseen crises that lead to indebtedness are well known to every debt adviser: redundancy, failure of self-employment, and the onset of chronic sickness or disability. Relationship breakdown and consequent separation of the household can bear similar consequences. Here, the resulting mental and emotional distress may distract from preparing for the impact on personal finances, even though the separation could well have been anticipated. In all these instances, the saying 'the bigger they are the harder they fall' holds true. Relatively high-income households can be living comfortably on generous levels of credit, but as soon as a personal crisis hits – such as divorce or personal injury – high spending commitments make what was affordable debt become utterly unaffordable in a short period of time, as can be seen in Sarah's case:

Sarah, a marketing professional, had taken out a total of 10 credit cards without her husband's knowledge. She was falling behind on interest payments on a total balance of £70,000, and risked being petitioned for bankruptcy by a creditor. Sarah approached MAC for help after the couple separated and Sarah had fallen ill, unable to continue her consultancy work. To solve her debt problem, we advised Sarah to sell her share of the joint property to pay off the debt.

Contextual reasons for debt: financial crisis and austerity

Apart from changes to personal circumstances that precipitate people getting into unaffordable debt, easily available credit and austerity have contributed to their problems in recent years. As the UK economy and economic confidence grew throughout the 2000s, so did the availability of personal credit and therefore the level of personal debt. The financial crisis of 2008 led to a reduction in public spending on services and welfare benefits, and caused people to lose their employment or suffer wage freezes. Prior to the so-called credit crunch of 2007/08, personal lending had reached record levels: 100% mortgages were common, and financial institutions were falling over each other to offer loans and credit cards to individuals. Creditors lent and people borrowed with insufficient regard for the possibility of being able to repay. The new Conservative–Liberal Democrat coalition government of 2010 implemented a programme of austerity to tackle the UK's national debt of around £1 trillion (ONS, 2016). Government spending as a share of national income was set to fall progressively through to the 2015 election, and, as it transpired, into the next parliament (IFS, 2015).

There is a distinction between victims of the 2008 financial crisis, on the one hand, and sufferers of 2010s austerity measures, on the other. This is reflected in two broad types of debt: 'middle-class debt' and 'working-class debt'. Middle-class debt is typified by credit from mainstream financial institutions, in the form of bank overdrafts and loans, credit cards and sometimes unpaid taxes. It is not uncommon for a client to have lost work as a result of the financial crisis, and then suffer increased difficulty in finding work due to the cuts of public sector jobs and services during austerity. Working-class debt is typically broader: council tax and rent arrears, unpaid utility bills, and so-called 'payday loans' (short-term, high-interest credit). Credit cards and substantial bank loans or overdrafts are relatively rare in this type of debt, but in their place are catalogue mail order purchases and other forms of 'buy-now–pay-later' credit. Middle-class debt is more likely to result from a personal crisis adversely affecting a client's financial capability, while working-class debt can result simply from living routinely beyond the household's means. A considerable amount of the long-term debt problem among middle- and high-income clients dates from the pre-2008 period of easy credit, while debt among low-income clients can often be attributed to austerity measures implemented from 2010. Austerity has caused MAC's clients to suffer cuts to their welfare benefits. In addition they may have had their family support and mental health services rationed or discontinued, as in the following example:

Mun Yin's disability rendered him virtually housebound. He lived with his partner and full-time carer, Angela, and their school-age son. The couple had borrowed from payday lenders to buy gifts for their son to compensate for not being able to take him on excursions. Their social worker had brought them to MAC because they had been taking out further loans to finance the original borrowing. By that time they had taken out nine loans for a total of £3,000, but owed a further £4,000 in front-loaded interest and had a further £1,500 in utility debts – they had been awarded credit without having to demonstrate any ability to repay. A few weeks into the work with MAC, social services withdrew support for the family. The absence of a social worker to facilitate communication between MAC and the couple, and to provide practical support 'down on the ground', led them to disengage from our debt advice.

Between July 2014 and April 2016, new MAC clients divided equally between those with middle-class debt and those with working-class debt. Predictably, average middle-class debt per household was higher than working-class debt, at £15,000 compared with £10,000.[1] Even the slightest downward change to benefit income has a disproportionately large effect on people already in financial hardship. Throughout the summer of 2013, further restrictions on benefits payments were introduced across the country. People fell victim to the benefits cap, which set a maximum weekly total benefit payment of £500 for childless couples of working age or lone parents with children, and to the notorious 'bedroom tax', which effectively fined people receiving Housing Benefit for under-occupied properties. The coalition government introduced the measures to reduce the overall welfare benefits bill, bring a greater degree of fairness (in the case of the benefits cap), and release under-occupied housing (in the case of the bedroom tax):

> Emily was a single mother living in a town outside Cambridge with five children, some of whom had special needs. Prior to the introduction of the benefits cap, she was receiving a total of £555 per week in unemployment benefit, benefits for children, and support for rent and council tax. When the benefits cap was introduced, £55 per week was deducted from her housing allowance. Since this sum had been paid in full and directly to her landlord, the shortfall meant she began accumulating rent appears. In autumn 2016, the benefits cap will be further reduced to £384.62 (£442.31 in London). Emily was told that, if she worked for a minimum of 16 hours per week, the cap would not affect her. Despite the pressure of having to reduce essential household expenditure by 10%, and then a further 23% three years later, looking after such a large family on her own rendered going back to work impossible.

Not only do we observe a class division in the causes of debt, but there is also a noticeable difference between the debt solutions accessed by the middle class and the working class. Middle-class debt tends to be resolved by setting up affordable repayments that pay off the balance in full or at an agreed discount. For the most part, middle-class people find it easier to solve their debt problem because they have more available funds each month than working-class people. Insolvency might be undesirable because of the threat of losing a mortgaged property, or impossible because the household income is too high to justify it. By contrast, working-class debt is often most satisfactorily resolved with a Debt Relief Order (DRO, a form of mini-bankruptcy). DROs were launched in 2009 for those unable to afford a repayment level that would pay off their debts in a reasonable length of time, and who have next to no assets:

> Jo had been a teacher until a workplace injury left her severely disabled. Unable to work and with impaired cognition, she ran up £20,000-30,000 in non-priority debts, which proved difficult to trace. The level of debt and difficulty in identifying the creditors rendered her ineligible for a DRO. However, MAC could put her forward for bankruptcy, seeking the £705 fee from her union's benevolent fund. The court granted the bankruptcy and Jo was able to rebuild her life, completely free of the burden of debt.

Though the two tiers of Cambridge society might fall into unmanaged debt for different reasons, depending on how they were affected by the country's economic fortunes in the last decade, what unites them is the squeeze on household budgets arising from post-2010 austerity. Whether it is a consequent loss of support services or income, particularly in public sector employment, or a reduction in welfare benefits, the 2010s has seen debtors become less able to manage or solve their debt. Worryingly, this has not deterred a slow but steady increase in personal borrowing in the middle of the decade. Bank of England figures show consumer lending (which excludes mortgages and student loans) reaching an all-time peak in 2008, followed by a decline through to a trough in 2012-13. It then began climbing again at a steadily increasing rate through to the present time. As of March 2016, total UK consumer debt is £183.2 billion, and it is increasing at 9.8% per year. Perhaps in recognition of the challenges faced by debtors in the age of austerity, recent legislation has made insolvency more accessible. The debt ceiling for eligibility for a DRO was raised from £15,000 to £20,000 in October 2015, the maximum value of assets (excluding vehicles) that could be owned rose from £300 to £1,000, and the fee of just £90 has remained unchanged since the introduction of DROs in 2009 (The Insolvency Service, 2015).

Austerity, community building and advisor–client relations

In a time of austerity, the gap between rich and poor invariably increases, with a subsequent negative effect on the sense of community in society. Some debt charities hold money management training sessions for groups of people in debt, which encourages a sense of peer community, but MAC only works with individuals and couples in isolation from their community. As such, we cannot claim to foster relationships between clients, although in any case this is never an easy task, as people in debt rarely share their problems beyond their close family and friendships. One might expect that a charity such as MAC – which tends to bring together volunteers of a predominantly middle-class background and a partly working-class clientele – might help to bridge the gap between rich and poor in British society. But we cannot claim to achieve this either. It is certain that advisers' casework grants them a profound and humbling insight into the lives people living in relative poverty. However, there are boundaries to our work: we do not visit clients in their homes or meet them outside the office, and, in any case, our data prevention and confidentiality policies prohibit us from the sort of social intercourse that promotes a sense of community. Most clients accept that they come to MAC to solve a specific problem, rather than to build relationships. Crucially, because of the stigma attached to being in debt and the sense of failure this entails, many find it helpful to treat the interaction with advisers in a relationally detached manner, maintaining a polite distance between themselves and their advisers.

When MAC communicates with creditors on behalf of clients, it helps to reduce the stress that most clients experience when having to deal directly with the people to whom they owe money. The downside of this is that some clients abdicate all responsibility for addressing their debts, in the naïve expectation that MAC can single-handedly resolve all their debt problems. Occasionally MAC is treated as a convenient mail drop, where the client's incoming mail is left with the team to sort through and respond to. Depositing a pile of mail with us can be a client's way of taking the opportunity to dump mounting debt problems on someone else, and then walk away from them.

As will be explained later in the chapter, MAC's advisers are not particularly looking for open gratitude from their clients. While this is often forthcoming at the beginning of the casework, at the middle-phase stage of researching the clients' finances, a problem of failing to attend scheduled meetings or to follow through with a repayment plan can set in. Sadly, many cases end without any acknowledgment or communication of closure from the client, even though he or she may well have reached a satisfactory conclusion:

> Dale and Sophie had been running their business at a loss for some time, but had not sought any help until their debt problem had reached a frightening scale. They were personally liable for a total debt of £25,000, but had barely £40 spare each month to offer creditors. They were behind with their rent and had not paid their council tax for five years. One creditor had already obtained a county court judgement against them, and the council had appointed bailiffs. Out of desperation, they came to MAC, and we were able to help them apply for benefits that they had not claimed, and negotiated affordable repayments. However, after two missed appointments and failure to respond to all attempts to make contact with them, we had to close the case without resolution, unsure of the reason for non-engagement. We could only hope that another debt advice service would somehow make more progress.

One explanation for this variable degree of interaction with MAC is that clients can view us as simply part of the spectrum of state support. Even though we receive no financial assistance from the state sector, maybe meeting advisers across a desk and answering detailed questions about their finances frames a particular kind of interaction in which clients regard their advisers as agents of the state, invested with the power to forfeit as well as provide. Nonetheless, bringing together advisers of a predominantly middle-class background and a partly working-class clientele helps bring different parts of the population in cities such as London or Cambridge into closer contact. Advisers from a relatively wealthy background – usually in education, healthcare, research, engineering, finance or law – admit that they know or meet few people from disadvantaged backgrounds, even in their own churches. Undertaking debt advice grants them a humbling insight into the lives of people living in relative poverty. This experience forges a greater understanding of the dire consequences of indebtedness and poverty, and perhaps even heightens a sense of solidarity and of community cohesion in an otherwise divided city, even if at a relational distance.

Given the degree of frustration experienced by volunteers, what keeps them motivated to work at MAC? Faith plays a key part in keeping advisers motivated in wanting to address clients' difficulties and bridge societal gaps. Christian-based motivation works on two levels. Taking a highly theological perspective, some of MAC's founding members argued that freeing people from debt is a living liberation metaphor of Christ freeing people from the burden of having to obey a set of rules to try to earn their salvation. In submitting to the sacrifice of dying on the cross, Jesus bore the punishment (of separation from God) intended for everyone who falls short of God's perfect standards. A more practical perspective holds that supporting people who are disadvantaged for any reason is a way of extending to them Christ's compassion for underprivileged groups, and indeed love for all people. The latter view is currently more prominent among volunteers. It is true that some good deeds mirror Jesus's strategic ministry (such as liberation) or match his works of compassion and miracles (such as healing the sick or, in our case, reducing mental distress). However, most people, including myself, would not prefer these over any other good work (such as welfare provision, which is not found in the New Testament miracles) as somehow more authentically Christian. But whatever the Christian inspiration, be it spiritually high-minded or pragmatic, the MAC team members share a common objective: to help solve clients' money problems in a sensitive and person-centred fashion, without any kind of judgement.

Christian service is best carried out in gratitude to God by someone who has already experienced his love. It is easy to fall into the trap of thinking that because you do not meet God's standards, in doing good works you can somehow appease him. As well as discouraging such inappropriate motivation, New Testament teaching promotes a Christian fruitfulness that uses the gifts and opportunities that God has given people to make a positive difference to others' lives. This allows them to continue working with clients, despite the frequent lack of recognition and respect. After all, it is a little easier to cope with frustrations and knock-backs when you believe you have God behind you. Furthermore, our advisers enjoy the sense of an ecumenical community that develops among MAC volunteers. Consequently, I need put little effort into praising the MAC volunteers – instead, my duty is to concentrate my efforts on ensuring that their work is fruitful.

In an ironic twist, austerity can also have a positive impact on external forms of community building, by increasing partnerships and collaboration between various welfare and social action organisations. This is something that is necessitated by government cuts to state welfare benefits and services. Ultimately, all these successful facets of increased community cohesion bear fruit in improving the holistic care provision for vulnerable people in the city:

Mary came to MAC with significant debts that had reached advanced stages of collection. Not only did we help her maximise her income by applying for unclaimed state welfare benefits, but we also linked her up with three other Christian organisations that provided a food parcel, a Christmas hamper and a birthday gift basket for her son.

Conclusion

As a faith-based grassroots initiative, MAC makes an enormous contribution to a relatively small number of people using its services. It cannot promise literally to free people from debt – unless they are eligible for insolvency – but it is able to help people break the cycle of spiralling debt and make the seemingly unmanageable become manageable. This goes a long way towards restoring clients' dignity, hope and control over their lives, taking away the paralysing stress and stigma of being in debt. The nature of our work is highly pragmatic and entirely focused on the individual client. As such, MAC does not necessarily aspire to develop a strong sense of community among people in debt – the stigma attached to indebtedness hinders this anyway. Nonetheless, in an era of austerity, MAC's work has never been more important to the many isolated individuals who live with unmanaged debt. The sense of community with which we are working does not mean that we seek to create an enduring kind of connectedness – rather, we attempt to give the many isolated and distressed people who live among us a sense of not being alone in their strife. Support is always on offer, and those in the grip of debt can rely on our long-term help. Reassuring people in need that they can access a supportive internal and external network is one of our key aims, as we seek to reach out to an ever-increasing number of Cambridge residents.

MAC is a very long way from its ultimate aim of eradicating debt in Cambridge. Small charities like ours do not have the economy of scale to undertake meaningful debt prevention work. In fact, too often clients only come to MAC when their finances have reached crisis point, with eviction orders hanging over them, court action being taken out, or bailiffs visiting to procure their household goods and vehicles. We would prefer to offer budget coaching to people even before they fall into debt, and, in any case if they are in debt, we are far better placed to negotiate with creditors before debts get out of hand. Still, many people are unwilling to face up to their problems, defaulting instead to denial and paralysis until they are shocked out their inactivity by their creditors' recovery activities. The stigma attached to indebtedness makes many people deny their situation until it completely overwhelms them, and hinders us from achieving much purposeful debt prevention. Instead, too often we feel like an emergency or crisis charity.

People will always want to access credit, and, lacking influence over their income, it is their level of expenditure that will decide whether or not their debts will be manageable. MAC could do more to address patterns of excessive spending preventively, but its advisers are reluctant to tackle this issue out of fear that clients will feel judged and shun the safety and welcome that the charity offers. However, we must do more to address the emotional obstacles that cause clients to resist debt advice, both at the outset and at all stages in the process. When clients do not engage with us, it is easy to attribute their behaviour to poor self-organisation or an over-dependency on the advisers, who are then expected to solve the debt problems with little actual client input. More often than not, it is anxiety about being required to face up to their situation that makes clients hide from both creditors and advisers. This fear is a societal issue – austerity politics labels our clients as undeserving or a failure – but, if overcome, would markedly improve clients' motivation and progress to becoming debt-free.

Occasionally, clients visit the office to thank the team after a successful insolvency or completion of their debt repayment plan. This experience more than compensates for the feeling of emptiness when a client's outcomes remain unknown. To see a client's mood lifted so far above his or her starting point, and witness a renewed confidence in engaging with city life, is an enduring privilege of debt advice that outweighs all the woes of false starts and poor client engagement. Taking part in neighbourhood activities is the kind of new community we want to see our clients feeling able to be a part of, without a sense of shame or worthlessness. We might achieve this through getting them out of debt, but it would be so much better if being in debt was not nearly so stigmatised in the first place.

Note
[1]   The average debt of all clients from this period is £12,700.

References
Cambridge City Council (2014) *Key Issues: Anti-Poverty Strategy 2014-2017*, Cambridge City Council, [Online] Available at: www.cambridge.gov.uk/sites/default/files/documents/Key%20Issues%20APS.pdf [Accessed 01 May 2016].

IFS (2015) *Total UK Public Spending*, London: Institute for Fiscal Studies, [Online] Available at: www.ifs.org.uk/tools_and_resources/ fiscal_facts/public_spending_survey/total_public_spending [Accessed 12 December 2016].

Money Advice Service (2016) *A Picture of Over-Indebtedness*, Money Advice Service, [Online] Available at: www.moneyadviceservice. org.uk/en/corporate/a-picture-of-over-indebtedness [Accessed 12 December 2016].

ONS (2016) *Dataset: Government Deficit and Debt Return*, Office for National Statistics, [Online] Available at: www.ons.gov.uk/economy/ governmentpublicsectorandtaxes/publicsectorfinance/datasets/ governmentdeficitanddebtreturn [Accessed 12 December 2016].

Rickard Straus, R. (2015) *Britain's in love with borrowing again: Household debt hits record £9,000 and is growing at the fastest rate in a decade*, Thisismoney.co.uk, [Online] Available at: www.thisismoney.co.uk/ money/cardsloans/article-3007368/Household-debt-hits-record-high-9-000-says-PwC.html [Accessed 01 April 2016].

The Insolvency Service (2015) *Getting a debt relief order*, First published 28 Aug 2015, updated 1 Oct 2015, GOV.UK, [Online] Available at: www.gov.uk/government/publications/getting-a-debt-relief-order/ getting-a-debt-relief-order [Accessed 12 December 2016].

The Money Charity (2017. *The Money Statistics*, The Money Charity, [Online] Available at: http://themoneycharity.org.uk/money-statistics/january-2017 [Accessed 13 March 2017].

SIX

Community finance: the emergence of credit unions in London

Paul A Jones and Michelle Howlin

In the United Kingdom (UK), credit union interventions to serve the poor and financially excluded have been recognised by local and regional government and supported, from the beginning of the 1990s, by grant aid and in-kind support (Jones, 1999). Tackling financial exclusion through credit unions became UK government policy and strategy from around 1999 (HM Treasury, 1999) and, by 2006, credit unions were receiving significant financial investment from local government to expand their reach in low-income communities. Credit unions have also been supported through multiple partnerships with churches and faith organisations, housing associations, community associations, trade unions and employers, all of which have acknowledged the important role of credit unions in serving less well-off members of society. The Most Reverend Justin Welby, Archbishop of Canterbury, for example, famously advanced the role of credit unions in combatting high-cost, payday lenders, which he maintained caused severe detriment to financially vulnerable individuals in low- and moderate-income households. For the Archbishop, credit unions offered an ethical and practical alternative.

Yet, this focus on serving financially excluded individuals and communities has proved to be a two-edged sword for most British credit unions. On the one hand, credit unions have realised their social goals and succeeded in engaging many thousands of people alienated and marginalised from mainstream financial services provision. This success undoubtedly raised political support for and expectations of the sector. Seen as being able to reach out to the poor, they are now regarded by government and others as being able to play a major role in supporting low-income families and, more recently, assuaging the impact of the UK government's welfare reform programme through the provision of affordable and supportive services. However, the rub is that success in serving people on low incomes has often resulted in the weakening of credit unions as financial institutions.

The reality is that serving high-risk vulnerable individuals, commonly demanding additional staff time and resources, is a high-cost endeavour. Restricted by law and by ethics from charging higher rates on loans and fees, credit unions serving mainly low-income communities can struggle to ensure their own economic sustainability. As such many remained dependent on external grant funding to serve these groups (Myers et al, 2012).

Endeavouring to reconcile social objectives and economic sustainability within the context of increasing political expectations has become a constant challenge for credit unions in Britain. External grant support from local government is disappearing in the age of austerity and credit unions have had no choice but to generate sufficient income from trading to survive.

This chapter focuses primarily on the development of credit unions in London, and explores how they are trying to resolve the tensions of remaining true to their mission to serve the financially excluded but at the same time ensure their own economic success and independence. It discusses the background of credit unions in the capital, the challenges they have faced over the years and how currently they are endeavouring to reform as professional financial cooperatives serving the entire community. Credit unions have had to face the paradox that to serve the poor, they must first successfully serve more moderate- and higher-income members.

For some commentators, of course, the tension between social objectives and economic sustainability is unresolvable: they claim that there are always going to be in-built limitations to the viability of achieving financial inclusion objectives through voluntary mutualism (Sinclair, 2014). They question the role of credit unions in promoting government policy and their capacity to respond to the needs of financially excluded communities. This chapter takes a contrary view and argues that with modernisation and reform, credit unions can go a long way to resolve such tensions and make a significant contribution in low-income communities.

Credit unions within the social economy

Credit unions are voluntary, member-owned, not-for-profit financial cooperatives found in 109 countries with some 223 million members worldwide (www.woccu.org). Wherever they exist, they provide savings, credit and other financial services to their members, and offer them a socially responsible alternative to the for-profit, investor-owned banking sector. Alongside a wide range of cooperatives, mutuals, not-for-profit and voluntary organisations, credit unions form an important part of the social economy, characterised by the attainment of social objectives through enterprise (Campos and Chaves, 2012). Based on the principles of self-help, cooperation and social justice, and through the active engagement of their members, credit unions endeavour to deliver affordable financial services, to build the social and economic fabric of society and to advance democracy at a local level.

In different countries, credit unions follow varying paths of development. In the United States, for example, they grew primarily among employee groups (Thompson, 2013), whereas in Ireland, they have focused on creating accessible community-based financial services embedded within neighbourhoods, villages and towns (Jones, 2013). In Britain, credit unions also serve employee groups and local communities, but, inspired by a strong sense of social mission, since their creation in the 1960s they have played a distinct role in tackling financial exclusion and poverty through offering people on low incomes and often on welfare benefits a pathway to financial health and stability. This is not a role that has been undertaken, in any real way, by banks and mainstream financial providers, or directly by the state. Banks have for a long time fled to serving quality customers and exhibit little interest in or capacity for developing products and services for low-income groups. Low-value savers and borrowers are just not profitable for the for-profit banking sector. It has been left to credit unions as third sector, voluntary organisations to reach out to and serve the financially excluded with ethical and affordable financial services.

The emergence of credit unions in London

Credit unions first appeared in London in the 1960s, when newly arrived immigrants from the Caribbean settled in the capital and found it difficult, if not impossible, to obtain credit from mainstream financial providers. At the time, often their only option was to use sub-prime loan companies that charged high, if not extortionate, interest rates on loans (O'Connell, 2005). In the early days, these credit unions were small, intimate community organisations. In many cases, they operated from church or community halls, or even from members' private homes, and high priority was given to the engagement of members as volunteers to run the organisation. Members tended to know one another, and maintaining strong social bonds took priority over any real focus on economic growth and development. Throughout the 1960s, for example, Hornsey Credit Union in London only had about 200 members at any one time.

Nevertheless, by the early 1970s, the UK government had recognised the potential of these grassroots, community-based credit unions to reach out to people not served, or poorly served, by banks and mainstream financial providers. This led to the passing of the Credit Unions Act in 1979, when the government saw that legislation was central to any effective long-term development. Following the Act, there was increased interest in credit unions in London and in their potential to offer not only local communities, but also associations and groups of workers, access to savings and loans products appropriate to their needs. London taxi drivers – cabbies – were one group that had routinely struggled to borrow from banks. Consequently, in 1979, the Licensed Taxi Drivers' Association Credit Union was the second credit union to be registered under the new Act. Through the 1980s and 1990s, the social and economic deprivation faced by many low-income communities in London encouraged the continued development of community-based credit unions, often supported by local authorities as a strategic response aimed at combatting poverty (Jones, 1999).

Political support for credit unions grew and they became increasingly seen by central government as vehicles to offer affordable financial services to people on low incomes, those that banks and financial institutions were unwilling or unable to serve (Thomas and Balloch, 1994; Donnelly, 2004). By 2001, with the support of grant aid mainly from local and regional government, around 60 small credit unions had been established in London, the majority serving low-income neighbourhoods.

Community solidarity and action

These early community-based credit unions arose out of the grassroots experience of people struggling to make ends meet on low incomes. Even when assisted by grant aid or other local authority support, credit unions were always created by local people responding voluntarily to the financial needs of their own communities. Local activists established them as third sector organisations committed to self-help, mutuality and social purpose. Many of the early credit unions had much more in common with community development initiatives than they did with any recognisable formal financial institution. Social goals were often much more evident than economic ones. There was a strong focus on the mobilisation of volunteers, on their education and training, and on their participation in a movement based on solidarity and collective action. In fact, research in 1999 revealed that 83% of community credit unions described themselves as community development projects to tackle poverty or to provide services for disadvantaged people (Jones, 1999).

Throughout the 1990s, and into the new century, many local authorities throughout Britain, including the Greater London Authority, in addition to grant aid, supported the development of credit unions through the employment of credit union development workers to mobilise and train volunteers (Jones, 1999). The focus was on empowering people, marginalised from the financial system, to take collective action to transform their own lives and that of their communities (Ledwith, 1997; Fuller and Jonas, 2002). Research into the motivations of over 1,000 of these volunteers revealed the strong social ethos that underpinned their commitment (Jones, 2005). Most felt part of a social movement committed to justice and societal transformation. The widespread commitment to achieving social goals among volunteers explains why so many people from churches, trade unions and community organisations became involved freely in running credit unions. In 2005, it was estimated that there were some 10,000 volunteer directors, committee members and operational staff working in credit unions throughout the country. These are not people who would have ever volunteered in a bank.

The engagement of volunteers was much more significant to credit unions than any cost savings through using unpaid labour. Volunteers, whether as directors, committee members or operational staff, were regarded as a key factor in enabling credit unions to engage at a grassroots level with people in communities in a way that mainstream financial institutions would find impossible. The social networks of volunteers were seen as important in understanding members, in responding to their financial needs, and in contributing to the social fabric of the local community.

Credit union reform

By the end of the 1990s, however, serious concerns were raised within and outside of the credit union movement regarding the long-term economic viability of this social model of credit union development. These concerns came to a head in 1999, when research undertaken by Liverpool John Moores University revealed that most credit unions in low-income communities were financially weak, vulnerable and served less than 200 members (Jones, 1999; see also Goth et al, 2006). The development of credit unions serving employee groups, which followed a similar model, was stronger, but still relatively modest. Even though social model credit unions benefited their members, and undoubtedly the volunteers who were able to develop new skills and commitments in a community setting, their impact within wider society was marginal. Local authorities and government continued to support credit unions, and were ready to make grants available for their development, but policymakers' expectations and demands were increasingly that credit unions should be able to reach out to many more people, especially in low- and moderate-income communities.

From 1999, credit union activists and public funders began to question the traditional approach to development based on small, tight-knit fields of membership, volunteerism and informal collective action. The Liverpool John Moores University report (Jones, 1999) called for a paradigm shift in credit union development and for the introduction of more business-focused approaches, based on robust business planning, suitable premises, the introduction of computerised accounting systems, and the hiring of staff to eliminate complete dependence on volunteer labour. The shift called for, in fact, a move away from understanding credit unions as community development projects, to seeing them as community-based but professional financial institutions. Subsequent to the 1999 report, research undertaken by the World Council of Credit Unions (WOCCU) in Latin America reinforced the view that, if British credit unions were to build the capacity to make a real impact and expand significantly within low-income communities, a greater reform than the introduction of basic business practices would be required (Richardson, 2000a, 2000b; Jones, 2004a, 2004b). The long-term stable development of credit unions, it was argued in the WOCCU studies, required a more radical organisational and operational restructuring, known as the 'new model' of credit union development (Richardson, 2000a; Jones, 2004a, 2005).

The move from social model to new-model credit union development was based on what Richardson (Richardson, 2000b) defined as seven key 'doctrines of success'. These were serving the financial needs of a more economically diverse membership, rather than focusing entirely on low-income and financially excluded communities; the maximisation of savings, product diversification, operating efficiency, financial discipline and effective self-governance; and assimilation, the process of bringing financially excluded groups into the mainstream economy by providing comparable financial products and services to those offered by mainstream financial institutions. The shift from a social to a more business-like and commercial model of development was not uncontested. Some pundits (Fuller and Jonas, 2002, Fuller et al, 2006) argued strongly that the professionalisation and expansion of credit unions would inevitably undermine their social and community ethos, and, instead of being a radical alternative to mainstream banks and financial institutions, they would become paler versions of the same.

However, despite such criticisms, credit unions in London and Britain generally embraced a process of organisational reform in order to take the benefits of membership to a much wider population, while at the same time endeavouring to preserve and strengthen their historic social and community values. In many places, this resulted in a reworking of the concept of volunteering, away from operational tasks, now often undertaken by paid staff, to a greater focus on the roles of volunteer directors and committee members and that of credit union champions or representatives, who are able to communicate the value of credit union membership directly in local communities and workplaces. Organisational reform undertaken since 1999, accompanied by advances in legislation and regulation, has resulted in the significant strengthening of credit unions both in London and nationwide. This involved, however, an increase in the number of mergers, as credit unions endeavoured to benefit from economies of scale. From 2001 to 2014, despite the registrations of new credit unions, mergers together with some closures resulted in an overall decline in the number of British credit unions, from 686 (the maximum at any one point) to 371. In London, the number of credit unions also halved between 1999 and 2014, to around 30. However, between 2001 and 2014, overall membership of British credit unions rose from 365,934 to 1,046,623 members, and total assets from £318 million to £1.2 billion. Recent total membership figures for London credit unions are not available, but community credit union membership in London grew from 4,943 in 1999 to 55,206 in 2011 (Jones and Ellison, 2011). This figure will have increased since.

Credit unions and financial inclusion

Recognised as serving a market unserved by mainstream financial providers, credit unions were often supported by local authorities with grants or in-kind support as part of their anti-poverty strategies. In London in the 1980s and 1990s, credit unions were directly supported by the Greater London Council and London borough councils. They funded a regional organiser for the Association of British Credit Unions Ltd, as well as a development worker and five development programmes to support traditional social model credit union growth. An influential report published by the Local Government Association in August 1999, following the Liverpool John Moores University report published earlier in the year (Jones, 1999), set out the vision of new model credit union development. It strongly urged credit unions to reform their business models and operations to ensure a wider reach into the low-income population and to achieve long-term financial sustainability. At the time, many credit unions were still dependent on grant aid from local authorities and other sources to ensure the stability of the business.

By the mid-2000s, credit unions were showing sufficient strengthening and promise of reform that they were being increasingly regarded by local government as capable of providing the appropriate range of financial products and services to tackle financial exclusion. Collard and Kempson (2005), Rossiter and Cooper (2005), the National Consumer Council (2005) and McKillop and Wilson (2003) all argued that the needs of the financially excluded would be best served within strengthened, new-model credit unions. The UK government was also growing in confidence regarding the capacity of credit unions to serve low-income communities. It knew that the banks would neither have the will nor the wherewithal to tackle financial exclusion, and so looked to credit unions to fulfil this important role in society. From 2006-11, the Labour government created a Financial Inclusion Growth Fund to expand the availability of affordable credit through credit unions and other social lenders. The primary aim of the programme was to assist financially excluded borrowers to avoid taking out sub-prime, high-cost loans, but rather to access credit through credit unions or social firms. Nearly £100 million was invested into the fund, which provided credit unions with capital for lending and revenue to cover administrative costs.

Through the growth fund, 405,134 affordable loans to low-income members were made, to a total value of over £175 million. Collard et al (2010) in their evaluation of the fund demonstrate that the average (mean) amount originally borrowed was £478 and that the majority of loans (93%) were provided at an annual percentage rate (APR) of 28% or less. Thus a £478 loan repaid at £10.52 per week for 52 weeks results in an interest charge of £59.71. In comparison, at that time, a £478 loan from a home credit company, repaid over 52 weeks at £16.73 per week at an APR of 272.2%, would accrue an interest charge of £391.96. The impact of a saving of £332 on a £478 loan on the budget of a household struggling to make ends meet on a low-income can be considerable. Typically when faced with having to buy basic household items or clothes for the children, with loans from high-cost, sub-prime lenders, the result is over-indebtedness and increased financial vulnerability. Around 90% of growth fund loans were through the circa 100 credit unions contracted to deliver the programme.

The growth fund had a significant impact on participating credit unions, of which there were 11 in London, granting over 35,000 loans to a total value of £15 million. There were at least three major benefits for credit unions – the fund promoted the development of products and services in the low-income market, it strengthened organisational capacity and efficiency, and expanded membership significantly among low-income groups. There was, however, one significant drawback: the scheme entrenched the focus of credit unions on low-income and financially excluded individuals. Of course, serving economically disadvantaged groups has always been regarded as a key mission of credit unions from the beginning, but new-model development, aimed at the stability and financial sustainability of the sectors, requires that credit unions serve a more economically diverse population. The growth fund tended to push back on that key sustainability goal.

On products and services, the growth fund required credit unions to make significant changes to their lending products, particularly removing the requirement of members to save before obtaining a loan and charging higher rates of interest. It also involved moving into transaction banking services, whether through the opening of a credit union current account or the use of a pre-payment debit card. Increasingly, credit unions were accepting the welfare benefits of members into the credit union, and they required a way of accessing cash easily and of making payments. The focus on offering transaction accounts involved credit unions moving to electronic channels for deposits and payments. Unlike previous grant aid programmes, growth fund contracts were only open to credit unions with demonstrable organisational capacity to deliver credit to large numbers of low-income people and payments were dependent on credit unions meeting targets and operating standards set by the Department for Work and Pensions. This had a significant strengthening effect on credit unions. An independent study revealed that 80% of growth fund lenders improved operations and business practices as a result of programme delivery (Collard et al, 2010).

On membership expansion, the majority of managers interviewed in a study into the development of London credit unions (Jones and Ellison, 2011) regarded their credit union's participation in the growth fund as the single overriding factor stimulating credit union growth. Some London credit unions changed significantly. In the years 2005–10, for example, Lewisham Plus Credit Union grew from 1,385 to 5,001 adult members (261%). With growth fund support, it developed a comprehensive range of products and services, including transaction banking with the current account. It has since expanded operations to serve two additional London boroughs, opening a new branch in Bromley. Overall, the UK government regarded the delivery of the growth fund a success. As a result, in March 2011, it announced the creation of a new credit union modernisation and expansion fund of up to £73 million, to replace the Financial Inclusion Growth Fund, which ended that month. For reasons that will become clear later, this new fund was not designed to provide further capital for lending, but rather to modernise and upgrade the credit union business model and operating systems, so that credit unions could extend their reach in the low- and moderate-income population, and ultimately be strengthened and stabilised as sustainable businesses.

Economic and organisational challenges

Many credit unions in London have transformed significantly over the past 10 to 15 years (writing in 2016), both through and after the growth fund period. London Mutual Credit Union, for example, was established in 1982 to provide financial services to council employees, but since has changed its field of membership to serve anyone who lives and works in Southwark, Lambeth, Westminster or Camden. From 1982 to 1997, a period of 15 years, it grew to serve just 1,600 members and accumulated £1.8 million in assets. With growth fund support, from 2005 to 2010, its membership grew from 4,454 to 11,500 (160% growth). In 2016, it served over 21,000 members with a wide range of products and services from its five branch offices. It is a full-service financial institution, offering savings, loans and a current account, with full electronic access for members. It now has over £25 million in assets. Similar transformation and development can be seen in London Capital and London Community Credit Unions, among others.

However, significant economic and organisational challenges remain for credit unions more generally. A 2011 research study into credit unions in London (Jones and Ellison, 2011) revealed a range of difficulties that credit unions face in establishing themselves as strong and efficient cooperative institutions. In London, as elsewhere, credit unions faced major challenges in maximising income and in reducing costs, and in attracting savings and in ensuring effective lending. A significant number of London credit unions were not yet generating sufficient income to sustain and develop the business. Indeed credit unions are still endeavouring to develop efficiencies in operational systems, but this is not easy, since many credit union directors and managers lack the experience, staff or resources to make rapid progress in re-engineering the business. The result was that, in 2011, most London credit unions still depended to some extent on external financial or in-kind support to cover basic operating costs.

Long-term sustainable development depends on attracting an increasingly economically diverse membership, through offering the kinds of quality products and services that people want, and through the kinds of modernised, electronic delivery channels that more moderate-income members find attractive. Even though there are exceptions, most individual credit unions in London lack the resources to develop an attractive range of products and services, and to introduce modern IT and electronic systems. A particular challenge is to develop effective lending at realistic prices, both to attract higher-value borrowers and to meet the cost of serving high-maintenance borrowers with low-value loans. In 2011, for most London credit unions, the lending business was not performing at a rate or size to achieve optimum financial return. The average loan-to-asset ratio among community credit unions was around 56%, whereas 70-80% of assets need to be out on loan in order to achieve financial stability (Jones and Ellison, 2011). Despite growth and expansion, most credit unions overall were still finding it difficult to break through as major players in the financial market. The problem was that development depended on each credit union independently strengthening its own management and operational systems. This is resource-intensive and expensive, and it results in developments in processes and procedures having to be replicated time and time independently in each credit union.

One solution to this problem could to be found in greater collaboration and in the development of an integrated system of shared services. It was for this reason that, in 2011, the UK government agreed to fund a new credit union expansion project, aimed at the development of a collaborative integrated system, containing a core electronic banking platform that would assist in driving greater professionalism and efficiency throughout the credit union movement. The implications of the credit union expansion project for credit unions are discussed next.

East London Credit Union

East London Credit Union (ELCU) is open to everyone who lives or works in one of six boroughs in east London and Epping Forest district. It was registered in 2003 as Waltham Forest Community Credit Union, but changed its name in order to expand its area of operation.

Its development typifies the issues faced by many credit unions in London and elsewhere. Like many credit unions, it arose out of a group of socially motivated individuals, coming together to respond to the needs of people on low incomes or experiencing financial exclusion. Their aim was to provide affordable financial services, to offer financial education, and to enable people to free themselves from high-cost, sub-prime lenders. The founders were inspired and motivated by their Christian faith to make a difference in the local community. They were active in churches across Waltham Forest, and it was through their invention that other residents in the borough and stakeholders from local government and other community organisations were motivated to become involved in the project and to persist through the three years of planning it took to form the credit union.

The development of the credit union was not easy; the volunteers faced many challenges and hurdles. Initially, the credit union received grant aid from the local authority and was able to open up in high-street premises and employ a small staff team. However, growth was not as expected, and with increased rental costs and the non-renewable of funding in 2006, the credit union lost its premises and employees. For the next four years, volunteers ran the credit union initially from a room in a local community centre. It was only through their dedication and patience that it survived. Slowly, with the support of new grant aid and some growth in income from lending, it was able to rebuild its staff team and returned to high-street premises in 2010. Like many credit unions, ELCU has been strongly supported by external grant aid, mainly from local government, initially the London Borough of Waltham Forest, but also from other sources such as the Big Lottery Fund. Though local authority support, it was able to access regeneration funding from a variety of sources. The reason for the funding was always the commitment of the credit union to serve financially excluded individuals, whom the banks and mainstream financial providers have no interest in serving.

The single most significant external financial investment in the credit union, however, was the Financial Inclusion Growth Fund. In 2006, at the outset of the growth fund, the credit union was going through a period of strategic and operational difficulty, but external funding enabled the group to stabilise and reach out to many more people in the community. In the first financial year of the growth fund, in 2006-07, 896 loans were issued, totalling £426,000 (£125,000 directly from the growth fund scheme). Less than five years later, in the financial year 2011-12, the credit union issued 2,367 loans, totalling £1,194,800. The credit union has lent out over £3.5 million, underwritten by the fund; the investment has strengthened the credit union's capital adequacy ratio and the income on loans has improved the credit union's bottom line. Through the growth fund period, 2006-11, credit union membership increased from 935 to 4,024. As in other participating credit unions, the growth fund strengthened the financial position and organisational capacity of ELCU, but left the credit union with large numbers of low-income members, many on welfare benefits, who save little and required low-value loans. These generate little income and are expensive for the credit union to serve. In order to continue to fulfil its social goal of serving low-income, financially excluded communities, the credit union recognised that it had to diversify its membership base and attract people on moderate and higher incomes into membership.

Beginning in 2011, the credit union endeavoured to implement a programme of organisational reform. It strengthened its governance structure through the recruitment of skilled and competent directors to the board, as it recognised that leadership from the top is fundamental to any successful organisational change (cf. Jones et al, 2016). It reworked its business and strategic plan to ensure its sustainable development over the medium to long term. Alongside this, it enhanced management processes and procedures with a particular focus on introducing an effective risk management framework. As part of its approach to organisational reform, the credit union invested heavily in new infrastructure, including digital delivery channels, and in staff training and development. The credit union also moved into new purpose-built premises with improved back-office facilities.

However, the credit union also recognised that more fundamental changes to its business model were required. It accepted that the need for significant digital infrastructure investment to achieve growth and provide the digital access to quality products and services that consumers today expect and require. Consequently, the credit union joined the Credit Union Expansion Project (CUEP) in 2012-16. The implications for this transition to the CUEP programme are discussed later in the chapter.

The credit union also focused on rebranding itself as an ethical, cooperative financial institution for the population at large, and as a socially committed alternative to the for-profit banking system. It remains focused on serving people who are marginalised and excluded from mainstream financial providers, but seeks to broaden its appeal through the provision of competitive financial services. This involved generating marketing messages around the credit union being a source of ethical, fair, community finance, as well as a provider of the kinds of high-quality products that the modern consumer would expect from any professional financial institution. As a sign of growing confidence in the capacity of the credit union to deliver alternative financial services to the population at large, in 2015, the London Borough of Waltham Forest made a £500,000 investment to deliver a range of initiatives, including business lending. However, even though the credit union has often been supported by local government, it remains an autonomous, independent and voluntary financial institution firmly within the third sector. It is clear that it owes its existence to the commitment of numerous volunteers, motivated by social, ethical and Christian values, and dedicated to improving the lives of people on low and moderate incomes. Even though it now employs a chief executive officer and staff team to manage the organisation, ELCU strongly retains its volunteer ethos and values highly the volunteers who serve on the board of directors and who still participate in many of its operational tasks.

In 2016, the credit union undertook research into the motivations and expectations of its volunteers. The research involved a survey of 18 volunteers and a series seven in-depth, structured interviews with current and previous volunteers. As to be expected, a commitment to the social purpose of the credit union to serve people unserved by mainstream providers remained strong among volunteers. Fifty per cent of those responding to the survey said that they volunteered to make a contribution to the community, and 40% said they wanted to be involved in something worthwhile. However, the main motivating factor for current volunteers was to gain or develop experience and skills: 78% wanted to use or develop existing skills, and 83% wanted to gain new skills. The second most important factor was to find employment: 57% stated that they wanted their volunteering experience to help them find a new job.

For the credit union, offering people in a low-income community the opportunity to develop skills and experience to enhance their employability is in itself a social goal and part of the credit union's reason for being. Fifty-six per cent of volunteers said they were involved because they hoped to meet new people through volunteering. This also forms an element of the social focus of the credit union. Through promoting social interaction among volunteers and a sense of local community, the credit union sees itself as contributing to the building of social bonding and bridging in the neighbourhoods it serves. Interestingly, in the interviews, none of the volunteers had heard of credit unions prior to their involvement in ELCU. For the most part they had been referred to the credit union by Jobcentres and partner organisations keen to enable individuals in the community to gain work experience. It was only through the opportunity to volunteer that people became aware of the benefits of social and community finance, and of the active contribution of the credit union to the local population. Typical comments of the volunteers included:

> "Keeping busy, social interaction, and feeling you are contributing towards the community."

> "Putting something back into the community – the number one factor."

> "It makes you feel good as you are doing something for the community; it lifts your spirit. You feel your achieving something: you're part of the team."

> "Volunteering is a way of gaining experience and helping the community. It helps me to build my confidence and my personality."

ELCU is committed to recruiting volunteers to serve on its board of directors, to assist as operational staff, and to promote and champion the credit union in the community. It recognises that its volunteers are key conduits of inculcating the values of cooperative and community finance within the population at large. Through their commitment, the credit union can preserve its position as an alternative to the for-profit banking sector.

Tackling austerity through business success

Like many credit unions, ELCU retains its historic commitment to serving the financially excluded and vulnerable in society, and for this reason both central and local government continues to support its development.

For government, credit unions are particularly important within the context of the introduction of welfare reform. The Welfare Reform Act 2012 introduces a wide range of reforms to the benefits and tax credit system – many of which entail recipients needing to be more financially capable and to have access to products and services that meet their needs. In this respect, government sees an important role for credit unions, insofar as they can enable access to transaction, savings and budget accounts, and offer the financial support people need.

They are also seen by government and other agencies as enabling people on lower incomes to manage their finances in a time of austerity and, often, of reducing incomes. As austerity affects communities throughout the country, people have more and more need of financial services that support rather than undermine stability. The temptation for many people squeezed on low incomes is to resort to high-cost lenders with the constant inherent danger of over-indebtedness and financial hardship (cf. Ellison et al, 2011).

Fulfilling these expectations will be challenging. Under austerity politics, associated with successive governments in the UK since 2010, external and publicly funded grant aid for credit unions will undoubtedly disappear. In the past, some credit unions have also received financial support though various European Union (EU) initiatives, which will disappear with the withdrawal of the UK from the EU. If credit unions are to tackle austerity and to achieve their social objectives, they will have no choice but to succeed first and foremost as businesses. Business success is the *sine qua non* for the achievement of the credit union's social purpose.

This has resulted in credit unions having to make some hard choices. There are some high-risk or already over-indebted consumers that they are just not able to serve and paradoxically they have had to increase interest rates on some loans to remain in business to serve financially excluded groups in the long term. In April 2014 legislation was introduced to raise the interest rate ceiling on credit union loans to 3% a month (42.6% APR). At first sight, this seems high, particularly to readers in other EU jurisdictions, but it compares with the 399.7% APR charged in May 2016 on a £400 loan over 32 weeks by home credit companies.

In order to achieve business success, alongside other credit unions in the UK, ELCU is in the process of transforming its business and operating model through participation in the government-sponsored Credit Union Expansion Project. The aim is to develop as a fully autonomous financial cooperative, independent of any external grant aid or financial support, which has the capacity to serve financially excluded and vulnerable people into the future.

Expansion and modernisation: tackling exclusion in the future

The UK government realises that ELCU will not be able to undertake its role of serving financially excluded groups if it does not expand its appeal to the wider population first. Only thus can it achieve long-term financial stability as a financial institution. For this reason, the government in 2012 agreed a budget of up to £35.6 million to develop a collaborative business model for credit unions, structured as a programme of interrelated interventions to enhance credit union performance.

Becoming part of the CUEP was a major step forward for ELCU. It offers the opportunity to modernise and upgrade its systems and operating model, and to widen the appeal of their products and services within the population at large. It offers the real possibility of being strengthened and stabilised as a sustainable co-operative business, of becoming more comparable to mainstream providers, and thus of making a more significant impact within their local communities.

CUEP is organised and managed by Cornerstone Mutual Services, a subsidiary of the Association of British Credit Unions Ltd, and it brings together 35 credit unions throughout Britain, including ELCU, which have agreed to collaborate to transform radically their offer in the marketplace through the development of a shared business and operating model.

For the directors and staff of ELCU, the decision to join CUEP followed an operational and financial diagnostic of the credit union. It was clear that the credit unions' back-office systems required significant intervention, were time-consuming, inefficient and costly, and that each credit union on its own was ill equipped to develop the kinds of quality products that are attractive to the modern consumer. By joining CUEP, ELCU has gained access to enhanced, collaboratively designed products and services, automated account services, digital channels of access and delivery along with centralised business support, a new marketing strategy and back-office services. Its move onto a new electronic IT platform gives its members real-time access to their accounts through online and mobile banking, as well as unique sort code and account numbers, providing a better member experience.

ELCU went live on the shared platform in the summer of 2016. It remains committed to the development of a member-owned and local financial service, based on a high level of volunteer engagement and member accountability. But it accepts that its long-term sustainable development depends on attracting and retaining an economically diverse membership through offering competitive products that are delivered through modern, digital delivery channels that more moderate-income members find attractive.

ELCU sees no contradiction between development as a modern, professional financial institution and retention of the social, cooperative and Christian values on which it was founded at the outset. But undoubtedly such a move will bring its own challenges; in social enterprises, as Alegre (2015) has clearly demonstrated, there are constant trade-offs between social and economic objectives. It is the responsibility of the board of directors of the credit union to ensure that these two objectives are managed harmoniously in the interests of the member-owners of the credit union (see Jones et al, 2016). The board of ELCU is confident that its move to modernise the business will only result in a more effective and secure service for its low-income and financially excluded members.

References

Alegre, I. (2015) 'Social and Economic Tension in Social Enterprises: Does it exist?' *Social Business*, 5, 17-32.

Campos, J. L. M. and Chaves, R. (2012) *The Social Economy in the European Union*, Report drawn up for the European Economic and Social Committee by the International Centre of Research and Information on the Public, Brussels: Social and Cooperative Economy.

Collard, S. and Kempson, E. (2005) *Affordable Credit: The Way Forward*, Bristol: Policy Press.

Collard, S., Hale, C. and Day, L. (2010) *Evaluation Of The DWP Growth Fund Revised Final Report*, London: University Of Bristol and Ecorys. For the Department of Work and Pensions.

Donnelly, R. (2004) 'British Credit Unions at the Crossroads in Harafolos', in S. Karafolas, R. Spear and Y. Stryjan (eds) *Local Society and Global Economy, The Role of Co-operatives*, Naoussa: Editions Hellin, ICA: 25-54.

Ellison, A., Whyley, C., Forster, R. and Jones, P. A. (2011) *Credit and Low-Income Consumers*, York: Friends Provident Foundation.

Fuller, D. and Jonas, A. E. G. (2002) 'Institutionalising Future Geographies of Financial Inclusion: National Legitimacy versus Local Autonomy in the British Credit Union Movement', *Antipode*, 31, 85–110.

Fuller, D., Mellor, M., Dodds, L. and Affleck, A. (2006) 'Consulting the Community: Advancing Financial Inclusion in Newcastle upon Tyne, UK', *International Journal of Sociology and Social Policy*, 26, 255-271.

Goth, P., Mckillop, D. G. and Ferguson, G. (2006) *Building Better Credit Unions*, Bristol: Policy Press.

HM Treasury (1999) *Credit Unions of the Future*, London: Report of the Credit Union Taskforce.

Jones, P. A. (1999) *Towards Sustainable Credit Union Development*, Liverpool: Liverpool JMU and the Association of British Credit Unions Ltd.

Jones, P. A. (2004a) 'Changing British Credit Unions: Learning Lessons from Latin America', in S. Karafolas, R. Spear and Y. Stryjan (eds) *Local Society and Global Economy*, Naoussa: Editions Hellin, ICA: 69-94.

Jones, P. A. (2004b) 'Growing Credit Unions in the West Midlands – The Case for Restructuring', *Journal of Co-Operative Studies*, 37, 5-21.

Jones, P. A. (2005) 'Creating Wealth in the West Midland though Sustainable Credit Unions', *An Action Research Report*, Manchester: Association of British Credit Unions.

Jones P. A.(2013) *Towards Financial Inclusion – the expansion of credit union financial services for low-income households in Northern Ireland*, Belfast: Housing Rights and the Consumer Council.

Jones, P. A. and Ellison, A. (2011) *Community Finance for London, Scaling up the Credit Union and Social Finance Sector. A Report for Santander*, Liverpool: Policis and Liverpool JMU.

Jones, P. A., Money, N. and Swoboda, R. (2016) *Credit Union Strategic Governance*, Liverpool: Liverpool John Moores University.

Ledwith, M. (1997) *Participating in Transformation: Towards a Working Model of Community Empowerment*, Birmingham: Venture Press.

Local Government Association (1999) *Sustainable Credit Unions – Guidance Notes for Local Authorities*, London: LGA.

McKillop, D. G. and Wilson, J. O. S. (2003) 'Credit Unions in Britain: a time for change', *Public Money and Management*, 23, April, 119-24.

Myers, J., Scott-Cato, M. and Jones, P. A. (2012) 'An "Alternative Mainstream"? The Impact of the Financial Inclusion Policy Context on the Development of Credit Unions in Wales', *Public Money and Management*, 32, 409-416.

National Consumer Council (2005) *Affordable Credit, a Model that Recognises Real Needs*, London: The National Consumer Council and Policis.

O'Connell, S. (2005) 'Alternatives to Money Lenders? Credit Unions and Their Discontents', *History and Policy*, [Online] Available at: www.historyandpolicy.org/policy-papers/papers/alternatives-to-money-lenders-credit-unions-and-their-discontents [Accessed 1 March 2015].

Richardson, D. C. (2000a) 'Model Credit Unions into the Twenty-First Century', in G. D. Westley and B. Branch (eds) *Safe Money. Building Effective Credit Unions in Latin America*, Washington: John Hopkins University Press: 91-114.

Richardson, D. C. (2000b) *Unorthodox Microfinance: The Seven Doctrines of Success*, Calmeadow: Microfinance Bulletin.

Rossiter, J. and Cooper, N. (2005) *Scaling Up for Financial Inclusion*, London: Church Action on Poverty/Debt on our Doorstep.

Sinclair, S. (2014) 'Credit Union Modernisation and the Limits of Voluntarism', *Policy & Politics*, 42, 3, 403-419.

Thomas, I. C. and Balloch, S. (1994) 'Local Authorities and the Expansion of Credit Unions', *Local Economy*, 9, 166-184.

Thompson, P. (2013) *Development of the Modern U.S. Credit Union Movement 1970-2010*, Lulu.com, [Online] Available at: www.lulu.com/shop/paul-thompson-cude/development-of-the-modern-us-credit-union-movement-1970-2010/ebook/product-20567693.html [Accessed 24 August 2016].

SEVEN

Finding employment and living a good life in London

Chris Price

London, like all big cities, has a reputation for being a place of professional opportunity where it is possible to achieve social mobility. For the low-skilled population and those with low educational attainment, such aims, however, are difficult to achieve. Although there are many jobs available, a number of these now offer below-average pay, operate zero-hour or flexible work contracts, and provide no opportunities for progression, which renders the attainment of an income that guarantees adequate living conditions nearly impossible. The consequences of a growing conflict between living costs and earning opportunities often lead to debt, food poverty and homelessness, followed by more personal and social issues. The issue is exacerbated for long-term unemployed people and those with mental health issues. Even if they succeed in gaining employment, adjusting to the new routine of such contracts, with their shift work and flexible hours, can be difficult.

Pecan started in 1989 with a mission to support people, especially those with difficulties, into employment. The difficulties clients face may be related to education, confidence, mental health, age, criminal convictions or many other factors. For over 25 years, Pecan has worked with the people of Peckham, a long-term disadvantaged area of London. The charity was created by a group of local churches adamant that they wanted to meet the needs of the area. This desire was especially acute following riots in the neighbourhood during the late 1980s. The riots were an outpouring of feeling of being left alone by the government. People felt forgotten and blamed for the social and economic situation. Our goal has remained the same when addressing the employment needs of the community: supporting people to build their self-belief.

In this chapter, I describe how unemployed people often struggle to find jobs in London due to a lack of self-esteem and social isolation, or because of difficulties arising from changing life circumstances. I also illustrate the structural difficulties posed by labour and housing market policies in achieving social mobility. The chapter thereby argues that while Pecan does its best to help people find and stay in employment by providing expert advice and emotional support, the structural difficulties posed by labour and housing market changes, which result in income and housing insecurities, can prevent people from shifting to a more stable position in their lives.

We started our work at Pecan with a group of volunteers knocking on doors in a local north Peckham housing estate. It was designed in the late 1960s with an emphasis on concrete and blind corners. It looked drab and cold, and this had a significant impact on how people felt about living there. Pecan's receptionist Irene, a loyal supporter of our work, and one of the original volunteers, recalls the experience:

> "People were scared to answer the door. No one ever knocked on the doors for a good reason! But some people answered. They explained how they were scared to go out and felt isolated with nothing to offer."

Through multiple conversations, a prevailing theme emerged. People did not address their issues, search for work, or develop community because they did not feel they could. So Pecan formed around the desire to uplift people and encourage them to recognise their true worth.

Pecan started with a series of workshops to help people discover what they could offer in way of skills, experience and character, and how to get a job. People attended in increasing numbers as the word spread. The surrounding community became more in touch with itself, and employment figures rose. Soon, the local council heard about the impact Pecan was having, and in a short while a contract for services was offered.

Over the years, we have run an array of employability projects, including IT support for older people, volunteer placements in other organisations, and community-run initiatives, such as a launderette and a woodwork workshop. Additionally, we have run courses in English, Maths and English as a Second Language, and offered a number of different qualifications. As is always the case, projects, funding and jobs come and go, but Pecan has stood strong, and today continues to deliver initiatives that support vulnerable people in the local community.

Getting people into employment is still at the heart of our mission, but the way we approach it varies. We have head-on interventions that directly support people on a path towards a job. But we also have community programmes that tackle the repercussions of unemployment in the local area. For example, we currently host a Trussell Trust foodbank for the borough on behalf of local churches. This service allows us to support people at a time of immediate crisis. Although the project focuses on providing food, we also use it as an opportunity to provide information, helping people deal with the issues that initially led them to the foodbank. We work with Christians Against Poverty (a debt advice charity), Citizens Advice, Advising London and other agencies that provide in-depth support to vulnerable and disadvantaged groups.

We also run Hourbank, a time-banking service that aims to create a sense of community and reduces isolation. Hourbank gives people the chance to share skills and build community simply by helping one another. It is a unique social group that runs on a simple time-banking system. Members of Hourbank advertise their skills, hobbies and interests on a private virtual noticeboard. From here, fellow members can 'purchase' these skills, offering their own unique abilities as payment. Through giving, our clients are uplifted and can demonstrate that they have something to contribute to society. For example, 12 members came together to help out at Brimmington Festival. Most were either retired or unable to work, although one eventually did find work. Their conversation revealed how individuals in a vulnerable position benefit from both regular encounters and collaboration. One of the participants said:

> "The Brimmington Festival was wet! We also had to compete with another loud DJ. However, we soldiered on selling refreshments and hot cups of tea (despite the urn struggling for power), delicious home-made samosas, cakes and fruit punch. Twelve members came to serve, put up the much-needed gazebo, decorate, peddle cakes and chat to the Deputy Mayor."

Nearly all those who helped at the festival have struggled with some aspect of their lives. For example, Christina (all names in the chapter have been changed to secure the anonymity of our clients) regularly has severe panic attacks and learning difficulties, and Paul, who supports her, also has learning difficulties and has recently had his benefits sanctioned by the Department for Work and Pensions because he missed an appointment at the Jobcentre as a result of accompanying Christina to hospital. Ethan has recently found some part-time work, but before that, he also had problems because of sanctioned benefits and had enquired about the foodbank. Paul, who has health issues, is also facing loss of welfare benefits and is likely to need foodbank assistance. He helped all day at the festival, from 10am to 6pm. Stuart rarely comes out of his house, and Arthur used to be homeless. Mike has diabetes and has recently been in hospital for treatment for her finger and eyes. Peter has been unemployed for a long time, and Melanie has severe health issues. She had her benefits sanctioned for not turning up to Jobcentre appointments because she was in hospital. She also enquired about the foodbank. Nick suffers from obsessive compulsive disorder; he does not like to be touched and gets upset if asked anything personal. However, all these people helped on the day and gave their time. Time banking is about looking not at their problems but at what they *are able* to do.

An example of the group's success can be found in Rachel's story. Rachel had not worked for a long time when she arrived at Hourbank. She often wore the same clothes, talked about conspiracy theories, and had some disturbing stories about her family life. Yet, despite her struggles she is very creative and we wanted her to share her skills with others, building her own self-esteem and ability to give to others. In the summer, Rachel attended some creative writing sessions at Hourbank, and we saw that she had great skill in writing and performing. We encouraged her to share a poem of hers at the Festive Party. Her dramatic style and engaging manner was a hit, and we even printed her poems so she could give them to others. Rachel's involvement with Hourbank allowed her to tackle the difficult interpersonal problems that limited her employment options. Her story is exemplary for recognising the multiple directions from which we should aim to resolve unemployment issues.

Pecan runs two projects that solely support ex-offenders in addressing the specific obstacles that a criminal record or custodial sentence can present to gaining sustainable employment. Hands-on guidance and skills training, such as teaching how to budget, are fundamental components of the support systems provided. First, we run Empower, a mentoring scheme, which supports men and women who have been convicted of a crime and live in Southwark to find employment after their release from prison or while serving a community sentence. Finding employment is one of the biggest factors in reducing the reoffending rate. For many people a job provides a social landscape, practical purpose and routine. All of these are goals within successful rehabilitation into the community. Men who go through the prison system have a 50:50 chance of returning within two years. For women, the likelihood of reoffending is a lot higher, currently at nearly 70%. Employment dramatically reduces these figures to only 10%.

The following case study illustrates the success we had with one ex-offender, Jerome.

> Jerome used to work as a retail manager until he fell foul of the criminal justice system. He was made redundant and his inability to provide for his family led him to commit further crimes until he received a custodial sentence. On release, Jerome was referred to Empower. His adviser took time to explain how to disclose his conviction in a positive way, and he had help with updating his CV to show his experiences outside of work. Jerome was later invited to interview for the role of Gate Line Assistant with Network Rail. Although he was initially disappointed at the wage in comparison with his previous jobs, his mentor encouraged him to attend the interview, saying that it was a starting point to get him back into employment. He was later offered the post. After he started the job, he came back to Pecan to thank his adviser: "I can never forget how Pecan supported me." He still visits our reception occasionally and tells anyone there, if not for Pecan, he would not be where he is now. Since starting work, we understand that he has not re-offended and enjoys the new social and work opportunities that the job has opened for him.

Pecan's second ex-offender programme works solely with women and is called Moving On. This project supports women under 30 who are about to be released from prison. Our resettlement coaches start working with them while they are in the prison and continue the work when they are released and re-enter the community. The aim of this intensive resettlement coaching scheme is to help young women become independent, aspirational and secure in their surroundings. In the first three years of Moving On, the reoffending rate of our clients was 50% below the national average for the cohort.

In addition to teaching people how to work towards employment and financial stability, Pecan has invested in creating new ways to help people find jobs, one of which is SE Storehouse, a new social enterprise. With its core aim of providing training and work experience opportunities for clients, SE Storehouse has a three-pronged approach. First, it develops its own range of upcycled furniture and a variety of bags in culturally relevant designs that are currently made in Holloway prison. This offers clients opportunities to gain creative skills and work experience. Second, its retail arm, SE Storehouse, sells the items to the public from a pop-up shop. Finally, the overarching aim is to be a financially viable enterprise that generates an income stream for the charitable activities of Pecan.

Ignition is another Pecan project that directly tackles issues around unemployment in a new and creative way. This is a partnership programme and social franchise owned by Pecan and Jericho Foundation in Birmingham (www.jericho.org.uk). We have pooled our resources of over 40 years' experience of supporting people into work and developed a model of support that can be delivered in a variety of community settings such as churches, mosques and prisons.

Ignition equips representatives of community groups with the knowledge, tools and training to support unemployed people in their community. This model is designed to be delivered flexibly to meet the time constraints and patterns of activity at the different centres. It covers topics such as job aspirations, CV preparation, employers' perspectives, work etiquette and interview skills. The advantage of this programme is that it enables both Pecan and Jericho to reach a wider audience of people than they would normally have access to. Unemployment can often wrongfully lead to feelings of shame, which inhibits a client's will to seek support. By creating an initiative that provides a support network in the familiar setting of a potential client's own community, we increase the probability of their attendance.

Martha's story provides an example of this. Martha had been the receptionist of a large motor sales garage for 25 years. But when the company decided to centralise the reception to a new location she was made redundant. When she went to her local Jobcentre she burst into tears on seeing from the window the garage where she had worked for so long. At this low ebb, Martha attended a local job club set up by a community representative who had attended an Ignition course at Pecan. A year later, the work club leader received the following letter from Martha:

> Hi Brian,
>
> Many thanks for your help over the past year, especially with my CV.
>
> Thought you would like to know that I have found myself a job at a garage at Beckenham. I started there 2 weeks ago and I just love it, have fitted in extremely well. It was good to meet you, as you were a life saver for me. Hope you all continue with the excellent work that you do.

The diversity and success of each of Pecan's projects show that to effectively support those dealing with unemployment, we have to look past their general need for a job and focus on their individuality. It is unreasonable to approach an ex-offender with the same employment support strategy that we would use for a middle-aged woman recently made redundant. Over the past 26 years of charitable works, we have learnt that we have to tailor our support to different social groups, treating unemployment from multiple angles. The organisation creates different activities and evolves according to the various problems that arise, which in turn reflect people's personal experiences.

While Pecan invests in innovative, diverse ways to tackle unemployment among particular social groups, one of London's biggest problems, it also operates within existing structures such as the National Careers Service (NCS). This service provides anyone, regardless of gender, race or social status, with an entry point to other services, training and job opportunities. This project helps people to develop their CV in more creative ways: they are encouraged to explore what they want to do and how their experience outside of work can help to convince an employer to offer them an opportunity. Operating within the NCS means that everyone can receive support from us, whether through one of our tailored projects for certain demographics, or through a walk-in appointment. Our range of projects offers diverse, direct support on both practical and emotional levels for people struggling with unemployment. We do not just offer a product, but rather we create an environment of kindness that encourages people towards a more hopeful career path. Unlike the approach taken by many recruitment agencies and Jobcentres, unemployment cannot be treated without emotion. It is a deeply personal situation and can only be effectively tackled when this is taken into account.

Philippa's story proves the value of the appropriate environment for supporting efforts to find a job. Philippa visited NCS after being out of work for a couple of years. She had aspirations to work in health and social care, and previous work experience as a receptionist. Our staff at the NCS encouraged Philippa to get some voluntary experience, helping her to update her CV and highlighting Pecan's own need for volunteer receptionists. She eventually began volunteering with us. Alongside this work, she enrolled in a training course in health and social care. It was not long before she was offered two jobs, one as a receptionist in a social care company and the other as a sales assistant for a large chain retailer. In her spare time, she still volunteers with Pecan, remaining grateful for the support we gave her.

The difficulty in dealing with unemployment is that beyond an individual's complex, personal issues, there are external factors that exacerbate the problem. One of these is the lack of employment offering a decent wage. According to Joseph Rowntree Foundation's minimum income standards for 2014 (Padley, 2014), the amount of income needed to survive in the UK has risen sharply since 2008. The key research findings showed the following:

- A lone parent with one child now needs to earn more than £27,100 a year, up from £12,000 in 2008. In a dual-parent household with two children, each parent needs to earn £20,000. Single working-age people must now earn more than £17,100.
- Despite social and economic change, the list of goods and services is very similar to that of the original study in 2008, but people's ability to afford them has declined. Overall the cost of a basket of essential items has risen by 28% over six years, while average wages have increased 9% and the minimum wage by 14%.
- Increased tax allowances have eased the pressure somewhat for some households, but the freeze to child benefit and ongoing cuts in tax credits have outweighed this for low-earning families with children. Out-of-work benefits have fallen further and now provide 39% of what single, working-age people need to reach a minimum income standard. On the other hand, pensioner couples who claim all their allowances receive 95% of the amount required.

Finding a job that pays enough to live on is hard enough, but finding a job that pays enough to buy a house is nearly impossible for most of our clients. A regional analysis on home ownership in 2015, conducted by the consulting firm KPMG, shows that in Pecan's geographical area, the South East, a first-time buyer would need an annual wage of £46,010, against the actual annual average wage of £24,391 (KPMG, 2015). The principal types of employment people secure through Pecan are elementary and entry-level jobs that often pay below the average wage. Moreover, most of these people work part-time or flexible hours. Table 7.1 shows the types of jobs Pecan beneficiaries typically find and the average full-time salary for these jobs in February 2016, according to adverts placed with Reed, a national jobsite (www.reed.co.uk).

Table 7.1: Typical jobs and salaries of Pecan's clients

Post	Average salary
Hospitality	**£ per annum**
Waiting staff	19,834
Barista	18,332
Porter	15,509
Customer service	**£ per annum**
Customer service adviser	19,988
Switchboard operator	18,245
Call centre handler	17,991
Social care	**£ per annum**
Child care worker	25,039
Home carer	20,335
Support worker	19,612
Retail	**£ per annum**
Assistant shop manager	23,863
Team leader	20,682
Sales assistant	19,450

If people cannot afford to buy a house, they must rent. However, rent figures correspond with rising house prices, with the average rent being £1,849 per month in the area of Southwark (Home, no date). The yearly cost of renting is higher than the income for the posts listed above, and this figure does not include the extra living costs of tax, electricity, water and, of course, food. This means that, in general, individuals and families on lower incomes are being priced out of the area, complicating even further the task of finding a job. The centre of the city is the hub of the job market, yet to travel in for work is also a growing expense. The final alternative is social housing, where supply is extremely short (LSE, 2015).

The problem is worse for individuals on flexible/zero-hour contracts, which are on the increase (Farrell and Association, 2016). Furthermore, the combination of living on a low income and working on a flexible or zero-hours contract makes financial planning extremely difficult. An effective and consistent budget requires a secure and regular minimum income. Hours that vary from 40 one week to eight another week mean that employment no longer resolves difficulties with saving money, as the following case study shows.

Judith faced a dangerous scenario of the type that many zero-hour contract employees fear. She was referred to Southwark Foodbank in March by the local Citizens Advice Bureau. Before Christmas, she had been working in customer services and had secured a reasonable amount of hours, which provided her with a liveable income. To celebrate Christmas, she bought a selection of presents for her family and young grandchildren. To buy the presents, she went to a legal high-street lender to obtain a short-term cash loan, which she had planned to pay off by budgeting in future months. However, after Christmas, Judith's hours were significantly reduced. She was struggling to pay her housing and utility costs, and her loan became even more crippling. As many people do, she had transferred the loan to another company to pay off the first one. She then transferred it again. By this time, the monthly payments were rising and rising. She finally visited the Citizens Advice Bureau, which helped her negotiate a new payment plan. But in the short term, she was referred to the foodbank to create a financial plan to get back on her feet. Judith had done her financial planning before taking out the loan. Sadly though, her job stability had changed. In this situation, earning a low income means not having the reserves to overcome financial hurdles.

Many people think employment alone is the only answer to sustainable living. Unfortunately this is not true. Appropriate levels of income and expenditure are also needed. Income levels are in the hands of the employer, and employees have little influence over them. Many overhead expenses are also out of individuals' hands, such as the standard payments for rent and council tax.

There are a number of organisations that help people to budget and manage any debts, but many of these, including Christians Against Poverty (www.cap.org.uk), Community Money Advice (www.communitymoneyadvice.com), Advising London (www.advising.london.org.uk) and Citizens Advice, have come to realise that for many people on low income managing money is not the problem. The issue is having enough money for sustainable living.

A related issue is a lack of knowledge regarding cooking. Through our foodbank, it has become apparent that there are a large number of people who have never learnt basic cooking skills or the key food groups that make a balanced diet. Many clients buy ready-made meals rather than cook for themselves or their families. A number of parents do not know how to cook rice, or what to do with lentils. These are great bulk foods that are low in fat and high in nutrients, but do not form part of people's diets because of a lack of knowledge. People need access to good, unprocessed food that is available at affordable prices, and generally cheaper than ready meals and fast food. However, although individuals may be motivated to learn how to cook, they lack teaching and support systems.

One group attending foodbanks in increasing numbers is older men, many of whom had their meals cooked for them in the past by wives or partners. Now they are on their own, either through death or separation, or, for some, even because a parent on whom they still remained dependent has died. Many of the men who come to Pecan rely on ready meals and cheap local fast food, or at least until their health is damaged from an unbalanced diet.

Many of these men worked in Southwark in various manufacturing firms such as Peek Freans, the famous biscuit maker. At one time, the local factory area around Bermondsey was known as Biscuit Town because of the wonderful smell of biscuits and the number of people working in the factory. Many other factories filled the river banks and the back streets from Bermondsey through Rotherhithe to Peckham. These enterprises employed vast numbers of local men up to the early 1990s in a wide variety of manual and production-based roles. However, since then, manufacturing and storage has moved out of central London, and the people who worked on the ground tended to stay behind after being made redundant.

Retraining for different industries has not been easy for these men. Those who have struggled the hardest have low levels of literacy and numeracy. They did not need these skills in their previous trades. Now, they are not as able to compete with the educational standards of someone half their age. Moreover, this does not take into account the practical difficulties of their ageing bodies and weakening stamina; their unemployment is reinforced from all directions. Another key barrier for these men is that they are often unable to work full time because of health issues. Added to this, the job market in London has changed dramatically. Many feel left behind and out of touch. They have virtually no experience of computers, so the idea of filling a gap in, for example, IT programmers from this group is not viable.

So what happens to them? Why are they referred to foodbanks? Many have been unemployed for a number of years. They have attended a government work programme, completed the requisite two years, and are now back at the Jobcentre. Then, leading back to the starting point for this example demographic, they lose their life partners and so begins the struggle to cook healthy single meals. This, plus the process of going through repetitive job rejection and feeling unable to gain work, leads to developing mental health conditions and a spiral into depression. At Pecan, we are developing new ways to work through the foodbank and educate clients about personal food economy. We also advertise the Hourbank and those community projects that attempt to resolve the knock-on effects of prolonged unemployment on our clients. This enables us to build friendships and teach people to shop carefully and eat appropriately. Ultimately, though, there is no way of avoiding the primary issue: our clients just do not have enough money.

When people have moved through the system and begin to suffer health problems, it becomes even harder to secure employment. The whole process becomes a catch-22. Due to a lack of education and low literacy and IT skills, people miss their appointments at the Jobcentre, or forgot to log their job-searching progress online. This means that they do not meet their contract with the Jobcentre, and thus their benefits are sanctioned. Once sanctioned, they are referred to foodbank. This is a palpable experience, and for many, although the foodbank volunteers are very welcoming, it confirms to them that they have hit rock bottom. This only exacerbates their mental health conditions.

Escaping this treadmill is hard. One such person is John.

John had worked for over 30 years in a timber merchant's yard. He kept everything tidy and was a favourite with many customers due to his knowledge of and eye for timber. Sadly he was made redundant in his late fifties. Since then he has been looking for other manual jobs, either in construction yards, factories or building sites. Most of the posts John looked at have gone to younger people who naturally have more strength. They also have the IT skills needed for modern warehousing systems. Alongside this trend, there has been a significant reduction in the number of factories and industrial units available in the area. Most of the old buildings have either been converted into 'loft-style' apartments or have been knocked down and replaced with housing.

John started volunteering at the foodbank in 2015 after over four years of unemployment. He has become a key part of the team, using his skills for sorting and teamworking. He has recently been told by the Department for Work and Pensions that he can retire in four months' time. Until retirement, though, he needs to keep applying for jobs. If he does not keep applying, his benefits will be sanctioned. I asked John what he felt his chances were for securing employment. A rough translation for his reply is 'none'. Sadly, he is right. He has come to the end of his working life, but through volunteering is able to still be an active member of the community. The volunteering has, in his words "brought me back to life". He had been depressed, had needed foodbank support, and felt he was not valuable to society. Now he recognises his value through volunteering, which he will continue in retirement.

The constant development of cultural and work environments illustrates the fact that just gaining employment is not a solution for many unemployed people. For those clients like Jerome, Martha and Philippa who do manage to secure employment, the fact is that they must then adjust to a new work environment. When people have been out of work for a long period of time, becoming used to a new routine can be difficult, especially if they are working shifts or on a flexible contract. Dealing with change is one of the hardest things for people to accept, and if they have a history of mental health issues, too much change is often an obstacle to their recovery. At Pecan we support people through the process of starting work. We help to highlight the likely issues for them. Many of our schemes provide follow-up support, as this gives clients the opportunity to ask the questions they do not want to ask a new employer.

There is more to a new beginning than just settling into a new role. Progressing is also important. When entering employment at an elementary or entry level, we encourage people to look at what they want to progress to. This is why we encourage self-belief from the very first time we meet a client. Most people do not start at the top of a profession, but work their way up. Promotion often comes with increased pay, which then raises the client's standard of living. This is why we continue to coach and mentor people once they have found employment.

Progression within employment is difficult. There is a significant growth in low-skilled rather than high-skilled jobs in London, which means the opportunity to progress is significantly limited. This will prevent a considerable number of people from moving beyond their current financial constraints. Still, employment is not the only goal. It is part of the journey and a proven factor in leading a more sustainable and happy life. The latter is the more critical goal for Pecan, and that is why its approach to the issues of unemployment and money management has garnered much success and attention. We do not just address these issues as a practical element in our clients' lives. We see them for the complex emotional dilemmas they truly are. Unemployment is a personal thing, and so to correctly deal with it we must look at the *person* involved. Our strap line of 'Kindness, Belief, Hope' is built on the experience that people receive at Pecan, rather than the practical service offered. What we can offer will change, but the way we treat people will only improve. What do we mean, then, by 'Kindness, Belief, Hope'?

- **Kindness.** At Pecan, kindness means that people will be treated with honesty, compassion and fairness. It does not mean to just say what people want to hear, but helps people to understand what needs to be said. Kindness provides reality to a situation and helps people deal with this reality whatever the level of trauma involved. Kindness is keeping with people when times are tough rather than denying the situation.
- **Belief.** We never stop believing in the potential of every person. All people are unique. All people are loved. We aim to help people on a journey to self-belief, to a place where they can see their value to the community around them. By helping people to see the good in themselves, we can help them to achieve good in the world. We believe in people so that they can believe in themselves. To believe in people, we recognise the need to build them up. This is not done through false praise, but through helping them to find and use their talents, knowledge and skills.
- **Hope.** Through kindness and belief we aim to inspire hope in our volunteers, staff, partners and visitors. Hope is a future object – we cannot hope for something that has happened, but we can hope for the future. It is by having hope that we can all focus on positive next steps in life.

Overall, this chapter has shown that living in London on a low income is difficult because of the high cost of living. Finding a job in London may not be difficult, but finding a job that can support your household in the long term is. The move towards zero-hour and flexible contracts exacerbates this problem. The benefits system is not flexible or quick enough to respond to the changing circumstances of people on such contracts, despite the words of former work and pensions secretary Iain Duncan Smith that the government wants to 'make work pay' (*The Spectator*, 2014). This can only be done if employers change their practice of low pay, which would make them uncompetitive against those that do not change. Alternatively the benefits system needs to look at a how it can respond better to the changing employment practices in today's economy.

With a growing trend in low-income employment, getting a job is not the golden answer it once was. People need to look to other ways of managing and thriving in their situations. Understanding money management is vital, along with building resources such as cooking skills to save money. With a culture of growing isolation exacerbated by the rise in social media and personal entertainment, people need to be encouraged to seek actual social experiences, through volunteering or other activities.

As a community charity, Pecan does not look at issues in isolation. We work with the whole person through providing a mix of services and support. We aim to continue to provide the current services, but also to develop further. Southwark Foodbank, for instance, is developing a series of courses and activities that will educate and provide opportunities for sustained living, such as cooking groups, holiday clubs and money advice sessions. Our employment support services are looking to develop more entry-level training programmes for people seeking employment. The support does not stop there. We will stay in contact with people to ensure that they are aware of opportunities for moving up the career ladder. Having hope for the future means that we believe in change.

Adjusting to the demands of the system is vital, so when the system needs to change to support its users, someone has to say something. At Pecan we regularly have the ear of politicians and decision makers in the community. We will continue to share the experiences we and our clients face on a daily basis with decision makers so that change can happen.

References

Farrell, S. and Association, P. (2016) 'UK Workers on Zero-Hours Contracts Rise above 800,000', *The Guardian*, [Online] Available at: www.theguardian.com/uk-news/2016/mar/09/uk-workers-on-zero-hours-contracts-rises-above-800000 [Accessed 20 April 2016].

Home (no date) *Peckham Market Rent Summary*, Home.co.uk, [Online] [Accessed 20 March 2016].

KPMG (2015) *Affordable Housing further out of reach, says KPMG*, KPMG, [Online] Available at: https://home.kpmg.com/uk/en/home/media/press-releases/2015/05/affordable-housing-further-out-of-reach-says-kpmg.html [Accessed 28 March 2016].

LSE (2015) *Housing in London: Addressing the Supply Crisis*, London: London School of Economics and Political Science.

Padley, M. (2014) *A Minimum Income Standard for the UK in 2014*, Joseph Rowntree Foundation, [Online] Available at: www.jrf.org.uk/report/minimum-income-standard-uk-2014 [Accessed 10 April 2016].

The Spectator (2014) 'Iain Duncan Smith's Speech on Welfare Reform – Full Text', *The Spectator Blog*, [Online] Available at: http://blogs.spectator.co.uk/2014/01/iain-duncan-smiths-speech-on-welfare-reform-full-text/ [Accessed 20 April 2016].

EIGHT

The Tafel and food poverty in Germany

Sabine Werth[1]

After the fall of the Berlin Wall in 1989 and the reunification of Germany in 1990, the country found itself caught in a state somewhere between euphoria and shock. For the majority of the population, 'that which belonged together had finally been brought together', to paraphrase the former West German Chancellor Willy Brandt. At the same time, the sheer dimension of reconstruction, restoration, and assimilation efforts to bring East German states on par with western standards became clear. The notion of 'recovery east' (*Aufschwung Ost*) coined by Helmut Kohl, the chancellor overseeing reunification, was on everyone's lips. The German parliament passed a law to introduce a new tax used exclusively for the redevelopment of public infrastructure in East Germany, called the solidarity contribution (*Solidaritätsbeitrag*). Being forced to adapt to West Germany's economic system, however, many private East German businesses were forced to close or restructure, which, in many cases, led to the dismissal of entire workforces.

In the former East Germany, there had never existed a shortage of jobs. Everyone had been employed, whether his or her position made sense economically or not. Job safety and equality had been cornerstones of East German society. With what many critics saw as a dangerous takeover of East German companies by western competitors, innumerable people became unemployed, as profit replaced employment as the principal aim. Throughout unified Germany, a growing feeling of loss and inequity began to take hold. Some West Germans felt they had been obliged to contribute too much to East Germany's recovery with the new special tax, while East Germans often lamented the loss of their society and country, alongside social security and a sense of self-worth. German society began to drift further apart. The West German social security system, in the form its citizens had become accustomed to, began to diminish, while the embracing welfare state of the former East Germany was abolished. Disenchantment with politics began to spread, and the feeling that those elected to represent the people had lost touch with their constituency became more prevalent. It was at this time that the Berliner Tafel came into being.

The Berliner Tafel's foundation

Founded in 1993 by the Berlin Women's Initiative (Initiativegruppe Berliner Frauen), an association of which I was a member, the Tafel (German for table) is based on the model of City Harvest in New York City, where volunteers collect food and redistribute it to those in need throughout the city. In Germany, too, we noticed both a surplus of food and many people in need, so we wanted to save food from being thrown away and give it to Berliners who needed it. This basic idea remains the driving force behind the Berliner Tafel. Originally conceived of as a simple way to help the homeless for a limited period of time, the Tafel rapidly developed into a long-term project. We began collecting food in February 1993. We asked bakeries and small markets to donate their unsold products, explaining that we were looking for quality food products to distribute to the less fortunate. Many merchants readily gave us their best baked goods, fruits and vegetables. We took the goods to various social institutions throughout Berlin. The amount of food that was collected from every corner of Berlin has been growing since. Today, the Tafel supplies over 300 social initiatives with food, including homeless shelters, addiction treatment centres, emergency shelters, outreach clinics for women, children, the elderly, and many more. Some schools in Berlin also receive food from the Tafel, specifically for children whose parents cannot prepare meals for school breaks.

At the end of 1993, I split the Berliner Tafel from the Women's Initiative so that more volunteers, including men and non-members, could participate. When we appealed to the public in our effort to recruit volunteers, more than 100 people responded. Around 50 of them then attended the first meeting and joined the new association. To this day, volunteer commitment has been unwavering. For many volunteers, helping out at the Berliner Tafel brings structure to their day. Whether they are early retirees or between jobs, they feel as though they have a purpose and belong to society at large. The press often accompanied us on our collection and distribution rounds, which is why the Berliner Tafel quickly became known beyond the municipal borders, inspiring other social initiatives to adopt our model. First, an initiative in Munich founded the Münchner Tafel, and the organisers followed my suggestion to copy the name to increase recognition. The Neumünster Tafel and Göttinger Tafel followed suit. But it was with the founding of the Hamburger Tafel that we truly had a big breakthrough, as the concept was now being replicated in another major city – which also happened to be the media capital of Germany. Thus, the Hamburger Tafel received an enormous amount of press coverage and became a role model for Tafels in many other German cities. Germany's Tafels in large cities primarily follow the early Berlin model, delivering food to established social initiatives, where it is prepared and served to clients. In smaller cities and towns, Tafels run distribution points. In some of them, food distributions are scheduled up to six times a week. Users sometimes refer to them as Tafel shops. Some Tafels are registered associations, others have private sponsors. (Approximately 40% are sponsored by Diakonie or Caritas, two of the leading faith-based social service organisations in Germany.) The German Tafels have established basic tenets that each Tafel must respect: for example, all Tafels primarily enlist volunteers, although paid employees may be hired for support, and Tafels do not purchase goods, but redistribute food donations.

The Tafel model has also been adopted in other German-speaking countries, namely Austria and Switzerland. In 2016, there were five Tafels in Austria. The first Swiss Tafel was established in Bern; 10 additional Tafels followed. More and more people contacted us in Berlin to enquire about establishing a similar initiative in their own country. In other countries, the term foodbank is often used. The main difference between Tafels and foodbanks lies in the fact that the standard foodbank model is a 'warehouse' model: the organisation receives deliveries from external organisations and stores the food. Various social programmes act as foodbank associates and usually pay for the food they receive. The Tafel's approach goes significantly beyond this.

In 2005, the Berliner Tafel extended its services by establishing Laib und Seele,[2] a project founded in cooperation with participating churches and Berlin's regional radio and television network, rbb. A total of 45 Berlin churches open their doors once a week to distribute donated food directly to people in need, whereby need is defined as concerning those who have a monthly income of less than 800 euros. Clients also have to present a document to show that they live within the postal code corresponding to the distribution point. The symbolic payment of a coin – between one and two euros – gives users a sense of engaging in a fair exchange, despite their difficult situation. The distribution always includes fresh fruit, vegetables and baked goods, and sometimes also staples such as preserves, pasta, or rice.

The fact that the founding of Laib und Seele and the introduction of a new social benefits programme in Germany, Hartz IV, took place in the same year is purely coincidental. Friederike Sittler – one of the people behind Laib und Seele, and head of the Church and Religion department at *rbb* – and I have always stressed the fact that we would have started supporting those in need regardless of social security reforms. Those who take the collection and redistribution of food seriously cannot aim to support social organisations only; rather, they must also strive to reach out to individuals across the population. In the years leading up to the founding of Laib und Seele, an increasing number of soup kitchens were being established, where anyone, homeless or not, could receive a midday meal free of charge or for very little money. For me, soup kitchens have always been the epitome of societal impoverishment. People eat their meals silently, and, when finished, solitarily return to their homes or the streets. From the very beginning, Friederike Sittler and I believed that the establishment of a sense of sense of community was essential – from the time waiting in the queue until after the meal.

Branching out

Today, the Berliner Tafel reaches approximately 125,000 individuals every month. Approximately 1,700 volunteers support us in this endeavour. The social value of this work is enormous. In addition to the redistribution of food, and sometimes books and clothing, the Tafel makes possible frequent cooperation among people within the community. Naturally, no one is happy to be dependent on donated food, and the first visit to Laib und Seele is surely uncomfortable for many. But that is exactly why we chose the name. We want to share a loaf of bread, but people's emotional wellbeing must also be considered. It is important to us that people can establish ties to one another, that they can feel solidarity or community. Due to the sheer quantity of clients, many distribution points have introduced a number system. Many customers arrive much earlier, however, as they enjoy speaking with one another during the waiting period. Often, coffee and homemade cake, baked by the volunteers, are offered to shorten the wait. Such gestures by volunteers and staff prevent a sense of shame or stigmatisation among clients. Instead, they create a sense of neighbourliness. Friendships have blossomed, and sometimes even relationships.

Food distribution is also purposeful for volunteers. They feel that they are doing something worthwhile, useful and purposeful. They often meet people with whom they would normally not have any social contact. Laib und Seele helps to mitigate two problems of modern society: social barriers and isolation. It fosters contact and connections among people across class, religious identities and ethnic boundaries. In this way, we have achieved at least one goal: that of conveying to people the feeling that they do indeed live in a community marked by solidarity. Many Tafel users ordinarily experience neglect by a society in which so many feel left behind, at best reduced to being reliable voters, but forgotten by the very politicians in whom they place their trust. In order to counter increasing isolation and solitude, the Tafel took the decision to expand its scope and shape tomorrow's society more actively.

We feel compelled to reach the children and youth of today, and to teach them something beneficial and practical for their future. We realised that we could not simply rely on parents, schools and the state to accomplish this, given that our daily experience had shown us that many young people were assuming the perspective of their parents and also felt left behind. When parents are without money, children cannot partake in activities such as school trips, summer camps, or excursions; when parents never cook, children will not learn how to cook either. We observed that children's interest in nutrition or in food and its preparation is not conditioned by their parents' social status. This is one of the reasons the Berliner Tafel expanded its mission to focus on children and youth through KIMBA (*Kinder Imbiss Aktiv*, or Active Diner for Children). KIMBA is there for everyone to learn about the value of food, good nutrition, and the importance of sharing a meal together, regardless of one's financial or social background. Specially trained Berliner Tafel staff teach children how to handle and cook food, explaining the benefits of healthy eating, in a double-decker bus retrofitted with a teaching kitchen (KIMBAmobil), a retrofitted train car also with a teaching kitchen (KIMBAexpress), or in school kitchens (KIMBAschule). The children – regardless of their financial background, country of origin, or their parents' educational background – learn how to prepare light meals on their own. Most kids recognise fruit (bananas, strawberries, apples) but often they do not realise that once fruit is diced and sliced and mixed together it becomes a fresh fruit salad – which does not have to come out of a tin. Most children have surely enjoyed fruit salad, but often they simply do not know how easy it is to prepare themselves. By equipping the next generation with the knowledge of how to cook with fresh fruit and vegetables, instead of just warming up ready-made meals in the oven or microwave, we can empower children and shape the future of our society. It must be made clear to everyone that one's own buying behaviour in the supermarket has an impact on more than just our personal lives. It is important to understand the origins of the food we buy, how it is produced, who is earning how much from its production, and the impact of our consumption.

It is also important to pay attention to seasonality and regionality. If you would like to purchase an apple from the local region in February, you must know that it has been refrigerated in a warehouse for months. Most likely, such an apple will have a larger ecological footprint than an apple that has been flown in from New Zealand to Germany. It is worth noting that life without an apple in winter can still be perfectly nice. With this aspiration, KIMBAmobil frequents primary and secondary schools as well as community programmes for children and youths. KIMBAexpress is situated on the property of the Berlin Wholesale Market (Berliner Großmarkt) premises, adjacent to the Berliner Tafel distribution facility and headquarters. During the winter months, when it is too cold to conduct courses in the two vehicles, KIMBAschule continues, as our staff and volunteers take lessons into the kitchens of local schools.

All the KIMBA services have been a great success, booked thousands of times. KIMBAmobil has found enormous resonance in German towns and cities, several of which are contemplating establishing their own KIMBA schemes. At the EXPO 2015 in Milan, the German pavilion exhibited our KIMBAmobil. The KIMBA team cookbook, funded by Berlin's municipal solid waste disposal agency (BSR), won a Gourmand World Cookbook Award in the category Children's Food Book. Many of Berlin's children have already had the proud pleasure of independently preparing a meal that they discovered in the KIMBA programme. KIMBA is a wonderful opportunity to hand over to the next generation our knowledge about food, healthy eating, the joy of cooking and the importance of community life.

Increasing need, declining provision

Food in capitalist countries is produced in excess. Full shelves are, and always have been, a sign of prosperity. The ability to purchase large quantities of food continues to signal social achievement and family or individual wealth. In Germany, the excessive amounts of available food have led to a throwaway culture. Retailers have traditionally thrown away surplus food, especially when it is close to, or past, the 'best-before' date. Thanks to the Tafel, this food can be redistributed to people in need. Today, the German Tafels support more than 1.5

million people out of an estimated 7 million people in need country-wide. But can this level be sustained – and is it enough? The Tafel's relationship with retailers is mutually beneficial. A retailer's priority is to sell. Every product sold becomes profit. Unsold goods represent a financial loss and must be disposed of, increasing disposal costs. For that economic reason alone, companies gladly accept the Tafel's help. The Tafel provides retailers with relief and at the same time enhances their public image. Less has been thrown away and retailers' contribution benefits some members of society – an apparent win–win situation.

A particular difficulty is Germany's *Mindesthaltbarkeitsdatum* (MHD), which translates as minimum-shelf-life date as mentioned above, or the 'best-before' label in Great Britain. After this date has passed, consumers are unsure about whether or not they can still eat or drink a certain product. In Germany, the reason for this labelling is very simple: the MHD is the producer's guarantee that a product's expected texture, colour and taste will not change before that date. If that is not the case, the consumer can return the product and demand a replacement. In general, a product remains perfectly edible after the MHD has passed. Products whose MHD has been reached are often specially labelled and sold for a reduced price. The consumer is thus made aware that a certain guarantee for visual quality no longer exists. The public, however, usually believes that the best-before date is akin to an expiration date. This makes it difficult to sell food past its best-before date. Instead, it is redistributed through the Tafel. Despite our work, there is still a large amount of food waste. Retailers do not generally donate unsold dairy products, meat or fish (because of health and safety concerns). This is, however, beginning to change slowly. Tafels throughout the country have demonstrated to retailers how much food they are unable to sell and, consequently, how high their losses are. In response, retailers have developed processes to reduce food waste: orders have become better planned, production has become more sensible, and trade has become more target-oriented. This means that over the years the amount of collectable food has been declining. A year ago, we were still collecting approximately 1,000 tons of food per month. This amount has been decreasing, and we have to drive to a greater number of supermarkets to collect the same amount as before. We have to deploy more vehicles and use more petrol. Rescuing food has become more work-intensive and costly. Some of our volunteers see this situation as threatening. They have a feeling that their clients might not be receiving enough in the future. But is 'more' really the end goal?

The important thing is to collect surplus food reliably. Over the years, the Berliner Tafel has been confronted with a situation in which the amount of food collected has decreased while, simultaneously, the number of people in need has increased, particularly that of the elderly poor and people in precarious employment situations. In addition, the social stigma attached to receiving assistance has waned. In 2015 and 2016, we saw a pronounced surge in clients at Laib und Seele, also due to the vast number of refugees settling in Berlin. In 2015 alone, approximately 4,000 refugees frequented distribution points across the city every month. Clearly, this puts strain on the distribution system. Nonetheless, organisers at Laib und Seele and the Berliner Tafel endeavour to take such disparate interests and needs into consideration. Happily, it works for the most part. This situation underlines why it is important for us to retain financial independence from state institutions. The Berliner Tafel is funded solely through membership fees and donations. Had we taken advantage of government funding, we would have been obliged to support an even larger number of people in need, straining our services beyond capacity. Our reasoning continues to be valid. We take from where there is too much and give to where there is need. This activity is carried out exclusively on a voluntary basis. Retailers donate the food, Tafel volunteers collect, sort and redistribute it. Nothing more, nothing less. The combination of voluntary action and flexibility accounts for the Berliner Tafel's success over the years, and for that of many other Tafel branches. We are not restricted by state regulations or red tape. Only a minority of Tafels in Germany see this differently, cooperating closely with state authorities and using public funding.

Our volunteers have noticed that state welfare agencies are sending low-income individuals to the distribution points more frequently, suggesting that they will definitely receive help there. The routine reassurance 'you are entitled to their support' is concerning: this statement is not correct, given that only publically funded charities are required to help those entitled to state benefits. The Tafel system offers employees at the unemployment office an option for their clients, but this attitude puts enormous pressure on volunteers at distribution points, struggling with large numbers of newcomers. This also concerns refugees who have been told that they will definitely receive food at a particular distribution point. However, some do not meet the requirements. For example, refugees who are living in shelters with regular meals are not eligible for Tafel support. The current situation (early 2016) can thus only be described as a crisis. It illustrates yet again the lack of flexibility on the part of the political system. Thousands of volunteers are stepping in where the state system has failed. The Berliner Tafel's financial independence from the state has always been, and remains, paramount. This gives the Berliner Tafel its vital autonomy to critique political failure and to signal to those in power that they should officially increase support for those in need, rather than rely on civil society to compensate for the state's retreat.

The future

Despite criticism, the Berliner Tafel's diverse activities have persuaded many people to support us financially. The minimum membership fee of 2.75 euros per month has been constant for years, which also permits lower-income individuals to support our mission. Approximately two thirds of our more than 2,000 members generously contribute more than the minimum. This crowd-funding approach has allowed our organisation to survive recent economic crises: we do not rely on large donations or corporate sponsors. It is very important that Germany's more than 900 Tafels, each with an individual history and context, find a common sense of purpose and establish effective communication channels. This is especially important in the area of seeking to influence social policy. Tafels are viewed by some with scepticism; others see them as hopeful, strong agents of change with a pioneering influence.

The Tafels have worked hard to build a strong reputation across German society. They are held in high esteem by the general population, the retail and economic sectors, and many other public institutions. Representatives often appear on talk shows, give media interviews, and speak in schools or at charity events. The Tafels' opinion carries weight. Initiatives critical of the Tafel movement, such as Twenty Years of Tafel are Enough, founded by Stefan Selke, invite Tafel representatives to take part in debates. These critical debates influence the Berliner Tafel organisation as well, inspiring lively and constructive discussion. The Berliner Tafel is a seismograph of societal developments, in which one can find a diversity of people: active volunteers or those in need of help, young or old. It is not a static entity, but an organisation engaged in constant change through reflection and thinking ahead. Of course, this does not always happen without friction. Some turn their back on the Tafel when they find that it does not conform to their ideas or ideals. It is also important to look closely at how people articulate such disappointment, and to learn from it. Only in this way can an organisation of this size grow in a healthy way. This raises a very fundamental question: does such an organisation have to grow continually to maintain its success? Or will other initiatives replace it some day?

There are notable projects committed to the idea of self-sufficiency, such as transforming unused plots of land into gardens for fruit and vegetables, or teaching people how to grow herbs on balconies. They can be great additions and illustrate fascinating, new directions, but people must continue to reflect on sustainability and nutrition, which is why initiatives like KIMBA – teaching young people about food – are important. More than 60,000 people in Germany are involved with the Tafel movement, paid or as volunteers. Over 1.5 million people receive food from the Tafel. German politicians are aware of the Tafels' enormous contribution. Tafel participants enhance the country's social fabric. While for years the Tafels have consistently been receiving fewer goods and the number of people coming to distribution points has increased, fewer goods can also be seen as a positive sign – supermarkets and others are more aware of food waste issues – but this development still has negative implications for us. Since local Tafels continue to be founded across Germany, more Tafels must share an ever-decreasing amount of food, faced with an ever-increasing number of people in need. The Tafels have agreed on regional boundaries, whereby each Tafel is permitted to collect food within a 20-kilometre radius. When Tafel workers are unable to collect sufficient food within their zone, they have two possibilities: they distribute less, or contact neighbouring Tafels and ask them to share their donations. Tafels should give voice to such problems, alerting the public to the difficulty resulting from dwindling food resources and other developments.

Public policymakers ought not to rely on the Tafels to continue with their job – in an ideal world, there would not be a need for such institutions. Thus, the closure of a Tafel should not necessarily cause alarm, but in most cases is probably an indicator that some people will suffer. In the case of a Tafel closure, supermarkets must consider new waste disposal strategies; those in need must learn to live without familiar support; and volunteers are likely to have a sense of failure or, at the very least, of not having acted early enough to prevent closure. In such a case, a Tafel would have to speak out publicly, explain the situation and offer a solution to all parties involved. Tafels have become a permanent fixture in our society, but still, even as the founder, I have always been clear about this: I would rather not live with the need for Tafels. It has become apparent to me, however, that the social circumstances that bring people to use Tafels will not change any time soon. Thus, many sides rely on the frictionless process of collecting, sorting and redistributing. Dependency among the parties involved has grown. It is particularly important for all Tafel participants to recognise these interrelations as well as their risks. It is also important to stress again that we ought not to act as a fig leaf for politicians, who reduce welfare provisions and expect organisations such as ours to step in, but should make them aware of flawed and detrimental political decisions.

Conclusion

Through their work, Tafel helpers have a special view on a variety of social ills. When distributing food, volunteers hear, see and experience the consequences of political decisions. Personal hardship, worry about one's children and money, and the precarious reality of everyday life are routine topics among clients. There are people visiting the distribution points who see their use of the Tafel as the low point of their lives, and whose greatest wish is for it not to be a necessity. Others complain about the quality of the food offered and blame the Tafel for their individual struggle. At the same time, there is a vast amount of people who relish their contact with others when visiting the Tafel, distribution volunteers included. Naturally, it will always be possible to criticise both the idea of the Tafel and its necessary existence, but what would be the alternative? Tafels are a reflection of our society. Active participants notice hardship and suffering around them; they notice when donations dwindle; they follow the news to inform themselves about political decisions they see as socially detrimental. They take criticism of their work personally. Nevertheless, they carry on. Everybody realises that through their work they can change very little regarding the existing political structure. Still, they persevere. The Tafel concept is easy to comprehend; its implementation, by all means, more difficult. For many, however, it is a truly enjoyable experience. In addition to that, statistics have shown that volunteers live longer. So, who would not want to remain involved?

There have always been people seeking active engagement in society. They notice an issue and jump right in – that is what Tafel volunteers are like: a community that acts in solidarity, looks beyond its own horizon, and stands in for humanity. Agonistic approaches cannot work in such a community, only mutual support. Those who accuse the Tafel of wanting to 'dumb down' people and impede self-improvement have an inhumane view of others. Such an understanding of human beings implies that people are not capable of distinguishing between support from generous volunteers and our constitutionally granted right of equality. Tafel is participation. There is no reason not to make that participation possible for everyone.

Notes

1 Translated by Sarah Richey, International Coordination, Berliner Tafel e.V.
2 In German the term *Leib und Seele* means body and soul. As a play on words, the homonym *Laib* means loaf.

NINE

Addressing food poverty in the UK

Sarah Greenwood

As London foodbank network manager for The Trussell Trust, I hear countless stories like this one from Lydia, who was referred to one of the network's 420-plus foodbanks in the UK after losing her job:

> "I've worked all my adult life. After working in a bank for 25 years and then in a solicitors' office, I was made redundant when my boss had to get rid of 15 staff members across the board. I got redundancy pay but I still had bills, rent to pay and a child to look after. My money was dwindling; my income had gone from £24K a year to £4K…. I went to my new support worker and she advised she could help by giving me a voucher for a foodbank. I was shocked – I never even knew they existed here. I looked at her and just cried, thinking: 'Is this what it's really come to?'"

As well as giving emergency food supplies, the network offers emotional support and a growing range of practical projects via its More Than Food programme to help tackle poverty-related issues. Our mission statement is: bringing communities together to end hunger and poverty in the UK by providing compassionate, practical help while challenging injustice.

We are passionate about what we do and work collectively to make a positive difference in the lives of others. We are inspired by The Trussell Trust's mission verse taken from Matthew's gospel:

> For I was hungry and you gave me something to eat, I was thirsty and you gave me something to drink, I was a stranger and you invited me in, I needed clothes and you clothed me, I was sick and you looked after me, I was in prison and you came to visit me. (Matthew 25: 35-36)

In order to fulfil its aim of ending hunger and poverty in the UK, The Trussell Trust gathers statistics on foodbank use and uses them to lobby decision makers to achieve social change. This chapter details the different programmes we have devised and examines some external challenges the London network faces. In this chapter, I propose that one of the reasons for accessing foodbanks in times of crisis is social isolation.

How The Trussell Trust foodbanks work

The Trussell Trust foodbanks provide three days worth of nutritionally balanced food supplies and support to people in crisis who have been referred by frontline care professionals, such as social workers, or by Citizens Advice Bureaux or children's centres. For example, a foodbank manager told me:

> "A woman was recently referred to our foodbank by her GP, because she needed to eat when taking medication and could not afford any food. When she arrived, the woman told me that she had no food in the house apart from a bag of sugar. She had been surviving for days on nothing more than water mixed with the sugar. I could smell it on the client's skin, as her body had started to break down. The lady was offered a nutritionally balanced three-day supply of emergency food from the foodbank. She sobbed when the food was brought to her. She left feeling much more comfortable and positive, and able to take her medication safely."

Alongside food and support, many foodbanks also offer other items that clients need immediately, such as shower gel for a client preparing to go to a job interview, nappies for a baby, a winter coat on a cold day and sanitary items for women. A former television presenter, who could not find work and ended up being referred to a foodbank, was so moved when she was given some shampoo that she exclaimed: "I'll be able to wash my hair for my job interview now, I'll feel so much better."

The Trussell Trust foodbank model offers short-term emergency support and helps people out of pressing crisis. Beyond this, signposting to local organisations offering specialist support services and The Trussell Trust's More than Food initiative are a key part of The Trussell Trust foodbank model. We help Trussell Trust foodbank clients to locate local support services that can resolve the underlying causes of the crisis that brought them to the foodbank in the first place. Every foodbank client is referred by one of the 39,000 frontline professional agencies across the UK that issue our foodbank vouchers to clients they identify as being in crisis and facing hunger. More than 50% of these agencies are statutory. Each foodbank in London usually works with between 100 and 300 referral agencies in their local community. Trussell Trust clients may redeem three foodbank vouchers in a row, at which point the foodbank manager will contact the referral agency about putting together a support plan to help the client break out of poverty. At the discretion of the foodbank manager, clients can continue to access food from the foodbank. On average, our most recent research shows that each client needed less than two foodbank referrals to the foodbank network in a six-month period.

The Trussell Trust foodbank network's statistics show that between 1 April 2016 and 30 March 2017, 1,182,954 three-day emergency food supplies were provided to people in crisis by The Trussell Trust foodbanks across the UK. During this period, 111,101 three-day emergency food supplies were provided to people in London, with 40,679 of these three-day supplies going to feed the capital's children. This represents a small increase of 0.7% in foodbank use in London compared with the figure for the same period in 2015–16 (110,364). In London, benefit delays and changes remain the biggest cause of foodbank use, accounting for 42% of total referrals (27% benefit delay; 15% benefit changes) between 1 April 2016 and 30 March 2017, a rise compared with last year's 38% percent. Low income has risen as a referral reason from 21% to 24% over the same period.

Although there is usually a specific reason for triggering a foodbank referral, foodbank managers frequently find that multiple problems surface during conversations with new clients. As *Emergency Use Only*, our 2014 research with Child Poverty Action Group, the Church of England and Oxfam highlighted, the trigger cause of foodbank use is often the last straw in a line of crises when someone has exhausted all their usual coping mechanisms (Perry et al, 2014).

Communities coming together

The Trussell Trust is committed to community built on diversity, tolerance, cooperation and mutual respect, and to providing practical, non-judgemental support to people of all faiths and none. Our values are important to us, and we aim to live them out in all areas of our work and demonstrate social responsibility. All Trussell Trust foodbanks are community-driven, as they are set up by local people to help their own neighbours across Britain. At each foodbank centre, there are groups of local volunteers, often managed by a paid foodbank manager, who gather to welcome and offer hospitality to clients at their point of need. There are approximately 40,000 volunteers in the network.

Most of The Trussell Trust foodbanks are run in partnership with churches, and many are hosted in church property. Without the support of thousands of volunteers and food donors in London, all from a variety of faith traditions and none, the foodbank network would not operate. We have many volunteers from local Christian churches who are motivated by the belief that everyone is made in the image of God and therefore deserves respect and care, and we also have many volunteers from other faith backgrounds and of no faith. As one foodbank manager put it:

> "One of my Muslim volunteers loves the foodbank. She took one day off work each week to volunteer over several years. After moving away, she came back to visit and said she felt that the foodbank was a really safe environment – somewhere to come for comfort."

Another foodbank manager said: "A retired atheist man volunteers in our foodbank. His wife told me that he absolutely loves it."

Some Trussell Trust foodbanks offer the possibility of a Christian prayer to their clients, but only after they have been given their food provisions, so that no one feels under any obligation to accept. If the offer is refused, we respect the wishes of the client and do not proceed. If the client agrees, the volunteer offers a short prayer for one issue identified by the client. The Trussell Trust model explicitly prohibits proselytising in foodbanks. Clients are often vulnerable, and our primary purpose is to provide practical emergency support to people in crisis. Many clients, however, tell us that they appreciate the offer of prayer and some request it on subsequent visits.

Many foodbank clients would have never imagined they would need emergency food. We have learnt never to assume anything about people in crisis, because their journeys and personal circumstances are all so different, and we feel a great responsibility to produce our best efforts for them. One foodbank manager put it succinctly: "In the foodbank, we have to be very practical with the information we give. We never know who is coming through the door or their situation. We have to be prepared for all eventualities."

Our work is driven by the stories we hear, every day, of the daily struggle of living with poverty in London. The following real stories illustrate this diversity through a random sample of London foodbank clients:

- Lydia, who opened this chapter, was referred to the foodbank after being made redundant from her legal aid job in a solicitors' office. While she looked for a new job, the redundancy pay just would not cover the costs of bringing up her son and paying the rent and all the bills, and when she felt there was nowhere else to turn, the foodbank was there for her. She felt so welcome at the foodbank that she started to volunteer there regularly, and recently got a new job.
- An elderly blind man needed emergency food recently after he had his pension stolen from him at a cashpoint. He had no money for food. The foodbank helped him to report the case to the police. Officers even did a collection for him at the local police station to make sure that he would have a good Christmas.
- A couple who were both in low-paid work needed repeated help from the foodbank when the wife suffered from complications during pregnancy and her husband had to move jobs to be closer to home. Their flat was so mouldy that the whole family was getting ill, including the baby. The husband had to live with a friend for half the week because the mould aggravated his asthma badly.
- A successful journalist who had stopped working due to bladder problems that made her incontinent came to the foodbank before Christmas. She broke into tears when she found Christmas cookies in her food supply from the foodbank because she could offer this treat to her mother for Christmas.
- A London nurse came to the foodbank after her shift pattern changed. She had two school-aged children and her crisis occurred because the shift changes did not fit with the childcare she had already sorted out, and she could not afford to pay for different childcare until the end of her current childcare contract.
- A formerly successful businessman, who had been on a salary of more than £100,000 and had been in a stable relationship, came to the foodbank after his business had failed and his relationship had broken down. He began to consume lots of alcohol, lost everything, and ended up living on the street. He had recently been housed in a one-bedroom flat, but had no furniture or food. He was referred to the foodbank for assistance. The foodbank helped him with food and access to furniture.
- A man with chronic back pain after a career in construction came to the foodbank after having problems with accessing welfare benefits. He was living in a flat that was so unsuited to his needs that he had to travel to his friend's house to have a shower, simply because he could not lift his leg high enough to step into his bath. He had made friends with the volunteers at the foodbank who knew him

by name. He could not travel far because of his pain, so at Christmas the volunteers invited him to a meal at the church that hosted the foodbank so that he would not be alone. He gladly accepted.

Commonly, people who are referred for emergency food will have tried getting help to solve their social or financial problems by contacting family, friends and various local organisations. However, people in poverty cannot necessarily rely on their family or friends for support, as the latter are frequently struggling themselves. If they have relied on these networks and exhausted them, they often find themselves unable to access public assistance because of increasing demand on overstretched services. Many have already reduced their expenses to the minimum. Many parents tell us they regularly skip meals so their children can eat. Often they tell their children that they have already eaten or are not hungry, so their children will not feel guilty. Other parents survive by sharing one tin of soup as their main meal of the day. By the time clients arrive at foodbanks for the first time, they are often in a distressed emotional state. A foodbank manager explained:

> "Our clients have been everywhere else; we are the last place they come to. People have been sent from pillar to post. They are exhausted. One client rang and asked whether this was the foodbank. When I said yes, he burst into tears. They tell us how frustrated and hopeless they feel, how no one cares. Nine out of ten of my clients feel broken down. They need help. They turn to the system. No one listens. Automated telephone systems take the humanity out of the process. It seems like a tick-box exercise without any humanity. No one listens to their story."

Another foodbank manager confirmed:

> "Clients are often uncertain of what to expect and how they will be treated in the foodbank, so if we see people hovering around the entrance, we go out to them with a warm drink and offer them a warm welcome and hospitality inside, and they generally respond well."

The emotional help offered by the foodbank was emphasised by another one of our managers: "Often, foodbank clients tell us the emotional support is almost as good as the food." One single mother of two came to a foodbank before Christmas. She was a chef who had been out of work for a few months due to health problems and was living in a damp flat. She told us that her benefits had been sanctioned because she had filled in the wrong section on her benefits claim, and even though she corrected it on the form itself, her money had been stopped. She said: "there have been things that have happened in the last three years that have reduced me to a piece of rubble."

She told the foodbank manager that Christmas was going to be really hard because her children loved it but she could not afford to make Christmas special this year. A volunteer overheard and came and placed three prettily wrapped gifts, one for each of her daughters, on top of her food parcel. The mum broke down in tears, so moved by a simple act that showed some compassion. She thanked the volunteer: "I wasn't expecting that. It's so kind. You won't believe what this means." The foodbank manager elaborated:

> "As long as I know that our clients leave with hope [I am happy] … because people come without hope. They sometimes come like a zombie, they are so broken. They don't know what they will be given. People are often surprised by the amount of food given. Many say no one has listened before."

Social isolation in London and the lack of meaningful relationships affect many of our clients, who have no one else to confide in or ask for help in a crisis. One elderly client told us during a foodbank session that he had not spoken to anyone in many weeks. The manager of our foodbank in Richmond has seen many such cases:

> "Many of our clients have no community or family at all – which is shocking. Increasingly, people have no community to link to. It is a real show of fragmentation in our society. People don't even have social contacts. Any traditional behaviour of knocking on neighbours' doors to ask for help doesn't happen anymore. There is no common journey. People no longer feel they belong."

On my last visit to Brent foodbank, I noticed people staying at the session, not wanting to leave. They complained that they have no one to talk to elsewhere; some do not even have a television at home to make some noise and make them feel less lonely. If clients are lonely, they will often be invited back to the foodbank for a cup of tea and a chat. Sometimes, they come back to volunteer in the foodbank after their crisis is resolved. During our food collections at supermarkets, I invariably hear of someone who gives food saying they had been helped by a foodbank and wanted to give something back to say thank you.

Going beyond food provision

As previously mentioned, The Trussell Trust's vision is to end hunger and poverty in the UK. We work hard to give people in poverty a voice in the media, so that more people understand the reality of hunger in this country. The harrowing personal accounts of hunger and poverty we hear are not communicated widely in the UK press. Instead, the recent proliferation of reality television series such as *Benefits Britain* perpetuates myths of the undeserving poor. One foodbank manager explained:

> "Many people don't know anyone who has faced hunger and, as a society, many of us are not comfortable to acknowledge the existence of hunger in 2016 in London. It is much more convenient to overlook hunger and poverty overall by linking it to other countries, migrant communities, or the undeserving poor. This minimises the urgency to do anything to stop its spread."

The Trussell Trust is working to make politicians of all political parties aware of the realities of UK hunger, so they can create and influence policies to tackle poverty and help reduce the number of people needing emergency food. This is part of a long-term mission to reduce poverty in the UK – not only through our own work, but by influencing government to address the problem upstream, rather than expecting third sector organisations to take the place of a robust safety net. To do so, The Trussell Trust collates statistics about why people come to foodbanks, and shares this with decision-makers in the media and government. We also produce and commission research on the underlying causes behind foodbank use, for example, our work with the University of Oxford, the first phase of which found a strong link between sanctioning and foodbank use. We are keen to work with other independent foodbanks to collect data from a wider sample, to provide a more robust indication of the number of people accessing foodbanks across the country.

Since 2015, we have been piloting and rolling out our More Than Food programme to empower people to address the underlying causes of their food supply crisis. The programme, through co-locating practical services and advice, gives clients tools to build resilience in adverse conditions or rapid change in the future. Three of these projects quickly saw positive results in London.

The first is debt advice and money management, two areas in which there is enormous potential to help clients tackle not just hunger but also other social disadvantages. After initial pilots of placing debt advisers in foodbanks, we noted high levels of client engagement and problem resolution. Of those referred to advisers, 50% were still engaged with the agency after two months, and 40% had resolved their problem in less than that time period. Only 10% had not addressed their problem. We also noted that one in three clients did not think they were receiving enough help from the organisation that referred them to the foodbank, and therefore engagement with foodbanks may provide an ideal opportunity to introduce people to the additional help they need.

Second is the Npower Fuel Bank project, which sees fuel vouchers for gas and electricity pre-payment meters given to people at participating foodbanks, so they do not have to choose between heating and eating. Research conducted by Citizens Advice found that one in every six homes that uses a pre-payment meter has self-disconnected, meaning up to 1.62 million people go without electricity or gas each year. An Npower Fuel Bank voucher enables households that have run out of energy to get the power back on within a few hours and make sure there's enough electricity and gas for lighting, heating and cooking.

Third is Eat Well, Spend Less, a free six-session course that provides cookery, budgeting, hygiene and nutrition advice to help make tight budgets stretch further. It is an opt-in, entry-level course, so people do not need to know how to cook before they come. The atmosphere is informal and relaxed. Everyone cooks together, learning in a small group, so that people can share their skills and experience, and make friends. Building relations and new community are central parts of these new initiatives. Waterloo foodbank was one of the first projects in London to trial the project. This is the report from its foodbank manager:

> "In March 2015, we launched a fundraiser that we called the Lent Foodbank Challenge. The idea was that we would ask people to get sponsorship to live on a foodbank parcel for three days. My wife and I did this. Afterwards, we decided that we should try and get some fresh food into

the foodbank parcels, so I spoke to an organisation that tries to eliminate food waste by connecting food businesses with charities that are able to take their leftovers. They put us in touch with two traders at Borough Market, and for the last year we've been collecting fresh fruit, vegetables and bread to give to our foodbank clients. We were given so much food that we decided to use some of those ingredients and create a pay-what-you-can-afford weekly community lunch. We then heard about The Trussell Trust's Eat Well, Spend Less course, and thought it made sense to combine that with our community lunch. We quickly filled the course and the participants learned to cook low-cost, healthy meals, which we then shared at community lunch. The course was a huge success, so much so that we continued it for a fortnight beyond its usual six-week run because the participants were so keen."

Over 90% of foodbanks provide a diverse range of additional services within their foodbank centres, which has a positive impact on the local community. In The Trussell Trust London network these include: mentoring youths involved in gangs; offering counselling to local railway station staff after suicide attempts; working closely with street pastors; offering pregnant women the essentials they need for hospital and for the first few weeks of their new baby's life; running small-scale food growing projects, community meals, clothes banks and charity shops; and initiating partnerships with local organisations, such as advice sessions with pharmacists on the best way to take medication, and, at Norwood and Brixton foodbank, free legal surgeries with a local firm of lawyers. The project manager at Norwood and Brixton concluded:

"I never knew if the clients I referred would go to the legal service. However, when the legal surgery is inside the foodbank, this gives clients a chance to put their case and gain appropriate advice to resolve their situation. Through legal surgeries, we are impacting people's lives in more ways than before. People come into the foodbank and speak to us about their problems. Their situation is being helped."

The legal firm was so assured of the value of working with clients from this foodbank that it expanded its work to include another foodbank, whose manager said:

"A working single mother with a five-year-old son came to visit us just before Christmas. She broke down in tears as she explained that she was facing eviction and had no idea where she would go if that happened. She was working full-time as a cleaner and just couldn't make ends meet because her pay was so low. As well as giving her emergency food, she was also able to access advice from the welfare and housing adviser, and help from the in-house solicitor, both hosted in the foodbank, which would have otherwise been difficult to obtain due to her professional and childcare responsibilities. She left much better informed about what she could do to avoid eviction, and with emergency food and a fuel bank voucher."

Challenges

Foodbanks in The Trussell Trust network work to help build their local communities and increase resilience in vulnerable population groups. As for charities of all sizes across the UK, funding has become more difficult for foodbanks to access in recent years. Sustaining funding for foodbank manager salaries, storage costs for food, electricity, and transport costs for food collections are increasing concerns, especially as the need for emergency food shows no sign of decreasing. One foodbank with three centres, which distributed 1,913 parcels last year, had only one paid staff member (a manager employed for only one day a week), but is determined to do more.

The Trussell Trust receives no government funding, but some of the foodbanks in our network receive local authority funding as independent charities, and we have helped foodbanks to access such grant money, as well as donations from corporations and the general public, to cover running and capital costs. In many instances, foodbanks are reliant on a mixture of funding streams: grants from trust funds, donations from corporate companies, private donations, church collections, local businesses and school collections. They sometimes rely on the goodwill of church committees, which often decide to reject income-generating rentals in favour of offering premises free to foodbanks.

Fortunately, two London authorities have offered derelict buildings to two Trussell Trust foodbanks as working premises, each on a seven-year lease for a 'peppercorn' rent. Such support is invaluable for the recipient foodbanks and we hope it will continue for as long as there is need for it, even though there are hidden costs incurred through such generous gifts, such as renovations. But need is clearly increasing and there is a desire within the network to expand and do more for more vulnerable people.

One way in which the third sector is overcoming funding challenges is through strategic links with corporate partners. Recently, The Trussell Trust piloted a school holiday meals project for Southwark families, supported by a corporate sponsor. The foodbank manager ran several sessions, which were well attended by families struggling to feed their children during the school holidays. The session offered supervised play sessions for children, an opportunity for parents to talk and relax, and freshly prepared food for the families to eat together. This foodbank has contacts with several children's centres, whose staff have asked the foodbank to organise similar projects for them, since the foodbank now has the training and knowledge to provide this type of service. We are looking at ways to extend this vital service by raising money to fund staff, including play workers, and catering.

Conclusion

Poverty and hunger are often amplified through social isolation. These are real and widespread, not only in London, but across Britain. Foodbanks in The Trussell Trust's network provide immediate relief, as well as increasingly sophisticated support to help people out of crisis in the long term and thereby improve their lives. The Trussell Trust works to influence the development of communities that are more caring and better connected. As well as providing food in a moment of crisis or need, The Trussell Trust is seeking to expand its scope, providing services that empower people to move out of crisis. It also seeks to communicate the experiences of people in crisis to politicians, using stories and statistics to influence policy. We seek to work with local governments and industry, and partner with other charities.

As the report *A Strategy for Zero Hunger in England, Wales, Scotland and Northern Ireland*, by the All-Party Parliamentary Inquiry into Hunger in the United Kingdom (2014) highlighted, more work needs to be done in order to increase collaboration across sectors, and specifically between government, the third sector and businesses. The Trussell Trust has repeatedly called for government action on poverty, and maintains that it cannot alone end hunger in the country. There is an increased need for community life, and for greater fostering of social relations.

Finally, as Christians, I and many of my colleagues in the foodbank network look to the optimistic promises of Isaiah 58: 10–12 for inspiration for the future of The Trussell Trust network in Britain:

And if you spend yourselves in behalf of the hungry and satisfy the needs of the oppressed, then your light will rise in the darkness, and your night will become like the noonday. The Lord will guide you always; he will satisfy your needs in a sun-scorched land and will strengthen your frame. You will be like a well-watered garden, like a spring whose waters never fail. Your people will rebuild the ancient ruins and will raise up the age-old foundations; you will be called repairer of broken walls, restorer of streets with dwellings.

Note

This chapter includes excerpts from conversations between clients and managers of foodbanks in The Trussell Trust network in Richmond, Hammersmith and Fulham, Southwark, Norwood and Brixton, Brent and Waterloo. In order to hide the identity of clients, references to specific districts of London have been removed from the quotes.

References

All-Party Parliamentary Inquiry into Hunger in the United Kingdom (2014) *A strategy for zero hunger in England, Wales, Scotland and Northern Ireland*, [Online] Available at: http://cdn.basw.co.uk/upload/basw_74748-9.pdf [Accessed 20 November 2016].

Perry, J., Williams, M., Sefton, T. and Haddad, M. (2014) *Emergency Use Only*, The Child Poverty Action Group, Church of England, Oxfam GB and The Trussell Trust, [Online] Available at: www.trusselltrust.org/wp-content/uploads/sites/2/2016/01/foodbank-report.pdf [Accessed 20 November 2016].

TEN

Helping the homeless: a soup kitchen in London

Martin Stone

Muswell Hill is a neighbourhood in north London, identified by *The Sunday Times* as one of the five best places to live in London. It is known as the village on the hill. It has large, beautiful Edwardian houses, great views across the capital, exciting shops and restaurants. Muswell Hill is thriving socially and economically. The state schools have received 'outstanding' status, and there is a high demand to live in the catchment area of each school. It is a settled community, where many people have lived all their adult lives. There are 11 well-established churches and a thriving synagogue. These are communities within the community, but they still have a common social conscience, which often produces social action. One local example of this is the Muswell Hill Churches Soup Kitchen for the Homeless. It is strongly supported by all the faith groups and is hosted in Muswell Hill Baptist Church.

In 1994, a few people from the Baptist Church invited local homeless people for a warm evening meal. The volunteers cooked food in their homes and brought it to the church. The guests appreciated the gesture, and soon an established group of about 12 were eating at the church five evenings a week. Over the years, the project grew to offering 25 meals every evening. It thus became necessary to cook food on the premises. Appeals were made for help to other churches in Muswell Hill, and soon different churches were responsible for serving food different evenings each week. The local churches organised volunteers and provided the food. Much of it was generated by harvest festivals, and soon thousands of cans of beans and soup were arriving each October. This non-perishable resource enabled the soup kitchen to serve about 10,000 free meals per year (writing in 2016). Over time, our soup kitchen became widely known, and even schools and other community groups started donating non-perishable food.

This broad recognition is also reflected in our voluntary base, which is quite diverse. We attract volunteers from different faiths and non-faith backgrounds, across ethnic and age groups. Even companies have started sending us their employees to volunteer as part of their social responsibility initiatives. This large pool of about 80 volunteers provides food for up to 50 people, five evenings per week, throughout the year. Our client group consists mainly of single vulnerable men with alcohol and/or drug addiction, often exacerbated by mental health disorders. Many of them will die prematurely; self-harming through alcohol and drug abuse is quite common among the homeless population. We also invite people from the mainly middle-class Muswell Hill community along to share meals with our homeless guests. Accordingly, food is used to bring these two different groups of people together, who would normally not interact with each other. The shared meal is a way of breaking down the barriers and stigmas affecting the homeless population and particularly those suffering from mental health problems. In this way, soup kitchens like ours can assist in creating a more integrated community.

This chapter argues that charities helping vulnerable people can narrow the social distance between people of differing educational and financial status, and with different mental and physical abilities, thereby assisting in the construction of community, in terms of 'a social group with some degree of "we feeling" and living in a given area' (Bogardus, 1952, p 122). The chapter shows that a sense of belonging for vulnerable people can be achieved, first, by bringing them into contact with people from a different social stratum through specific activities to create common experiences, second, by encouraging participation in the soup kitchen group, which can then be extended to other groups, and third, by helping them to develop the social skills and self-confidence to confront social life more positively. The aim is that encounters with people from different social strata – such as our volunteers or Muswell Hill community residents – and the creation of a sense of belonging to the soup kitchen group will enable our vulnerable guests to reflect on their own lives and its opportunities, and to pursue positive change. We know from experience that their mental health and addiction problems, and well as their routine of living on the streets, make it difficult for homeless people to maintain attachment to what many of us consider normality: a home to live in, a family to care for, and purposeful employment. We thus seek to equip our guests with the right social skills and confidence that allow them to feel part of a group – our group – which then permits them to seek belonging in other communities also, discovering a path to becoming yet again a fully integrated member of society.

Social skills development

I took over the management of the Muswell Hill Churches Soup Kitchen in 2008. I had worked as a lecturer before and had no experience of cooking or working with vulnerable people who have various mental health issues and addiction problems, and whose basic needs are often not met. Initially, I was terrified of the cooking and meeting food safety standards, and of the guests, who often exhibited chaotic, challenging behaviour. I did take advice from mental health professionals and set myself three objectives: to ensure the health and safety of the guests and volunteers; to welcome and treat the guests as you would treat valued guests in your own home; and to help volunteers understand and interact with our guests.

My main aim was, however, to create social bonds between volunteers and guests, to achieve a sense of group belonging for both. I see this step as vital to allow homeless people to feel less isolated – and thus, ultimately, to get them off the street. Our volunteers are mainly in their early twenties and working in professional jobs. They would not usually engage with the homeless population. To enable more interaction, I started organising additional external and internal social activities, emphasised very personal interaction between volunteers, staff members and soup kitchen users, and changed the spatial layout of the soup kitchen.

We also planned excursions, such as a coach trip to the seaside. The whole group could decide the date and the destination: Brighton was the first choice. I will never forget the coach driver's face as he did a double take on a bunch of drunks sitting on a wall outside the Baptist Church. The trip meant taking a high risk. Little quarrels broke out over which channel to play on the bus radio, and participants constantly asked for toilets breaks on the motorway. It was a brief excursion to Hell, so to speak, but also, in some ways, very amusing. When we arrived eventually, I left the group members to explore the seaside by themselves. Nonetheless, I was worried that they would not return in time for the scheduled departure. I was wrong. They all returned, escorted by local street alcoholics with tags on their legs. My guys were being deported by drunks in Brighton.

The jokes and the experiences we shared during the trip were an important step towards developing a sense of group belonging. Talk of the trip continued for weeks and months afterwards. The group would not get tired of recalling the journey, incidents and funny situations. This is understandable. Such trips were not part of their daily routines at this point in their lives. The incessant talk about the trip also made it easier to move a lively conversation on to other issues. I could ask questions about the types of food that they would like, at what time of the day they were most hungry, or which aspects of the soup kitchen they enjoyed in particular. The trip also made the volunteers more engaged with our work. As a result of their participation, they felt a greater sense of responsibility for the wellbeing of our guests. After our shared trip, volunteers communicated more openly with me and with each other as team members; they also started planning changes in the soup kitchen together.

Such shared activities also encouraged our homeless guests to redevelop certain social skills that can be lost living on the streets, such as time management and a sense of obligation. During the trip, our guests were responsible for their demeanour in a new urban space, where residents had perhaps not become as used to antisocial behaviour as back in London. They had to organise lunch themselves. They also had to manage their time, making sure they did not miss the bus to return to London. Being part of a group activity also meant that they were not just responsible for themselves – instead, they also shared the collective responsibility to arrive on time so we could all leave together. On the whole, outings like the one to Brighton are vital, as they help break routine behaviour and open up the possibility of reworking everyday values. Another time, the general manager of the Hilton Hotel in Westminster invited our soup kitchen guests for a delightful afternoon tea. Some of them had never before experienced this unique English tradition. For others, it was the first time they had set foot in a hotel. In fact, a few had slept on the street outside the same Hilton; now they were being welcomed through the front door. The guests included Jack, a refugee fleeing the Zimbabwean government, and Jim, who was then in his sixties. When Jim first came to the soup kitchen, he wore ragged clothes; his skin was covered in sores. At the time he set foot in the Hilton, his skin had healed and he was wearing a fine suit, which had been stored away for weddings and funerals. Another guest was Peter. He had lived and worked in Manchester, and had spent much time on the streets. At the tea, I guided him through the art of spreading cream and jam on a scone. They loved the event.

Raising self-confidence

We also started many in-house activities, mainly to build guests' and volunteers' confidence to engage in social interaction with people different from themselves. The intention is always that such activities will help participants to carry over changes into their own lives. We started a series of poetry evenings, to which we invited people from the community, particularly those who would not usually interact with vulnerable people. What made the evening a success in community building was that you could not easily tell the difference between soup kitchen guests and local residents attending the event. They all sat together and interacted with each other casually. The exciting thing about poetry is that it provides a shared human experience. Every way of seeing the world expressed through poetry as art is equally meaningful. Residents, guests and volunteers enjoyed these emotional, moving events. For our soup kitchen denizens, it was an event they could actively choose to attend; they did not have to be present out of sheer need. They had even been invited. Self-esteem increased as their poetry was read out, acclaimed by keen listeners. They could become part of a new kind of group: not the poor and needy guys from the local soup kitchen, but the Muswell Hill community poetry group.

We also started film nights, using film as a medium to raise our guests' self-esteem and self-confidence. For example, I produced some humorous video clips that I wanted soup kitchen guests to comment on. They enjoyed the clips, which showed how a man overcame alcohol addiction, and applauded my efforts. I asked them to give me advice on the script and assess the acting, too. It would be wrong to assume that such activities can heal profound mental health issues. For many of them, unfortunately, the damage seems permanent. However, stimulation can still have a noticeable impact. Dignity and self-esteem can develop when you feel that others listen to you and ask for your genuine and appreciated advice. Another time, we went to see a film at the cinema, again with the intention of giving our soup kitchen guests positive memories of their time together. We watched the inspirational, true story of Eddie the Eagle – a British ski jumper who competed at the 1988 winter Olympics. Since 1929, no Brit had qualified for the discipline, and many of our soup kitchen guests had personal memories of the 1988 television coverage. The film transported them back to the days when they had been young men, with their lives still ahead of them. They were really engrossed in the film, and talked about it for weeks after. The acting inspired Nigel, one of our guests. He joined the Cardboard Citizens Street Theatre in London, a street theatre company, and started his own acting career. When he returned for meals, he talked about his performance on issues of homelessness; Nigel was excited about his ability to use his stories to move an audience. The objective of the kinds of activities that we pursue is thus to stimulate and challenge our guests, to provide them with social skills and confidence, and to give us the hope that some of them will eventually progress to new ventures – and perhaps even find permanent housing.

To encourage positive interaction among our guests, we have also made changes to the soup kitchen's spatial layout. We moved the eating area into a larger space in the Baptist Church, which functions as a nursery during daytime. This large space, easily accessible, constitutes a peaceful environment. The other area in the church, which we had used previously, had always been crowded, which contributed to shouting, pushing and shoving among the men. Now guests had the physical space to take their rucksacks off and place them next to their seats. They could choose a noisy or a quiet area, and if they chose to, they could move away from a potentially violent situation or confrontation. The new space influenced behaviour. If problems arose, they could be dealt with in one corner, without influencing the atmosphere across the room. Interestingly, we noticed that guests would nearly always share a table with the same group. This increased their sense of belonging; they were gaining in trust and confidence as meal times and the familiarity of the space brought comfort and routine to their usually unstructured lives.

Quality interaction

In our experience, frequent and deep interaction with volunteers is vital for redeveloping social skills – such as a sense of responsibility and time management – as well as the self-confidence to engage with others in a public space, following years out on the street. Mass feeding centres for the homeless in London are typically designed as temporary and anonymous support facilities to keep people going until they recover, turn their lives around, and embark on a new trajectory. However, this rarely happens – social isolation is rather perpetuated through such anonymous institutions, and change is very unlikely to occur there. In 2016, we served around 50 people in our soup kitchen every night during the week. The manageable number and the continuity among guests and volunteers are our project's strengths. While volunteers can engage with guests more frequently than at other soup kitchens, at times it can nonetheless be difficult for volunteers to interact meaningfully during dinner serving time, due to the succession of guests in the queue. In such situations, volunteers can struggle to find the time to sit down with guests, to eat and chat with them. To address this, I developed the concept of neighbourhood lunches, to overcome the problem of isolation and create a sense of belonging, nurturing social skills and self-esteem. Residents from different neighbourhoods in the area were invited to meet for lunch on a regular basis and join the guests I invited from the soup kitchen. I rented the lower hall at St Peter de Beauvoir Church. It was a place of beauty – a crypt that had been tastefully renovated: exposed brickwork, a courtyard and an open-plan kitchen. There were sumptuous sofas, a reading area, showers and modern toilets. It was a place of rest and recreation. Some of the guests told me that they came just for the sense of peace they could feel in this space. Such intimate venues have a very positive effect on homeless people who have not given themselves up yet, who are still fighting in the hope of finding a way out of their situation and leaving the streets permanently.

The lunch meetings work as follows: I invite soup kitchen guests for lunch at 2pm. I talk about the lunch during the week, and many conversations revolve around the topic. There are around a dozen guests who trickle in at around 2pm. Most of them are Polish. They came to England to find work, but ended up on the street. We drink tea and cook meals together. Such intimate events allow people to feel part of a proper group, in which they can be actively involved, rather than receiving generous assistance from volunteers. Our guests can thus become essential and valuable team members. We also invited a woman who usually organises Victorian children's parties. I was initially concerned that the guests would find her patronising, but the concern was unfounded. They loved the games, and thought long and hard about the quiz questions. As in many other activities, one core aim of those lunch meetings is stimulation. The guests feel inspired, and thus also enjoy meeting new people, while simultaneously retaining the security of their peer group. Feeling that they matter and belong also makes our guests more likely to open up and talk about their backgrounds and biographies. Sharing stories provides a mechanism to overcome isolation and signals self-esteem.

As mentioned, in a busy evening at the soup kitchen, there is often no time to talk to guests in depth. At those lunch meetings, however, with only a limited number of guests, there is enough time to sit down together. We can show that we care and are ready to listen, which, in turn, helps the guests to open up. On one such occasion, Andre told me his entire life story. He had been living in this part of London for eight years. He had worked in hotels and part-time for a charity shop. He was 56 years old and smart, often wearing business clothes. He was not dressed for life in a 'tent city'; instead, Andre used to rent a room in a house in multiple occupation (HMO) in Archway, inner north London. He talked to me about the colour of the room and the people in the house in great detail. For various reasons, he then left the accommodation, and found another HMO in a nearby district. This house was not licensed, however, and there were constant fights about stolen items; you could not trust people not to steal food from the fridge. After a while, he left this accommodation as well. Andre also had to give up his part-time employment due to sickness. With little money left, he could only rent a hostel bed for two weeks each month. The rest of the time, he was homeless.

At the hostel, he met several other itinerate workers of all nationalities, who talked about their respective plights. One acquaintance told Andre that he could share an abandoned, stolen car with him at night. Andre was very happy with this arrangement, especially since the car was a luxury one. One day, however, the police recovered the car. Andre was facing homelessness again, and at this time of year, it was freezing cold. He was told by another friend about a shack that he might be able to use. It had no windows, but at least provided some shelter. Armed with a sleeping bag, he went to the shack, hoping for a good night's sleep. In the middle of the night, a crack junkie burst in and told him to leave. Andre refused, stating that he was homeless. This night passed peacefully. The next one, there was more drama. A young Italian woman and a man came in at midnight and screamed at Andre to leave. "I am with a man and you must leave," she told Andre. The Italian woman was only 23 years old and a crack cocaine addict who sold her body to procure drugs. They also came to an arrangement for that particular night; the next morning, they had breakfast together, with 70p biscuits from Tesco supermarket. Suddenly, she told Andre that he had to leave and never return. Such unpredictable and precarious situations dominate the lives of homeless people. Depressed, confused and increasingly sick, Andre was hoping that he would be able to return to the hostel soon. Weekly special lunches give people like Andre the opportunity to maintain hope – they provide a routine occasion to which they can look forward.

Bridging the social gap

We not only encourage people from the community to interact with our guests by inviting them along to our activities, but we also provide volunteers through our training programme with the right skills to engage with vulnerable guests. As a result, homeless people can develop a sense of belonging to the soup kitchen group, and by extension to the Muswell Hill community. As you can see, we also believe that profound interaction between volunteers and guests will help homeless people to develop social skills and confidence, which can help them overcome a sense of stigma and social isolation. We thus encourage volunteers to engage purposefully with guests. As part of our volunteer training sessions, we both teach helpers how to maintain food and other health and safety regulations, and we show them how to welcome and treat our guests as they would those they invited to their own home. In our training, we emphasise the importance of engaging in conversations with our guests to decrease their sense of social isolation and raise their self-esteem.

Accordingly, we ask volunteers to address guests by their first name. While some occasionally prefer their names to remain private, the majority of our guests appreciate this more personal type of interaction. For those with an addiction to alcohol or drug, isolation and the inability to talk and concentrate are a constant challenge. Nonetheless, by continually trying to engage people in conversation, volunteers have been able to help some of our homeless guests to overcome difficulties. One of them is Gordon, a homeless man from Hampstead Heath. He had travelled around the world and drank extensively, but one day he stopped on the hills outside Swansea, in Wales. He came to London. A bricklayer by trade, Gordon lived on a tent in Hampstead Heath for seven years. He came for food at the soup kitchen and gradually progressed to be a very dedicated helper, washing up and managing the storeroom. We became friends. One day, I asked him what he would like to do in the future. He responded, "To walk from John o' Groats to Land's End" – from up north in Scotland to the most distant tip of southern England. I nodded, and we agreed a start date for the following summer. Subsequently, Gordon committed to training every day. He then completed the walk in 41 days. He trekked all day, every day, and then slept under a hedge or in a field at night. It was a great achievement, and Gordon has become known in the local community for his brilliant effort. He raised £6,000 for the soup kitchen, and newspaper clippings about his trip remain on display there. He finally moved into a shed on an allotment, and continued to manage the soup kitchen store cupboard. He is a recluse, living life on his own terms. A city such as London produces these quiet characters that no one notices, who have nothing and just live for the day.

An important part of our volunteer development programme is the reflective practice. Expressive and explorative writing, together with in-depth group work, assists in widening the perspectives of our volunteers. This work helps them to develop a clear sense of their values and the different roles and responsibilities they can take on in their lives. Each week, volunteers – and even I – take the time to write, learn and reflect on interactions in the soup kitchen, which are then discussed in small weekly meetings with other volunteers. We also meet in small groups for a writing session once per month. The experience of writing and sharing what we have written with others can be very moving. It is clear from the writing that issues regarding loneliness, fear of the future, and uncertainty about relationships affect volunteers as much as guests. To write and capture these experiences gives us all the strength to enjoy what we do and to develop ourselves via our personal stories. This reflective practice also gives us all the confidence to work with vulnerable people. Writing sessions serve as a safe space to deal with what we hear and experience. When sharing our written records with group members, we use the energy and support of the group to learn how to work with pressing human needs more effectively, planning for the future. Since reflective practice requires the participants to write and share many emotional experiences, and to listen effectively and with compassion to others, it allows us to expand our levels of empathy, particularly to the troubled lives of homeless people. Missy was a 25-year-old woman from Australia, who volunteered with us during her two-year stay in England. She loved volunteering and the reflective practice sessions so much that she planned to open her own soup kitchen back in Australia. I asked her what she had learnt from volunteering with us, and she replied: "To create an environment free of fear, in which guests and enablers can have a party together: just come, have food and celebrate life."

Conclusion

This chapter has shown that Muswell Hill Churches Soup Kitchen differs from many other emergency social institutions: it is not simply a place to meet people's basic needs, but a social site, in which community building – via the raising of self-confidence, and thus of the ability to engage with others – is a central objective. In this soup kitchen, we value encounters, which is why we organise activities that mainly surround food. Most of them take place at our soup kitchen and associated venues, but some of them are external and involve the community even more actively. We often invite residents, who tend to be mainly middle class, to join our guests. Thus, the sharing of food becomes a way of bringing people from different social strata, and often with different biographies and experiences, together. Many of our vulnerable guests are struggling with addiction or mental health issues, but that should not prevent us from engaging with them. 'many sufferers of mental illness feel lonely and isolated and can benefit from a friendly listening ear. Mental health training is not a prerequisite to listening and talking to someone in distress' (Melvin, 2012). The shared meal is a way of breaking down the barriers and stigmas relating to the homeless population, and particularly to mental health. Through these interactions with volunteers and local residents, our homeless guests can overcome social isolation and develop the necessary social skills to break the cycle of living on the street. Participation and a sense of belonging help them to develop self-confidence.

Furthermore, our explicit focus on volunteer development is paramount to be able to support vulnerable fellow citizens. Reflective practice – expressive and explorative writing, together with in-depth group work – allows our volunteers to widen their perspectives and remain sympathetic. It also helps them to develop a clear sense of their values and the different roles and responsibilities they assume when working with vulnerable people who seem so much unlike themselves. Due to the availability of limited financial and staff resources, volunteer development is often neglected in social initiatives. I hope this chapter has shown its importance in helping vulnerable people to feel good about themselves and about their contribution to social initiatives. I hope that our example encourages other charities to pay more attention to the importance of volunteer development.

We have also realised, however, that enabling our guests to break the cycle of living on the street is more difficult. A process of habituation regarding homelessness and its daily routines exacerbates the consequences of mental health problems and drug addiction. Thus, our work's focus is on providing guests with social skills and the necessary confidence to encourage them to develop a sense of belonging to a social group, and to extend that sense of belonging to a wider community and society as a whole. More than being simply an emergency solution to hunger, our soup kitchen seeks to support those who have lost a sense of societal belonging and relevance to feel needed and appreciated once again.

References

Bogardus, E. S. (1952) *Principles of Cooperation*, Unknown Binding.

Melvin, P. (2012) *Mental Health and Homelessness: Guidance for practitioners Opening Doors Project Guidance*, London: The Queen's Nursing Institute.

Part III
Social change and neoliberalism

ELEVEN

Social initiatives and social solidarity under austerity

Christina Fuhr

The 2008 financial crisis resulted in a protracted recession in Europe of a kind not seen since the Great Depression (Colley, 1992). The United Kingdom's (UK) politics of austerity has led to dramatic cuts to social security and public services, and has been accompanied by falling incomes, a continual increase in living costs, growing unemployment and precarious employment (Oxfam, 2013; Slay and Penny, 2016). The combination has, in turn, contributed to a rise in poverty (Irving, 2013). In Germany, austerity-related labour market and welfare reforms were implemented between 2003 and 2005 as a continuation of the *Sparpolitik* (budget and austerity reduction) path. They were aimed at welfare readjustment to ensure international competitiveness and fiscal sustainability in a situation of high unemployment levels and repeated failure to stabilise and ensure economic growth. These policies continued and have worked effectively in Germany to limit negative economic impact in the aftermath of the 2008 financial crisis (Eichhorst and Hassel, 2015).

Austerity policies in both countries have increased the presence of and need for social initiatives such as foodbanks (Bunyan and Diamond, 2014; Forsey, 2014; Loopstra et al, 2015; Selke, 2015) and, with them, civic engagement (HM Government, 2013; Selke, 2013). In the media, foodbanks have largely been depicted as the epitome of social solidarity during austerity. *The Oxford English dictionary* (2016) defines solidarity as 'unity or agreement of feeling or action, especially among individuals with a common interest; mutual support within a group'. Thus, solidarity is 'a feeling of togetherness and willingness to take the consequences of that' (Komter, 2004, pp 1-2). At present, however, it seems unclear to what extent foodbanks can create solidarity in society. The investigation of this topic is of societal relevance, since the economic crisis and the consequent call for austerity have contributed to the appearance of a new public concern over welfare abuse and a renewal of 'anti-scrounger' sentiment (Behr, 2010) across

Europe (Romano, 2015). In the UK, a political narrative around the reinvigoration of the 'benefit scrounger' myth and of the notion of the 'undeserving poor' appeared post-2008 (Brianta et al, 2013). This trend has paralleled the political legitimisation of social policy reforms that reduced social entitlements and increased workfare incentives in many European countries (Ghimis et al, 2014). Studies have, furthermore, illustrated how austerity has contributed to social segregation and inequality between high- and low-income groups in Europe (Seetzen et al, 2014; Copeland et al, 2015) and among marginalised groups and individuals (Clark and Heath, 2015). Considering that Germany and the UK have both seen a considerable expansion of foodbanks in recent years, this chapter, using the method of ethnography, will examine to what extent and thereby how foodbanks in Germany and the UK can construct social solidarity under austerity.

This chapter focuses on the largest foodbank networks in Germany and the UK, the Tafel and The Trussell Trust respectively. The Trussell Trust is a Christian charity with over 424 outlets that hand out non-perishable food to people in need directly (TT, 2016e). The Trussell Trust works as a franchise, with local branches paying joining fees to obtain training, their own web space and quality assurance checks (Caplan, 2016). In Germany, the first Tafel was founded in Berlin in 1993. It developed into a franchise model in which local community organisations, particularly church communities, collect food from local supermarkets and shops and offer it to other social initiatives and to vulnerable people directly. The Tafel now has 900 branches regularly serving around 1.5 million people, one third of whom are below the age of 18 (Tafel, 2016b). Post-2008, similar numbers have emerged in the UK. In 2014/15, The Trussell Trust gave out over one million food parcels to UK people in crisis (TT, 2016e). The focus on the Tafel and The Trussell Trust has allowed me to examine carefully the major differences and similarities between foodbanks in Germany and the UK.

The data for this chapter were collected between December 2014 and October 2015. I conducted seven interviews with academics in the field of social welfare and foodbank use in Germany and 10 interviews with volunteers and staff from the Tafel in Berlin. Fourteen interviews were conducted with volunteers and staff at various foodbanks in the United Kingdom, of which eight interviewees were from The Trussell Trust. Regarding the observational part of the study, I conducted most of the observations in foodbanks in Berlin and in London, along with major cities in its vicinity including Cambridge and Oxford. Where applicable, I also refer to observational data about foodbanks that I collected at other social initiatives and events.

Overall, the chapter argues that while foodbanks may create a societal representation of solidarity, they may also reproduce social stratification and segregation on the ground. It shows that foodbanks can generate a public image of solidarity on the macro-level, meaning on the societal level, but may struggle to do so on the micro-level, in other words in the interactions between service providers and recipients.

The public image of social solidarity

While creating social solidarity is explicitly part of the mission of some foodbanks in the UK and Germany, it plays an implicit role for others. For The Trussell Trust, 'bringing communities together' (TT, 2016b) to stop food poverty is an essential part of its mission. By contrast, the model of the Tafel only refers to the construction of solidarity in an indirect way by ensuring that the actions of the Tafel foodbanks are based on the values of sustainability, humanity, justice, participation and social responsibility' (Tafel, 2016a).

In both countries, however, by helping people in need, foodbanks offer a sense of togetherness, and therefore solidarity, through their physical and thus visual presence in neighbourhoods. Foodbanks like the Tafel and The Trussell Trust have become a solid feature of the social fabric of neighbourhoods due to their franchise models and, particularly, by working together with local communities – mainly church congregations – and by being placed in social institutions, such as churches and community centres. For example, the Tafel deliberately wanted to work with churches, in order to be able to set up its franchise model. According to Tafel founder Sabine Werth:

> "I was clear about the fact that we cannot get that [a network of foodbanks] established via volunteers alone.... I gave an interview on the cultural radio programme on Radio Berlin Brandenburg and I have said ... that I had already thought about contacting churches to do this. Friederike Sittler, chief of the editorial team Church und Religion at rbb [Radio Berlin Brandenburg], heard the interview and called me and said 'I have contacts in the churches. You have contacts to the foodbanks. Shall we not get together?'...That's how Laib and Seele[1] developed.... We have gradually contacted the churches and built up 45 issuing locations. Every issuing location is autonomous. For example, one church community doesn't offer food in the church but in a youth centre, whilst another community

operates the foodbank directly from the church; if you go in there you can see the boxes are stacked up around the baptistery."

According to the London Development Officer of The Trussell Trust, The Trussell Trust places a similar emphasis on partnerships with churches and local communities:

"All Trussell Trust foodbanks are launched in partnership with local churches and communities, because local communities are best placed to meet local needs. We'll provide you with all the tools, training and know-how that you need to start a foodbank so that people in crisis in your town don't have to go hungry."

Collaboration with foodbanks can also be beneficial for churches and other faith organisations as a means of engaging their membership and gaining new members. At the William Templeton Foundation Building of Hope Conference – Exploring the Role and Impact of Faith-based Leadership in Local Communities in London, one Anglican vicar argued that the Anglican Church is in the process of 'turning church inside out'. With declining membership numbers, she argued that the church becomes a faith community that works outside of its walls and moves towards others through the provision of charitable work.

The physical and visual presence of foodbanks in communally shared spaces – like supermarket chains and community institutions – through collection points such as baskets, bins and trolleys with clearly distinguishable logos and strap-lines such as The Trussell Trust's *Stop UK Hunger* or the Tafel's *Essen wo es hingehoert* (putting food where it belongs) nurtures the perception of foodbanks as being community actors that help people in crisis in their neighbourhoods, and at the same time create direct engagement with citizens. In the UK, for instance, the major supermarket chain Tesco partners with The Trussell Trust and FareShare[2] and has permanent collection points in 600 of its stores where customers can donate food anytime (Tesco, 2016). Branding as a community organisation that creates social solidarity also takes place through collection-day initiatives, where volunteers from the local community ask for donations from shoppers outside supermarkets. Such initiatives assist in forming the image of foodbanks supporting the common good of the community and thus are part and parcel of the local community building social solidarity. The Foodbank Network Director of The Trussell Trust added:

> "We would ask the public to donate food to us – [it] had the added effect of educating people of the need in their community. It got the community involved in the foodbank so it's a community solution to what is a community."

These collection-day initiatives mainly take place in collaboration with big supermarket chains, whose wide publicity reach helps foodbanks to spread the image of themselves as projects generating solidarity. During Tesco's eighth Neighbourhood Food Collection for The Trussell Trust, Tesco wrote on its website that 'generous communities nationwide' had provided The Trussell Trust with food to serve 2.8 million meals to help struggling individuals and families. Tesco even topped up customer donations by making a 20% financial contribution to The Trussell Trust, 'meaning the collection has not only provided vital food for UK people experiencing crisis', but that funds will also help Trussell Trust foodbanks to 'develop their services and provide important support, beyond food, to tackle the root causes of poverty'. David McAuley, Trussell Trust Chief Executive, is quoted on Tesco's website:

> We want to say a massive thank you to everyone who participated in this summer's Neighbourhood Food Collection. Unavoidable circumstances such as illness, redundancy or an unexpected bill can all leave people facing hunger and needing help from a foodbank. In communities up and down the country parents are skipping meals to feed their children, which is why the incredible generosity shown by Tesco customers, store staff and volunteers is so valuable; it enables Trussell Trust foodbanks across the UK to be there to provide emergency food and support when anyone is hit by crisis. (Tesco, 2016)

Collection-day initiatives are also effective in assisting foodbanks to brand themselves as generating solidarity by engaging citizens on the ground to donate food to them, such as at the one organised by CEF Oxford that I came across first hand at Waitrose in Headington. Volunteers explained the work of the foodbank to shoppers who stopped to engage, and motivated them to buy extra items and then donate them. One volunteer remarked:

> "We had no idea it would be such a huge success for the foodbank... I guess because there is not a collection

trolley like in other supermarkets, shoppers see giving to the foodbank as more of a novelty and do not experience donation fatigue – as they are not expected to give every week."

A female shopper who donated two packages of porridge said: "I didn't know there were people in our community who did not have enough food. It [CEF Oxford collection-day initiative] raises your awareness of what is going on in our community so we can help." In this way, collection-day initiatives and the act of donating to foodbanks can actually build and reaffirm a sense of social solidarity in communities.

Accordingly collaboration between foodbanks and industry can be profitable for foodbanks in terms of publicity to portray social solidarity. A number of the big supermarket chains have adopted foodbanks as 'partners' and this may appear on their websites as part of their corporate social responsibility (CSR) remit. A foodbank network director from The Trussell Trust elaborated as follows on its partnerships:

> "Our corporate partners would usually want to give us some money to help us do what we do. We have a number of partners: the ASDA foundation supply us with some money, Tesco supply us with some money to help pay for some of our staff.... We work with Unilever; PG tips is one of their brands. You know the little monkey that's on the adverts? So he has just been doing a fundraising appeal, a text donate appeal for us. So the monkey has a huge following on Twitter ... so he has been tweeting about The Trussell Trust and about the work of our foodbanks and people have been donating and so we have had some money through that. Our corporate partners can also supply volunteers.... Others have helped us more practically, where we need help. It could be anything from human resources to our website. Those are often in-kind help. So Lloyds TSB has been helping our team thinking about workload, some of our management information reporting and helping us to build that and how to manage the calls coming in here."[3]

As the quote highlights, foodbanks do not only receive publicity from industry partners, but also support – including financial and in the form of goods and services. Tafel, for example, receives sponsorship from various established businesses such as Metro and Mercedes Benz (Tafel, 2016e).

However, cooperation with foodbanks can also be profitable for industry. By supporting foodbanks, businesses fulfil their CSR agenda and use it as a marketing tool to increase their own public profile positively by portraying social care. Foodbank support can also reduce their company costs. In the case of retail collections of fresh food that cannot be sold or is past the sell-by date, foodbanks save retailers high waste-disposal costs. Luise Molling, who has done qualitative work on Tafel foodbanks, argued in an interview with me:

> "For companies, it is great that there is the Tafel, as all their waste products go, which they had to dispose of beforehand for a lot of money. And through helping the Tafel they are also cultivating their image…. They can also be regarded as the great benefactors so for them the support works well. You meet social demands and at the same time lower the costs for your company, because they can donate it [their food] rather than having to pay for disposal. Nothing better than the Tafel that gives them even a donation receipt which is tax-deductible, and then they can say afterwards we are the donors, we are the benefactors, we take care of the poor."

Allowing for foodbank collection days or a collection point or trolley in a food retailer can also increase sales. For example, a Waitrose shop assistant answered in response to how the food collection day by CEF Oxford volunteers went: "The generosity of Headington shoppers has cleared our shelves." In this way, the clients of foodbanks are not only the users, but also the sponsors, including citizens, who donate goods and money to foodbanks as the costs of running each foodbank and the national networks need to be covered. Luise Molling argued in this regard: "They [Tafels] are aimed at retaining their sponsors, well donors generally … the national network of the Tafel has personnel costs alone of half a million a year." According to the yearly report of the Tafel, the entire administrative costs – including personnel costs – of the Tafel in 2014 were over 1.1 million euros, which were covered by the 4.2 million euros of donations (Tafel, 2014).

Foodbanks also have mutually beneficial relationships with politics and the media, which assist the foodbanks' dissemination of their own public image as creators and perpetuators of social solidarity. In Germany, Tafel's role as a community brand that perpetuates social solidarity is nurtured through political patronage, which, in turn, provides publicity (Molling, 2009). For example, the former Minister for Family Affairs, Renate Schmidt, justified her patronage of the

Tafel in an article for the members' magazine of the Tafel as follows: 'Bourgeois culture is closely connected to civic engagement.... It is the diversity of the freedoms and responsibilities, initiatives and commitments ... – meaning a civil society ready to be responsible – that keeps the community together' (Schmidt, 2004, p 4; Molling, 2009, p 165). Similarly, her successor, Ursula von der Leyen, referring to the Tafel and its volunteers, said: 'A civil society must be able to take on community care actively' (von der Leyen, 2007, p 5; Molling, 2009, p 159), and the 2016 political patron, Manuela Schwesig, explained her acceptance of the patronage with the following words: 'I was very impressed to see how from a basically simple idea a broad movement for more solidarity and humanity is created in our society' (Tafel, 2016d). This quote indicates that having political patrons voicing their support for foodbanks and their role in supporting the common good and generating social solidarity assists the cultivation of this image. At the same time, the association with foodbanks is beneficial for politicians as it allows them, efficiently, to demonstrate solidarity with people in need and thus social responsibility, characteristics that are important facets of their public office roles.

In the UK, it is uncommon for politicians to be patrons of foodbanks. Yet, some foodbanks still connect with politics actively. Engaging local MPs and other government agencies also generates publicity and helps foodbanks to cultivate their image as community actors that build social solidarity. The Trussell Trust collects statistics relating to its foodbanks and engages with politics by 'sharing the experience of people helped by foodbanks and our social enterprises with governing administrations across the UK ... [and thereby] engaging decision makers with the realities of poverty' (TT, 2016c). For example, The Trussell Trust submitted evidence in September 2015 to the Work and Pensions Committee inquiry into welfare delivery. The foci of this inquiry were ongoing problems with the benefits system, as well as new issues relating to benefit delays and changes, which are seen as being major drivers of foodbank use. The organisation also gives regular input into the work of the All-Party Parliamentary Group on Hunger and Food Poverty, specifically its Feeding Britain inquiry (TT, 2016c). Its collaboration with political agencies is beneficial to foodbanks, as it supports their overall goal of ending hunger and poverty (TT, 2016b), while also generating publicity that cultivates foodbanks' image as creators of social solidarity[4]

The work of foodbanks fits into a wider political agenda of supporting charities' work to create positive change in communities under austerity. In 2010 the Conservative–Liberal Democrat coalition government introduced a new political ideology called the 'Big Society' (Norman, 2010), which claimed to 'put more power and opportunity into people's hands' (Cabinet Office, 2010, p 1). By implementing 'a range of measures to encourage charitable giving and philanthropy' (Cabinet Office, 2010, p 2), the responsibility for providing solutions to health, financial and social problems shifted from the state to communities (Blond, 2010). The Trussell Trust has been regarded as a prime example of the government's political agenda. The Conservative Home (2012) called the network 'the epitome of the Big Society' and 'a fantastic Christian charity'. In the UK parliament in December 2012, the former Conservative Prime Minister David Cameron directly praised the work of volunteers in foodbanks as 'part of what I call the big society' (Wells and Caraher, 2014 p 1427). In his 2016 Easter address, David Cameron emphasised the importance of charities, and particularly faith-based ones, in creating, as he called it, 'good communities' (Cameron, 2016):

> Across the country, we have tens of thousands of fantastic faith-based charities. Every day they're performing minor miracles in local communities. As Prime Minister, I've worked hard to stand up for these charities and give them more power and support.

In a wider context, governmental support of charities such as foodbanks is seen as beneficial to politicians as it demonstrates their solidarity with people in need while at the same time creating support for their agenda of shifting responsibility for alleviating poverty from the welfare state to the charity sector (Kendall, 2000; Milbourne, 2009).

As indicated earlier by Sabine Werth, the founder of the Berliner Tafel, collaboration with the media can also be beneficial for foodbanks in generating social solidarity. This can also be seen by the high amounts of donations received through media fundraisers. For example, in a fundraising event in December 2013 the NDR (North German broadcaster) collected 1.4 million euros for the Tafel. In the UK, there is similar support from the media. Reports about foodbanks in the UK, particularly about The Trussell Trust, have become a regular occurrence. According to Saul and Curtis (2013), there is little critical analysis in the media regarding the operation of and even the need for foodbanks. Few questions are asked about other models or ways of distributing food and how to use foodbanks as the stepping stone to more essential and just changes (Wells and Caraher, 2014, p 1439). Wells and Caraher (2014) indicate that the media reporting of food poverty and the use of foodbanks can influence public perception.

Through their affiliation with and positive reporting about prominent foodbank networks, the media can strengthen their community voice. According to the Foodbank Network Director of The Trussell Trust:

> "I think our profile in the media has been very high over the last year. Most [media] people when they think of foodbanks have come into contact with us in some way.... We do have a corporate relations manager who manages those relationships and what we are finding is that from these relationships others spring up."

To conclude, this section has demonstrated that foodbanks have become institutionalised in Germany and the UK. Through their physical representation in the community and their mutually beneficial engagement with core actors of UK and German society – faith institutions, politics, industry and the media – foodbanks can brand themselves as building social solidarity and seem to be successful in this respect.

Social solidarity through social action

Exploring the social dynamics within foodbanks and analysing thereby how volunteers sustain their motivation to donate their time and labour to a foodbank over time, this section demonstrates how these charitable organisations can build positive social relations among volunteers and staff through the provision of collective action and thereby group solidarity, aiding a macro-level representation of foodbanks building social solidarity.

Much has been published about social capital construction and volunteering: social connections that help to build trust and collective action within communities (Putnam, 2000). Accordingly, collective action can contribute to a sense of community belonging among those who are involved. A study of Tafel volunteers in the German state of North Rhine-Westphalia analysed that the four most frequently mentioned motives for volunteering were to have fun at work, to fill one's life with meaning, to feel needed, and to expand one's life experience (Selke and Maar, 2011). These results are substantiated by another research finding that volunteering in Tafels provides helpers with structure, meaning, recognition, the possibility of compensation of their own debt of gratitude and compensation for power losses in other areas of their lives such as work and family (Selke, 2009, p 280; Scheller, 2014, p 8). With this in mind, I found that the motivation for people to volunteer in a foodbank was often directly referred to as a sense of wanting to belong to society through belonging to a social group, a network of social connections and relations. For example, the female leader of a Tafel located in a church in an affluent part of Berlin, where most volunteers are retired middle-class Germans, said:

> "[Our helpers] want to be part of the larger society … [they] do not want to walk with an old lady where they are relatively isolated or assist a child in learning to read where they only have this one-on-one connection. They want a place where more is going on, where they have the feeling that there's life."

According to this Tafel leader, the motivation for being part of a team was equally and, in some cases, more important than helping vulnerable people:

> "For most, the priority is not the feeling that they must help the poor. This may play a part but it is not the deciding factor."

In order to ensure the continual involvement of members in foodbanks over time, positive social dynamics seem to be essential. These can lead to positive social relations and by extension a sense of belonging, and thereby promote group and thus social solidarity among the service providers. The study found that regard, defined in this chapter as signs of attention, notice and giving of care, is a nuanced, but important mechanism underlying the construction of positive social dynamics. Signs of regard are not only embodied in goods but also in services such as providing care, notice and, at the very least, attention (Offer, 1997). Receiving regard is a basic human need, which is necessary to achieve a positive self-concept, for which everyone strives (Tajfel and Turner, 1979; Hogg, 2006). It presents a mechanism that responds to an innate need to be attended to in order to feel safe and secure (Maslow, 1999). A priest, whose church hosts a Tafel in a poor area of East Berlin, where most of the volunteers at the Tafel are in their thirties to fifties and mainly unemployed, noted in this respect: "People have a role here [in the foodbank]. Many of our volunteers live alone and feel lonely. Here, they feel that they are needed." Some of its volunteers simply had physical or mental health problems that prevented them from finding work, while others could not find employment, of which a few told me that they were trained in jobs that ceased to exist after the fall of the German Democratic Republic, such as *Molkereifacharbeiter* (dairy worker). For them, working in a foodbank where they felt needed and received recognition for their contribution was essential to their sense of self-worth. This was echoed by the female leader of the middle-class foodbank in West Berlin where most of the volunteers were retirees[5] and volunteered in order to have a place of belonging:

> "They [volunteers] have difficulties when they are not needed anymore. There is also the wish for recognition. You find a conglomeration of sensations: recognition, movement, life, conversations with the other helpers, sitting together.... The community aspect certainly plays a big role in this."

Signs of regard were found in subtle behavioural recognitions such as the foodbank leader saying 'thank you' to volunteers for their help, or volunteers making cups of tea and coffee for each other, or bringing food along that was then shared with other helpers. In the Tafel in East Berlin, after everyone had left, the workers finished off the day by sitting together on the terrace with drinks and nibbles and sometimes had barbecues there as well. The leader of this foodbank contributed the following observation in this respect: "It's like a family here; you belong. You sit together afterwards [after the clients have left] and talk." Accordingly, expressions of regard took many forms. For example, whenever volunteers did not attend their usual shifts, their colleagues expressed concern and were eager to inquire about them with fellow volunteers, or message them directly in order to make sure that nothing was wrong. A volunteer at one of the Tafels I visited said: "You are missed if you do not show up because people count on you. You are part of the team." Considering that volunteers are not paid for their time and help, such gestures were considered important. In this way, such gestures can also assist in creating a sense of togetherness among volunteers.

Moreover, I found that signs of regard were often expressed in work-related practices. In all of the foodbanks I visited food delivery was a team effort. For example, when I helped two Oxford foodbank volunteers collect donated food from supermarkets and deliver it to social institutions, I observed how they helped each other carry food in and out of the delivery van. Stocking shelves and preparing food parcels with other volunteers, as experienced at the London Muslim foodbank Sufra, was also found to be important bonding time, with volunteers working together in order to achieve the common goal of delivering food to vulnerable people. All of these group-related work practices provided opportunity for regard to be expressed and trust to be established. This could be observed when volunteers, who had not worked together before, started chatting to each other about their personal lives only after they had been working together for a little while. At one of my visits to Sufra, two young Jewish women came to volunteer. After a while of packing food parcels and stocking shelves together with a Muslim and a Christian volunteer, they started talking about their daily lives: what their families were like, their friends and relationships, how it is to celebrate and not celebrate Christmas, as well as the difference between the fasting ritual of the Muslim Ramadan and Jewish Yom Kippur and what it meant to them. These findings resonate with Avner Offer's work about the *Economy of Regard* in which he demonstrates, using secondary literature, how reciprocity is driven by the pursuit of regard. Offer (1997) argues that 'regard provides a powerful incentive for trust' and promotes 'sociability, and sociability facilitates cooperation' (pp 454-5).

The concept of building positive social relations among volunteers to help vulnerable citizens is often used by foodbanks for publicity, aiding the notion of foodbanks building social solidarity on the macro-level. For example, The Trussell Trust writes on its website that 'volunteers are the life blood of The Trussell Trust,' continuing the advertisement of its services with 'whether you're giving out food to people in crisis at a foodbank centre or helping sort clothes for our charity shops, we could not operate without people like you giving your time. An amazing 40,000 volunteers helped us last year' (TT, 2016f). The Trussell Trust also highlights its inclusivity in this regard, emphasising that it provides volunteer opportunities for people with mental, social or physical difficulties and those serving community service hours so that they can 'make a positive difference in their communities' (TT, 2016d). Even the volunteers are quoted, highlighting that positive social relations among volunteers are important in helping to stop UK hunger:

> I find it rewarding in many ways; good company, plenty
> of laughs and the chance to help those in society who are
> in genuine and desperate need. The hours I volunteer are
> ideal and I still have plenty of time to enjoy my retirement
> in other ways – Peter, Volunteer. (TT, 2016f)

The same accounts for the Tafel in Germany, which advertises that the Tafel 'brings people together across boundaries and generations' (Tafel, 2016c). This also helps publicise what foodbanks are known for on a public level. For example, Barbara Klepsch, Staatsministerin für Soziales und Verbraucherschutz (Minister of State for Social Affairs and Consumer Protection), said in an interview with the newspaper *Wochenendspiegel* that 'the Tafels bring completely different people together who like to help. The Tafels can only live thanks to their help and engagement' (Kaiser, 2016).

Overall, this section has argued that group and thus social solidarity among volunteers, in terms of a sense of togetherness in helping people in crisis – contributing to a macro-level representation of solidarity by foodbanks – can be created through positive social dynamics and sustained through the micro-mechanism of regard.

Social solidarity disrupted

This section explores the extent to which social solidarity is expressed by volunteers and staff towards foodbank visitors by looking at the social dynamics between service providers and service recipients. In Germany, a lack of social solidarity by service providers towards service recipients could be observed through a lack of regard and at times even disregard – meaning inattention, negligence and carelessness that could even take the form of resentment or disrespect – during service delivery.[6] When I was conducting observations for our project in a homeless daycare centre in Berlin, the social worker who regularly collects food for her centre from the foodbank in the affluent area of West Berlin noted the arbitrariness of resource distribution when she came back from collecting food from this foodbank. She specifically referred to the high level of authority and decision-making power the service providers have in terms of food they hand out to clients and how this can play out in a lack of regard: "If the helper likes your nose you get more and if he thinks you look like you need more courgettes you get more courgettes." I have observed this in this foodbank when some customers made food-related inquiries. One male client at a foodbank in Berlin, for example, felt the need to ask in a begging way and with a tone of voice that signalled deference, "Are there still any aubergines left by any chance?" The fact that he felt he had to plead for food indicates the existence of a lack of regard by volunteers.

This social worker also noted a lack of regard in terms of the derogatory and impersonal manner in which clients were sometimes treated by volunteers: "The volunteers give food to people without respect saying things like 'Here, take that' with a patronising tone of voice." I observed such behaviour when a female client at the same foodbank asked "Could I have only brown rolls, please?" The volunteer who was serving her replied with a simple annoyed sigh, a gesture of disregard, which made the customer feel the need to justify her question by explaining that she had diabetes. Only then would the volunteer pack a bag with brown rolls for her. A lack of regard, which could shade into disregard, was also witnessed in how customer demands were answered by staff and volunteers. Another client in this foodbank tried to obtain more potatoes by asking in a very submissive way: "Can I have a bit more, please?", which was answered with a disrespectful 'tut' by the volunteer and a rough "Go on then." Even in the foodbank where most – at times all – of the volunteers are on benefits, the same lack of social solidarity expressed in a lack of regard between helpers and clients existed. The priest whose church hosts a Tafel commented:

> "There are problems from time to time... Both are in need. Both have the same need. If one of them, however, has a position, he's the boss; he can use his position against the others – 'Now I am finally somebody' – and there is then a power struggle."

An absence of solidarity was also expressed in volunteers' reactions when their expectations of how customers should behave were not fulfilled. Some volunteers could feel frustration and thus resentment towards clients when they did not say 'thank you' on receiving food or complained about the standard or type of food they received. One of the volunteers at the foodbank in West Berlin told me during one of my observations that when one of the customers did not want to take the dented peppers she had offered him, she told him he should just go to their local Penny (supermarket) and spend a lot of money on buying perfect peppers, knowing full well that he came to the foodbank because of a shortage of money. Some of the volunteers also felt resentment towards customers when they threw away food they had been given outside the foodbank, or they did not like to take certain foods that were offered to them. The priest quoted earlier gave the following example:

> "The Russian-Germans, they often do not eat salad … and then the ones handing out food, say: 'Look, they always only take the best. And the salad? They don't want that, and those are the Russians, they are doing that.'"

This expression of behavioural expectations by volunteers and staff towards customers, indicating a lack of social solidarity, could also be observed in the West Berlin foodbank. When I asked the volunteers, for example, why they cut the discoloured bits off the cauliflowers, one volunteer said critically: "We have to do cosmetic surgery on our vegetables; otherwise the customers won't take them."

Interestingly, social solidarity seems to be more prevalent in foodbanks in the UK. Here, people tend to be issued a maximum of three vouchers in six months, of which a majority do not make full use, as foodbanks in the UK are regarded as an emergency service. According to The Trussell Trust, people need, on average, two foodbank referrals per year (TT, 2016a). The restricted access to foodbanks in the UK suggests that there is more opportunity for quality interaction. There is also an institutionalised service that is offered by most foodbanks that consists of a conversation with a volunteer or member of staff when people come to the foodbank, whereby regard is shown. The aim of the conversation is twofold. First, it helps customers identify what has led to their crisis. This allows the volunteers and staff to provide ideas about how the clients can help themselves and refer them to the appropriate service that can help them solve their crisis, or if the relevant agency that can help resolve their crisis is present – as many Trussell Trust foodbanks are now partnering with general or specific advice services – giving them support instantly. Second, the conversation should help clients relieve themselves of their distress and isolation. The London Development Officer of The Trussell Trust, for example, argued that much of its help is provided by simply listening to the clients' needs so they no longer feel isolated and instead feel supported. She suggested that service users positively change after having had a conversation with them:

> "They light up, they start sitting straight; they say things like: 'Oh nobody has told me that before.' Or they may cry and are relieved. By that time, volunteers will not have even given them food yet."

The London Foodbank Network Manager of The Trussell Trust contributed this observation:

> "We witness anxiety and suffering. We try to offer hope and stimulate determination to keep going for one more day... Most foodbank project managers and volunteers try to nurture, invest time and watch people unfurl and grow a little."

In addition to the prayer offered to their guests, the London Development Officer cited earlier argued that this 'relationship-building' exercise or 'befriending' is 'priceless'.

Such focused interaction offers the opportunity for volunteers to give attention, notice and care to foodbank visitors, thereby demonstrating social solidarity. This finding resonates with literature by Collins (2004), who argued that participants in interactional situations 'develop a mutual focus of attention and become entrained in each other's bodily micro-rhythms and emotion' (p 47). What Collins describes is a positive emotional energy that is constructed in social interactions. Positive emotional energy is attention that people interacting with each other give to one another, meaning they give time and, within that time, focus to each other. In other words, a mutual feeling of being paid attention to is created in interactions. Providing attention, notice and, by extension, care through focus in interaction signals a willingness to be there for the receiver and thus can assist in creating positive social dynamics and in communicating social solidarity.

The evidence indicates that the institutional focus of foodbanks in Britain is on the provision of quality service, whereas in Germany the focus seems to be placed on quantity, which may make the demonstration of solidarity more difficult. Financially vulnerable people in Germany can normally access their local foodbank once a week. Many of the foodbanks in Germany thus serve a high number of customers, which means a lack of time and thus focus for each client. In the German foodbanks I visited, the sheer volume of customers prevented most of the volunteers and staff from engaging meaningfully with them. One foodbank volunteer in the West Berlin Tafel said: "You just don't have the time to talk to customers. It works here like at a conveyer belt." Another volunteer from this foodbank commented: "Within two hours you are trying to serve about 300 people, you just do not have time to spend more than thirty seconds with each person." These comments should be read in the context of Maar and Eberlei's (2013) findings from their research about foodbanks in Germany that 'the emphasis [for volunteers] is on the practical assistance in the form of collecting and distributing still eatable foods. It is not about providing psycho-social assistance or social policy oriented engagement for the purpose of reducing social inequality' (p 27).

In the UK, the focus on quality interaction and support may also be associated with the fact that most foodbanks are faith-based, mainly Abrahamic faith-based, and thus have an institutional framework of religious ethics of altruism and helping the poor. For example, Sufra identifies itself clearly as a Muslim charity and The Trussell Trust is a charity founded on Christian principles. The latter's mission verse reads as follows:

> For I was hungry and you gave me something to eat, I was thirsty and you gave me something to drink, I was a stranger and you invited me in, I needed clothes and you clothed me, I was sick and you looked after me, I was in prison and you came to visit me. Matthew 25: 35-36. (TT, 2016b)

Many of the employees and volunteers I talked to from The Trussell Trust felt a sense of responsibility to help their customers in such profound ways rather than simply providing the basic need of food to clients. For example, the London Foodbank Network Manager from The Trussell Trust argued that "anyone could be a foodbank client and very few of us are immune to catastrophic circumstances which cause chaos to financial stability and our own wellbeing". Accordingly, for her, working at the foodbank was not just about the provision of food, but also about listening to the clients and trying to help them with associated needs that are not fulfilled. She gave the example of a young single mother with two children whose benefits were sanctioned for five weeks over Christmas. She explained how the foodbanks had helped this client not only with food provision but also with having her sanctions lifted and the outstanding money for rent refunded, and how the volunteers have continued to help her get her home refurbished, as she had had to sell her furniture in order to feed her children. This was only one of the many stories the manager told me, describing how she and other Trussell Trust foodbank managers and volunteers had given hands-on help with needs other than solely the provision of food. Accordingly, this desire to extend help beyond the provision of emergency food, whereby staff and volunteers want to provide more than just food charity, indicates a sense of solidarity with people who are marked by social difference.

In Germany, the Tafels do not follow a religious ideology. While Tafels are often situated in churches and other religious places, their institutional mission is non-religious and generalist. They focus on values of (1) sustainability – advocating against destruction of food; (2) humanity – treating everyone with respect; (3) justice; (4) social participation; and (5) social responsibility. Through their action, Tafels take on the responsibility to remind society of its commitment towards people in need and who are isolated (Tafel, 2016a). Considering that there is also a lack of solidarity between service providers and service recipients in Tafels, a faith-based institutional framework may encourage a more in-depth and hands-on approach to helping people and thus more opportunity to express solidarity.

In summary, this section has shown that there can be a lack of social solidarity between volunteers/staff and service recipients, often expressed in lack of regard, which can even take the form of disregard. A lack of social solidarity was found in foodbanks in Germany but not in the UK. This may be associated with differing institutional approaches to engagement with vulnerable people. The institutional emphasis by German foodbanks seems to be on quantity interaction of volunteers and staff with clients by focusing solely on the provision of the basic need of food on a weekly basis. In the UK, the institutional focus is on the provision of quality interaction, enabled by clients' restricted access to foodbanks and the institutional practice of a sit-down conversation between service providers and service recipients. Considering that most foodbanks in the UK identify with the Abrahamic faiths, the chapter suggests that religious ethics of altruism and helping the poor may cultivate an institutional focus on quality interaction and thus support.

Conclusion

Foodbanks are often viewed as social solidarity organisations that usually distribute donated food among people in need (Martins et al, 2010). This chapter has explored the extent to which, and how, foodbanks in Germany and the UK can help to create social solidarity during austerity. It has detailed how foodbanks can portray a public image of togetherness in helping people in need and thus social solidarity. This is achieved through their physical presence in neighbourhoods and cities accompanied by their branding as community actors fostering the common good, as well as their mutually beneficial engagement with core actors within UK and German society, including faith institutions, political bodies, industry and the media.

The chapter has demonstrated how foodbanks build positive social dynamics and by extension social relations among volunteers and staff through the provision of collective action, thereby creating a sense of group solidarity, aiding a macro-level representation of foodbanks building social solidarity. By exploring how volunteers sustain their motivation to donate their time and labour to a foodbank over time, the chapter has shown that continuously expressed regard, defined as signs of attention, notice and care giving, is important in this respect. Regard allows for the construction and maintenance of positive social dynamics and in this way social solidarity. These findings resonate with Adam Smith, who notes in his book *The Theory of Moral Sentiments*

(Smith, 1976 [1759]) that activities are driven 'chiefly from this regard to the sentiments of mankind':

> What is the end of avarice and ambition, of the pursuit of wealth, of power, and preheminence?... To be observed, to be attended to, to be taken notice of with sympathy, complacency, and approbation, are all the advantages which we can propose to derive from it. (Smith, 1976 [1759], p 50; Offer, 2013a)

Not negating the importance of self-interest, Smith emphasises the relationship with the innate capacity for sympathy. It is not the sympathy for others that matters, but rather the sympathy of others: '*Nothing pleases us more* than to observe in other men a fellow-feeling with all the emotions of our own breast' (Offer, 2013a, emphasis in original). This need for acknowledgement by others is an underlying driver for cooperation and collective action 'which is comparable in its intensity with selfishness' (Offer, 2013b, p 285). Thus, future research should look further into the impact of micro-mechanisms on collective action, as I have shown that they can provide a more nuanced understanding of how social phenomena, such as social solidarity, may be perpetuated in society.

The chapter has also highlighted that there may be lack of social solidarity between volunteers/staff and service users. This can be expressed in a lack of regard by service providers towards service recipients, which may even take the form of disregard – signs of inattention, negligence and carelessness – or may shade into the expression of resentment or disrespect. A lack of social solidarity was found in foodbanks in Germany but not in the UK. The chapter suggests that this is associated with differing institutional approaches to the engagement with customers. The institutional emphasis by German foodbanks seems to be on quantity interaction of volunteers and staff with clients by focusing solely on the provision of the basic need of food on a weekly basis. In the UK, the institutional focus is on the provision of quality interaction, which I have proposed to be linked with the limited access to foodbanks by clients and the institutional practice of a sit-down conversation between service providers and service recipients. Considering that most foodbanks in the UK are faith-based, primarily Abrahamic faith-based, the chapter suggests that religious ethics of altruism and helping the poor may nurture an institutional focus on quality interaction and thus support. These findings resonate with Buckingham and Jolley (2015), who found that the Christian theology of foodbanks – based on their observations and experiences at the Aston and Nechells Foodbank in Birmingham, which is part of The Trussell Trust – can have a positive impact on the quality of the interactions between service providers and recipients.

By looking at the Tafel in Germany in comparison with a similar network in the UK, The Trussell Trust, my findings are able to add to the work of Selke (2013) and Schoneville (2013), who found negative sentiments created among Tafel users, including shame, disrespect and humiliation. This is done by suggesting that the institutional framework with its social structure – whereby service providers focus primarily on the provision of food on a regular basis – can create negative social dynamics such as those expressed in a lack of regard or even disregard by service providers towards service recipients. This may lead to negative feelings among users, thereby nurturing segregation and social stratification. These findings must be read in the context suggested by Ehlert (2013) that the professionalisation of charitable organisations in Germany – where acts of humanity have become quantified and the provision of help has become a game of interests, partially in order to be marketable and receive funding – contributes to participants losing social warmth. In view of the findings, I suggest that, when scholars seek to understand the reproduction of social divisions in society, looking at not only how charitable organisations provide basic needs, but also at the overarching institutional structure and the underlying social dynamics within such organisations in the face of an unequal society, is enlightening.

Notes

[1] Laib und Seele is the official name of the Tafel outlet that hands out food to vulnerable people directly.

[2] FareShare (http://www.fareshare.org.uk/) collects surplus food from wholesalers and the food industry, and redistributes it to other social organisations and community groups.

[3] ASDA and Tesco are both supermarket chains, PG tips is a brand of tea manufactured by Unilever, and Lloyds TSB is a bank in the UK.

[4] In this context, it should be mentioned that The Trussell Trust has been criticised as being pro-Labour because its chairman Chris Mould has a party affiliation and has been open in his criticism of welfare reforms.

[5] This age spectrum of the volunteers at the Tafel in West Berlin resonates with a study about Tafel volunteers in North Rhine-Westphalia, which found that 80% are female, on average 63 years old, and that 77% were Catholic, which was attributed to the confessional distribution in this area (Selke and Maar, 2001).

[6] Please note that while not all of the volunteers and staff I came across in German foodbanks expressed a lack of regard or disregard, the pattern found indicates that there is an existing lack of solidarity between service providers and service recipients that is worth reporting.

References

Behr, R. (2010) 'Labour needs to find a Retort to Osborne's Anti-Scrounger Rhetoric', *The Guardian*, [Online] Available at: www.theguardian.com/commentisfree/2010/aug/15/rafael-behr-cameron-benefits-cheats [Accessed 22 August 2016].

Blond, P. (2010) *Red Tory: How Left and Right Have Broken Britain and How We Can Fix It*, London: Faber and Faber.

Brianta, E., Watsona, N. and Philoa, G. (2013) 'Reporting Disability in the Age of Austerity: The Changing Face of Media Representation of Disability and Disabled People in the United Kingdom and the Creation of new "Folk Devils"', *Disability & Society*, 28, 874-889.

Buckingham, H. and Jolley, A. (2015) 'Feeding the debate: a local food bank explains itself', *Voluntary Sector Review*, 6, 311-323.

Bunyan, P. and Diamond, J. (2014) *Agency in Austerity: A Study of Fairness Commissions as an Approach to Reducing Poverty and Inequality in the UK*, Project Report, Ormskirk: Edge Hill University.

Cabinet Office (2010) *Building the Big Society*, London: Cabinet Office.

Cameron, D. (2016) *David Cameron's Easter Message to Christians*, Premier Christianity, [Online] Available at: www.premierchristianity.com/Topics/Society/Politics/David-Cameron-s-Easter-Message-to-Christians [Accessed 15 June 2016].

Caplan, P. (2016) 'Big Society or Broken Society? Food banks in the UK', *Anthropology Today*, 32, 5-9.

Clark, T. and Heath, A. (2015) *Hard Times: Inequality, Recession, Aftermath*, New Haven, CT and London: Yale University Press.

Colley, L. (1992) *Britons: A Forged Nation 1707–1837*, New Haven, CT: Yale University Press.

Collins, R. (2004) *Interaction Ritual Chains*, Princeton, NJ: Princeton University Press.

Conservative-Home (2012) *Food banks ARE part of the Big Society – but the problem they are tackling is not new*, [Online] Available at: www.conservativehome.com/localgovernment/2012/12/council-should-encourage-food-banks.html [Accessed 10 May 2016].

Copeland, A., Bambra, C., Nylén, L., Kasim, A. S., Riva, M., Curtis, S. and Burström, B. (2015) 'All in it together? The Effects of Recession on Population Health and Health Inequalities in England and Sweden, 1991 to 2010', *International Journal of Health Services*, 45, 3-24.

Ehlert, W. (2013) 'Professionalisierung: Traum oder Albtraum für Helfen?' *Sozial Extra*, 37, 15 17.

Eichhorst, W. and Hassel, A. (2015) *Are There Austerity-Related Policy Changes in Germany?* Paris: Institute for the Study of Labor.

Forsey, A. (2014) *An Evidence Review for the All-Party Parliamentary Inquiry into Hunger in the United Kingdom*, London: The Children's Society.

Ghimis, A., Lazarowicz, A. and Pascouau, Y. (2014) *Stigmatisation of EU Mobile Citizens: A Ticking Time Bomb for the European Project*, EPC Commentary, Brussels: European Policy Centre.

HM Government (2013) Charitable Giving Indicators 2012/13. *Charitable Giving Indicators*. London: Department for Culture Media and Sport.

Hogg, M. A. (2006) 'Social Identity Theory', in P. J. Burke (ed) *Contemporary Social Psychological Theories*, Palo Alto, CA: Stanford University Press: 111-136.

Irving, Z. (2013) 'Themed section: work, employment and insecurity', *Social Policy Review*, 25, 203-206.

Kaiser, A. (2016) 'Barbara Kelpsch "Die Idee der Tafeln lebt, weil..."', *Wochenendspiegel*, [Online] Available at: www.wochenendspiegel. de/10055-2/ [Accessed 28 August 2016].

Kendall, J. (2000) 'The Mainstreaming of the Third Sector into Public Policy in England in the late 1990s: Whys and Wherefores', *Policy and Politics*, 28, 541-562.

Komter, A. E. (2004) *Social Solidarity and the Gift*, Cambridge: Cambridge University Press.

Loopstra, R., Reeves, A., Taylor-Robinson, D., Barr, B., Mckee, M. and Stuckler, D. (2015) *Austerity, Sanctions, and the Rise of Food Banks in the UK*, London: UK BMJ

Maar, K. and Eberlei, C. (2013) 'Wer hilft in der neuen Mitleidsökonomie? Der Sozialraum der Lebensmitteltafeln aus Perspektive der ehrenamtlichen HelferInnen', *Sozial Extra*, 37, 5, 25-27.

Martins, I., Rama, P., Tchemisova, T., Pawluszewicz, E., Tania, G., Mira, M. and Ramos, J. (2010) *Report on "Food Distribution by a Food Bank among local Social Solidarity Onstitutions"*, 74th European Study Group with Industry, 26–30 April, Department of Mathematics, University of Aveiro, Portugal.

Maslow, A. H. (1999) *Toward a Psychology of Being*, New York, NY: Wiley.

Milbourne, L. (2009) 'Remodelling the Third Sector: Advancing Collaboration or Competition in Community Based Initiatives?', *Journal of Social Policy*, 38, 277-297.

Molling, L. (2009) 'Die Tafeln und der bürgergesellschaftliche Diskurs aus gouvernementalistischer Perspektive', S. Selke (ed) *Tafeln in Deutschland: Aspekte einer sozialen Bewegung zwischen Nahrungsmittelumverteilung und Armutsintervention*, Wiesbaden: VS Verlag für Sozialwissenschaften: 157-172.

Norman, J. (2010) *The Big Society: The Anatomy of the New Politics,* Buckingham: University of Buckingham Press.

Offer, A. (1997) 'Between the Gift and the Market: the Economy of Regard', *Economic History Review*, 3, 450-476.

Offer, A. (2013a) *Reciprocity and Regard. 'Regard' takes many Forms and powerfully influences Economic Exchanges*, Melbourne: Insights. [Online] Available at: www.insights.unimelb.edu.au/vol13/06_Offer.html [Accessed 20 May 2016].

Offer, A. (2013b) 'Regard', in L. Bruni, S. Zamagni and A. Ferrucci (eds) *Handbook on the Economics of Reciprocity and Social Enterprise*, Cheltenham: Edward Elgar: 285-294.

Oxfam (2013) *The True Cost of Austerity*, Oxford: Oxfam.

The Oxford English Dictionary (2016) *Solidarity*, Oxford Dictionaries, [Online] Available at: www.oxforddictionaries.com/definition/english/solidarity [Accessed 30 August 2016].

Putnam, R. (2000) *Bowling Alone: The Collapse and Revival of American Community*, New York, NY: Simon and Schuster.

Romano, S. (2015) 'Idle Paupers, Scroungers and Shirkers: Past and New Social Stereotypes of the Undeserving Welfare Claimant in the UK', in L. Foster, A. Brunton, C. Deeming and T. Haux (eds) *In Defence of Welfare*, Bristol: Policy Press: 65-67.

Saul, N. and Curtis, A. (2013) *The Stop: How the Fight for Good Food Transformed a Community and Inspired a Movement*, New York, NY: Penguin Random House Llc.

Scheller, E. (2014) *Welche Rolle spielen die Tafeln und ihre Akteur_innen bei der Armutsbekämpfung in Deutschland?* Armutszeugnisse.de. [Online] Available at: www.armutszeugnisse.de/themen/themen_21.pdf [Accessed 23 August 2016].

Schmidt, R. (2004) 'Beitrag zur Übernahme der Schirmherrschaft', *Feedback 1*, 4-5.

Schoneville, H. (2013) 'Armut und Ausgrenzung als Beschämung und Missachtung. Hilfe im Kontext der Lebensmittelausgaben "Die Tafeln" und ihre Konsequenzen', *Soz. Passagen*, 5, 17-35.

Seetzen, H., Ramsden, M. and Goldsmith, C. (2014) *Divided communities at a time of austerity: a visual ethnography of the experience of social division, community and place in a London neighbourhood* [Online] Available at: www.inter-disciplinary.net/critical-issues/wp-content/uploads/2014/09/seetzen-goldsmith-ramsdensppaper.pdf [Accessed 23 August 2016].

Selke, S. (2009) 'Die Leiden der Anderen. Die Rolle der Tafeln zwischen Armutskonstruktion und Armutsbekämpfung', in S. Selke (ed) *Tafeln in Deutschland. Aspekte einer sozialen Bewegung zwischen Nahrungsmittelumverteilung und Armutsintervention*, Wiesbaden: VS: 273-296.

Selke, S. (2013) *The Rise of Foodbanks in Germany is increasing the Commodification of Poverty without addressing its Structural Causes*, London School of Economics and Political Science, [Online] Available at: http://blogs.lse.ac.uk/europpblog/2013/07/11/germany-foodbanks/ [Accessed 25 May 2016].

Selke, S. (2015) *Despite Low Unemployment, Large Sections of German Society remain at Risk from Poverty. London School of Economics and Political Science*, [Online] Available at: http://eprints.lse.ac.uk/71469/ [Accessed 23 August 2016].

Selke, S. and Maar, K. (2011) *Grenzen der guten Tat. Ergebnisse der Studie Evaluation existenzunterstützender Angebote in Trägerschaft von katholischen und caritativen Anbietern in Nordrhein-Westfalen*, Freiburg: i.Br. Lambertus.

Slay, J. and Penny, J. (2016) *Surviving Austerity: Local Voices and Local Action in England's Poorest Neighbourhoods*, London: New Economics Foundation.

Smith, A. (1976 [1759]) *The Theory of Moral Sentiments*, Oxford: Clarendon Press.

Tafel (2014) *Die Tafeln verbinden Bundesverband Deutsche Tafel e. V. Jahresbericht 2014*, Tafel.de [Online] Available at: www.tafel.de/fileadmin/pdf/Publikationen/Jahresbericht_2014_klein.pdf [Accessed 25 June 2016].

Tafel (2016a) *Das Leitbild der Tafeln in Deutschland*, Tafel.de [Online] Available at: www.tafel.de/die-tafeln/leitbild-der-tafeln.html [Accessed 25 July 2016].

Tafel (2016b) *Die Tafeln – eine der größten sozialen Bewegungen unserer Zeit*, Tafel.de [Online] Available at: www.tafel.de/die-tafeln.html [Accessed 29 July 2016].

Tafel (2016c) *Meldungen*, Neustadter-Haßlocher Tafel e. V [Online] Available at: http://neustadter-hasslocher-tafel.de/aggregator/categories/1 [Accessed 28 August 2016].

Tafel (2016d) *Schirmherrin der Tafeln: Bundesfamilienministerin Manuela Schwesig*, Tafel.de [Online] Available at: www.tafel.de/der-bundesverband/schirmherrin.html [Accessed 21 May 2016].

Tafel (2016e) *Spender & Sponsoren – Jeder gibt, was er kann*, Tafel.de [Online] Available at: www.tafel.de/foerderer/spender-sponsoren. html [Accessed 25 May 2016].

Tajfel, H. and Turner, J. C. (1979) 'An Integrative Theory of Intergroup Conflict', in S. Wochel and W. G. Austin (eds) *The Social Psychology of Intergroup Relations*, Monterey, CA: Brooks-Cole: 33-47.

Tesco (2016) *Food Collection*, Tesco [Online] Available at: www.tesco. com/food-collection/ [Accessed 25 June 2016].

TT (2016a) *Foodbank Use Remains at Record High*, The Trussell Trust [Online] Available at: www.trusselltrust.org/2016/04/15/foodbank-use-remains-record-high/ [Accessed 25 May 2016].

TT (2016b) *Mission and Values*, Trussell Trust [Online] Available at: www.trusselltrust.org/about/mission-and-values/ [Accessed 30 July 2016].

TT (2016c) *Policy & Government*, The Trussell Trust [Online] Available at: www.trusselltrust.org/news-and-blog/policy-government/ [Accessed 20 May 2016].

TT (2016d) *Supported Volunteers*, The Trussell Trust [Online] Available at: www.trusselltrust.org/what-we-do/social-enterprises/supported-volunteers/ [Accessed 29 August 2016].

TT (2016e) *Trussell Trust Foodbank Use remains at Record High with over One Million Three-Day Emergency Food Supplies given to People in Crisis in 2015/16*, Trussell Trust [Online] Available at: www.trusselltrust. org/news-and-blog/latest-stats/ [Accessed 29 July 2016].

TT (2016f) *Volunteer with Us*, The Trussell Trust [Online] Available at: www.trusselltrust.org/get-involved/volunteer/ [Accessed 25 May 2016].

Von Der Leyen, U. (2007) 'Wir brauchen bürgerschaftliches Engagement mehr denn je', *Feedback 1*, 5.

Wells, R. and Caraher, M. (2014) 'UK Print Media Coverage of the Food Bank Phenomenon: From Food Welfare to Food Charity?' *British Food Journal*, 116, 1426-1445.

TWELVE

The new economy of poverty

Stefan Selke

There is no shortage of news coverage in Europe and abroad on scarcity, deprivation and austerity in wealthy countries. And there are lots of reports about life in a society of austerity, such as Great Britain (O'Hara, 2014; McKenzie, 2015) or Germany (Bude, 2008; Selke, 2008, 2013a). One can even assume that amid growing wealth, there are also established 'poverty cultures' within which affected people arrange themselves in order to preserve last shreds of dignity. For people without the necessary resources to fulfil the demands of an ideologised meritocracy (Distelhorst, 2014), the consequence is that 'arranging oneself is possibly the only alternative in order to find a way of life, to some extent' (Lutz, 2014, p 13). New ways into exclusion start in the middle of contemporary societies, long before they reach the trap of peripheral precarity.

Societal conditions under which poor people have to prove themselves as acting subjects are increasingly based on the anticipation of individual failure, framed in terms of general suspicion. The fact that complete segments of society are collectively stigmatised – for example, recipients of unemployment benefits are called *Hartzers*[1] in Germany – indicates the reversed burden of proof of the representation of one's own social respectability. Social exhaustion emerges as a newly established semantic field that groups people as 'worthy' or 'unworthy' individuals. This semantic field leads to a pre-modern moralisation of poverty and neo-feudalistic forms of poverty reduction.

In this chapter, I discuss German foodbanks (Tafeln) as a prototypical example of such phenomena, which I call 'economy of poverty'. In this economy, the main questions are: is a new culture of poverty subtly forming, based on the systematic and long-term presence of poverty? Does the emergence of new private actors, purportedly seeking to fight poverty, suggest that some people benefit financially from austerity? Are we witnessing the establishment of an economy of poverty that uses austerity to produce private profit? If this were so, it would at least explain why poverty is not being fought in a sustainable manner. In this chapter, I analyse whether certain services are *systematically* offered to the poor, and whether this supply is based on the existence of *structural* poverty. My central questions are: how is poverty becoming a business, and what is the central control mechanism in this economy of poverty?

So far, there have been no concrete proposals for a sustained fight against poverty that originate in a profound sense of outrage caused by the very existence of poverty in a wealthy society. Fostering this kind of outrage would permit sustainable political engagement with the roots of deprivation. Instead, it actually seems that societies have forgotten what sustainable poverty reduction is, even though there are elaborate analyses on the topic (Opielka, 2016; Sedmak, 2013). In Germany, the guiding principle of social sustainability was extensively negotiated for the first time in the German Federal Parliament (Deutscher Bundestag) within the context of a specially appointed expert commission that offers policy advice (Enquete-Kommission) about the principles of sustainability (Enquete-Kommission, 1998). The commission declared that social justice is a constitutionally protected good (civil right) and that it is the state's duty to ensure humane living conditions as well as protected spaces of social security, and that these duties are not to be delegated to private charities. But this is exactly what is happening. Furthermore, those responsible for social imbalances are applauding this development.

The chapter begins with a short introduction to German foodbanks, based on four basic narratives (part 2). This is followed by an explanation of the principles of the new economy of poverty (part 3), in order to apply these narratives to the case study of German foodbanks (part 4). My discussion moves away from a common pattern of listing the advantages and disadvantages of German foodbanks, instead examining more causal phenomena. The chapter's main thesis is that poverty has become a (fictitious) commodity that allows the systematic generation of profit. Although German foodbanks are merely one prominent example, they consider themselves the seismograph of society, and are therefore legitimately and appropriately chosen to illustrate key facets of a wider emerging economy of poverty.

This chapter illuminates the contours of this new economy of poverty, which were outlined in a recent edition of *The Society of the Spectacle* (Débord, 1996). In this kind of society, poverty is only reduced symbolically. Poverty management turns into a mere backdrop and serves the purpose of safeguarding the provisions of the economy of poverty and their environment. The focus on self-referential content of organisations makes it possible to gain profit from poverty in the first place, without fighting the root causes of poverty and without a bad conscience. Austerity – by which I refer to government policy that values budgetary balance above everything else – is the prerequisite for provisions within an economy of poverty.

Four basic perspectives on German foodbanks

As an instrument for poverty relief imported from the United States to Germany (Werth, 1998, 2004, 2009), German foodbanks supply an increasing number of people with food that is left over from the primary consumer market, donated by clients, or purchased by the foodbanks with donated funds. What appears to be a functional support system for social or individual emergency periods, such as political austerity or poverty, has become part of the basic food supply for a growing part of the population. Few topics are as emotional or moral as the debate over foodbanks. Even self-critical foodbank volunteers have been outspoken in questioning this approach, revealing inner conflict (see, for example, Wimmer, 2010, p 5). Since 2008, however, public debate in Germany has underlined the fact that foodbank volunteers are not to be held personally accountable for social grievances, especially the causes of poverty; at the same time, they do not engage critically enough with the wider ramifications of their limited local actions and with the implications of a national foodbank system in terms of sustainability (see Lorenz, 2012). An aggravating factor is the virtual hegemony of the federal association of German foodbanks (Bundesverband Deutsche Tafel).[2] The lack of competition or choice can mean that critical foodbank clients are discouraged from voicing negative opinions publically – even though some of these opinions have been published online or expressed in confidential communication.

Four main perspectives on foodbanks emerge from public and scientific discourse. Such foodbank narratives can be paired into two groups: two of the narratives are affirmative, which means that they endorse the existing conditions and stabilise the common sense of the foodbanks in media and politics. Two counter–affirmative narratives do not reflect popular opinion; they are predominantly critical. In the following section, I outline the content of different foodbank narratives, and analyse their ambivalences.

The voluntariness narrative

The voluntariness narrative is mainly cultivated by the media, and thus popular with the public. Its central claim is that committed citizens voluntarily solve problems within their neighbourhood instead of merely discussing problems and waiting for the authorities to fix them, therefore replacing state social responsibility. An illustration of this narrative can be found in the quantitative dimension of civic engagement. The popularity of volunteer work has been particularly manifest in foodbanks. The voluntariness narrative can only be understood against the backdrop of the value change in the logic of the political philosophy of communitarianism that has been empirically observed over a period of many years: the motivation for volunteering changed from altruism to projects of social recognition (Pinl, 2013; Opaschowski, 2014).

Despite its positive orientation, this narrative exhibits ambivalences. Civic engagement has turned into a factor for securing one's social status in society and has been made calculable (EU, 2007, 2010). In a neo-welfare state, the relationship between the state and its citizens, as well as the relationship among citizens themselves, have drastically changed (Lessenich, 2008, 2012). This narrative falls into line with this idea.

The commitment of foodbank volunteers reduces the burden on the state, which can lead to contradictory results. In the long run, the successful foodbank movement might lead politicians to believe that they have been relieved of their duty to implement social reforms to expand basic security benefits. Both the foodbanks themselves (Häuser, 2011) and external observers support this critique, although from different angles (MSAGD, 2009; Segbers, 2010; Lorenz, 2012; Selke, 2013b).[3] At the same time, the work of foodbanks relies on political recognition and partly on financial support by municipalities and private sponsors. The foodbank movement defines itself as an expression of civil charity and private benevolence, and is slowly becoming a substitute for long-standing civil rights. The foodbank system is exemplary for how responsibility for providing livelihood security shifts from the state to citizens.

Foodbanks can help bridge an economic gap (Martens, 2010) and they can provide short-term relief. However, as measured by the human right to adequate food, the right to social and cultural participation as established in Germany's constitution, and by the concept of human dignity (Segbers, 2013), foodbanks are, at the most, tolerable, but not desirable. Nevertheless, politicians' statements give the impression that the use of foodbanks does not have questionable connotations. The Green politician Katrin Göring-Eckhardt has even referred to foodbanks as 'small, lived utopias' (Göring-Eckhardt, 2010, p 151). This is, however, a social utopia based on foodbank users becoming used to being associated with social stigma. The commodities they receive do not compensate adequately for their negative emotional experience, as I have illustrated in my book *Schamland* (which would translate as *Land of Shame*) (Selke, 2013a). Furthermore, my research suggests that this sense of shame is common at foodbanks (see also Becker and Gulyas, 2012). Additionally, foodbanks do not address the structural roots of poverty. They predominantly secure their own existence: foodbanks want to be needed.

The save-our-food narrative

The original idea of foodbanks as 'emergency meals' for the homeless (Reidegeld and Reubelt, 1995) has transformed into ecological strategies of legitimisation within the context of which foodbanks no longer define themselves primarily as a social movement, but rather as an environmental one. They propagate the save-our-food narrative. At first glance, the plausible main statement consists of the recognition of an affluent consumer society, in which food is thrown away unless it is saved by the foodbanks, which distribute it to those in need. To understand this narrative, one must consider the (very few) studies on the (roughly estimated) amount of food that is disposed of in households and by industry. The food-saving argument is based on the assumption of a win–win situation: consumers clear their bad conscience, supermarkets cut their special waste cost, foodbanks collect free food, and those in need receive nutrition that they would not be able to afford otherwise. The redistribution of food is described as rescuing and takes place according to ecological principles.[4] At the same time, foodbanks rely on the fact that wasting food is a taboo with religious connotations, and thus morally charged.

This narrative also contains ambivalences. Foodbanks are part of an alliance of food-savers, organised by Germany's Ministry of Food and Agriculture.[5] The corresponding distortion of perspectives and euphemistic exaltation of the foodbank volunteers as food savers is problematic. The foodbank model has elevated debates about how to handle the waste problem above societal worries regarding its socially excluded members. Importantly, however, there have been serious doubts about the quality of studies calculating the amount of food thrown away in private homes: according to some researchers, the amount has been greatly overestimated (Fischer, 2013). Therefore, the influence of foodbanks on the total amount of recycled material might be far less than foodbanks claim.

With the diffusion of the save-our-food narrative, foodbanks have also invoked a sustainability bias, referring routinely to the ecological sustainability of their actions, while at the same time neglecting the importance of social sustainability (self-determination, participation, protective spaces free from paternalism and so on).[6] The core of social sustainability means self-determined consumption, which could be a guiding principle for a successful fight against poverty. But foodbanks establish a system of heteronomous consumption, which is illustrated by the foodbank users' obligation to accept what is offered to them, framed by an extremely restricted right to complain (Selke, 2013a, p 152). The main critique of this narrative is that it makes people lose sight of foodbank users. Foodbank clients do not feel like mature consumers. Instead, they describe an experience of poverty consumption, with associated social stigma producing a sort of broken self, as a number of clients' statements illustrate. In *Schamland*, I listed some of the derogatory terms with which foodbanks clients report being labelled, such as beggar, second-class citizen, a mere number, the fed (Selke, 2013a).

The image of the food saver is based on argumentative exaltation and, although it legitimises foodbanks, it does not improve the consumer status of its customers. On the contrary, charity is praised as an innovative form in this economy of poverty, as this statement by a former Tafel president makes clear: 'Those who are supplied with food from us are not receiving charity, they are doing something for climate and resource protection. That is an achievement of society that we must recognise' (Hartmann, 2013, p 59). The result is a problematic connection between two issues in the save-our-food narrative that are not causally related: the waste of edible food and the needs of citizens in precarious circumstances. It is implicitly assumed that the relief of one problem (addressing the throw-away society) could automatically solve the other problem (poverty). But this connection is based on incorrect assumptions. The alarmist emphasis on food waste merely serves to increase the legitimacy of foodbanks. Reducing the amount of excess food does not alleviate poverty. Getting rid of surplus food through foodbanks saves the food industry money by reducing the cost of waste disposal, and the industry's image also receives a boost. It does not, however, solve the problem of having surplus food in the first place or underlying problems of poverty.

The precarisation narrative

The question of what kind of a society made foodbanks possible at all, and how it was able to get used to foodbanks, is necessary to broaden the horizons of the much too narrow debate on foodbanks. This is a society, for example, in which the philosophy of the Tafel is printed in schoolbooks as an uncommented description of the social.[7] This is also a society in which an increasing number of people from an increasing number of social circles are using foodbanks.

Along with unemployed individuals, migrants, children and retirees, students have joined the list of those at risk of poverty that have started using foodbanks.[8] On the one hand, foodbanks have been expanding in number as well as in what they offer, from children's restaurants, cooking classes, and meals on wheels for the elderly, to the new student foodbanks. Yet on the other hand, an increasing number of foodbanks are complaining of a shortage on food donations. Some have already had to declare a halt in distribution and limit the number of clients because there is simply not enough food, despite additional food purchases and foodbank collection campaigns. The situation was exacerbated over the course of 2015, when 'a rapidly growing number of refugees and asylum seekers in Germany started frequenting foodbanks, too' (TAZ, 2014). Simultaneously, few people are talking about those who do not use foodbanks, although they are poor enough to qualify. When it is said that 1.5 million people use German foodbanks, it is easy to forget that 6-8 million people do not use foodbanks even though they would pass the local foodbanks' poverty definition.

Only few research papers on foodbanks make a point of keeping the focus on foodbank users. Instead, foodbank volunteers are the ones who receive significant public attention in the media and in political debate, captured by the voluntariness narrative. The main thrust of the precarisation narrative lies in the realisation that poor people are being regulated and, on different levels, dominated and punished by new control mechanisms. This change in perspective makes it clear that, under the dictation of omnipresent precarisation (Lorey, 2012), the governmental treatment of the poor is a politically willed form of isolation and control through self-control. The process of the democratisation of poverty in depoliticised 'society' can be used to illustrate this narrative. For it is within this context that citizens are expected to take on the role of the 'entrepreneurial self' (Bröckling, 2007) and are increasingly expected to assume responsibility for their own risk management.

In the end, this narrative can only be appropriately understood from the perspective of foodbank users. Relevant empirical data was produced through the research project Tafel-Monitor. The choir of foodbank users in *Schamland* is an experiment in polyphony to describe a social reality and to give the poor a voice (Selke, 2013a, p 121).[9] The quotes are not used as an ornament for academic analysis, but rather to emphasise the intrinsic value of their aesthetics and content. The ambivalence of this narrative therefore becomes visible. The foodbank users' perspective and their experience with the temporalisation of poverty in the foodbank system form the background to the precarisation narrative, which underlines the role of a sort of societal usher that the foodbanks have taken on. These make it clear that, instead of a sustainable and politically forced fight against poverty, mere poverty relief within immediate social proximity has prevailed as socially willed and politically acceptable. The criticism of this narrative emphasises that the application of a pre-modern alms logic has led to the neglect of the idea of providing for oneself. However, if one loses one's status as a *consumer*, one's status as a *citizen* is also affected. Ultimately, this regime will lead to the individualisation of blame through its orientation towards the principle of personal responsibility and socially desirable self-optimisation. Perceived individual failure leads to a chain of humiliation along different stages of life, at the end of which foodbanks stand for a space charged with symbolism in the middle of an affluent society. Foodbanks illustrate new social imagery that is found in the discrimination of the so-called losers.

The economy-of-poverty narrative

The main idea of the economy-of-poverty narrative is that foodbanks are always synchronised with economic, political and media interests and that this network builds a market from which many profit – except for foodbank users. Foodbanks act as moral entrepreneurs in this market, and the main service they offer their clients is a sort of moral reputation in the way of symbolic capital. Economic thinking and the principle of an open market have become established in civil society initiatives shaping the public sector: civic engagement and economic principles merge.[10] The consideration of an economy of poverty originates from the fact that foodbanks predominantly find their resonance in the economic system. Politics may grant foodbanks legitimation and the media may give foodbanks more attention, but in the end, it is private sponsors that provide foodbanks with the necessary resources.

This fourth narrative in particular is key to analysing foodbanks. Therefore, it is necessary to develop a basic understanding of how the market has entered the field of poverty relief as well as the corresponding principles of this economy of poverty. The idea of a modelling of a new economy follows the key question of how economic profits can be gained from poverty. At first glance, foodbanks do not seem to fit into this category, for they do not market poverty or directly profit from the poverty of foodbank users. On the contrary, they even try to relieve the poverty of their clients. In order to understand foodbank activities as an example of the new economy of poverty, it is necessary to have a broader understanding of profit. This understanding orientates itself on Bourdieu's (1983) theory of forms of capital, and places the focus on reputation as symbolic capital – a reputation cultivated by poverty reduction that is visible for society.

A requirement for the formation of an economy of poverty is that the market must enter the field of poverty. According to John Brewer (2013), marketisation is 'captured neatly in four "C"s – choice, cost, competition and commodification' (p 94). Markets can be understood as mechanisms that react to people's desire for more choices. How these choices are made accessible creates artificial competition in order to meet these needs in a cost-effective way. The use of the rhetoric of choice disguises the introduction of competition, the consequence of which is commodification, which describes the transformations of non-commodities into commodities, which can be traded on the market according to the basic rules of supply and demand.

Thus, the concept of an economy of poverty relies on the link between four different processes that form a functional chain. According to this theory, it can be explained how profit is gained on the basis of societal poverty. Together, the four parts of the process result in a 'moral market' (Stehr, 2007). On a cultural level, the process of boundary dissolution forms the breeding ground for the restriction of choices. On an organisational level, rationalisation processes allow amateur aid projects to develop into perfectly run enterprises that operate according to the principle of increased efficiency. At the symbolic level, against the backdrop of increasing competition over highly functional attributes within companies, moral consumption leads to added value and thus creates a moral market. At the economic level, poverty becomes a fictitious commodity as it passes through a number of transformation processes. This then leads to a stable relationship between supply and demand that has been established just for this commodity. The analysis in this chapter focuses on the cultural and the organisational level.

The principle of the economy of poverty is comprehensively based on the rationalisation of interpersonal behaviour that can be described in every conceivable area with usefulness-efficiency reasoning as well as with cost-benefit analyses. The 'terror of the economy' (Forrester, 1999) also manifests itself in the rationalisation of civic engagement (national engagement policies, EU-wide standardisation, professionalisation through volunteer trade fairs, branding, insurance and gratification systems) and in the rationalisation of poverty management (the principle of demand and support, bureaucratisation, sanctions to increase efficiency and as a means of control). Both the rationalisation of volunteers and those affected by poverty follow the same principle of McDonaldisation, which are spelled out in four primary dimensions: efficiency, calculability, predictability and control (Ritzer, 2013).

Foodbanks: a case study of markets in an economy of poverty

In the following, the principles of an economy of poverty are applied to the case study of foodbanks in order to show that they have greatly distanced themselves from their original image of a social movement (Stern, 2003; Selke, 2013b).[11] They must meanwhile be seen as a moral enterprise. The case of foodbanks makes the double activation of volunteers, on the one hand, and that of those affected by poverty, on the other, visible. A result of the activation of volunteers is the erosion of livelihoods through rudimentary transfer payments and the delegation of social policies to private charity systems with a pre-modern touch. Aspects of double-boundary dissolution are found at the level of local micro-politics: for one person (foodbank volunteer) this represents a life programme (self-fulfilment through volunteering) and for the other (foodbank user) it represents a survival programme (poverty relief through foodbanks).

The specific background here is the Hartz IV legislation: in October 2004, the German Parliament approved the relaunch of the Federal Employment Office (Hartz III) and the merger of unemployment compensation and welfare benefits (Hartz IV). In 2005 the German government implemented a package of policies known as Agenda 2010, which reformed the country's welfare system and labour market following paradigms previously institutionalised in the UK. An alarming development is the link between welfare state institutions and foodbanks. Those who receive Hartz IV unemployment benefits are referred to the foodbanks by the unemployment office, for example, when there have been cuts in individual funding. This begs the question of where state obligations end and civic engagement begins.

Now that the foodbank system has proved itself stable, there has been a dissolution of boundaries between norm and value systems, defining new tolerance limits. As early as three years after the introduction of the first foodbank in Germany, lawyer Falk Roscher (one of the first academic observers of the emerging German foodbanks) indicated that private charity was a threat to legal entitlement, saying that when such a system establishes itself, the limits of basic needs dramatically erode. Regarding the quality of the goods as being below the level of the market, the poor are represented as 'those to be provided for' (Roscher, 1996). A foodbank user expressed this in her own words thus:

> "The foodbanks cannot, in any way, substitute necessary social services. Often, foodbank users realise that the food supply is not of consistent, decent quality. In addition to socio-cultural participation, the required minimum subsistence level is hardly guaranteed in Germany. Sometimes, information on foodbanks is even contradictory. This is partly due to the fact that negative aspects, which are in fact a reality, are not mentioned in public. Thus, occasionally, foodbank users' freedom of speech, as established in the [German] constitution, is effectively forbidden under penalty of exclusion or even legal consequences. In the long run, foodbanks will not be able to substitute a crumbling welfare state."

However, foodbanks are only the end in a chain of processes that are recognisable by an ever-present tendency to teach, as well as the comeback of *Volkspädagogik* (educating the public), with its low-threshold offer of assistance and consultation. Foodbanks create substitute spaces that have been uncoupled from society. Based on qualitative interviews with foodbank users (150 participants) for the research project Tafel-Monitor (2011-14), the foodbanks' social environment can be characterised by a three-zone model. There are three prototypical patterns of foodbank use. Each zone represents a type of social integration of the foodbanks into the lifestyle regime of foodbank users. According to the (mis)conception of the system and experiences, each user drifts into one of the three zones. Therefore, each zone represents a typical way of dealing with the cognitive dissonance that is caused by foodbank use. Users drifting into the first zone habitually integrate foodbanks into everyday life without cognitive dissonance (stabilisation zone). Users who regard foodbanks as a form of pragmatic support are ambivalent – they see benefits as well as dissonances, and their view undergoes constant revaluation based on novel experience (negotiation zone). Finally, users who feel disappointed by forms of social interaction and other issues drift into the boundary dissolution zone – they try to distance themselves from foodbanks as soon as possible.

Orientation towards an economy of success

In this institutionalised substitute space, there is an increasingly clear orientation towards economic principles. In individual cases, ethical principles may motivate volunteers (Bell, 2000). Basically, numerous exogenous and endogenous types of rationalisation coexist in the case of foodbanks. In practice, what occurs within the framework of a situational economy is an orientation towards principles of the economy. Foodbank representatives imitate the economy, meaning that they refer to their users as clients and play the role of a salesperson. Attempts to overcome cognitive dissonance caused by the different social statuses of volunteers and users are most successful when reliable horizons of meaning and experience are imitated. Against this background, establishing relationships with the economy and economic settings has become standard.

In the field of foodbanks, there are numerous exogenous rationalisation processes. The political control of volunteer management within the foodbanks has reached a preliminary peak. This form of engagement has been celebrated (for example, by the European Union) or institutionalised in the form of the national engagement policies of the Federal Ministry for Family Affairs, Senior Citizens, Women and Youth, and professionalised (volunteer trade fairs, volunteer management). For the volunteers, foodbanks are a prototype for a field where they can participate as volunteers, in which they can experience themselves as self-efficient, where they receive gratitude from the foodbank users, and also get positive feedback and symbolic recognition from the political and public spheres.[12] An element of endogenous rationalisation lies in the fact that behavioural economics has become the leading science of a supply that is necessary for the support of many people's existence, which has gone almost unnoticed. Behavioural economics tries to motivate individuals to make better decisions through reward and penalty systems, irrespective of whether or not we are talking about civic engagement, nutrition, health, or lifestyle choices.

However, when seeing foodbanks as moral enterprises, the main argument is that the 'self-professionalisation' of foodbanks is based on an external orientation towards an economy of success. This can be demonstrated by different factors. The federal association of German foodbanks protects the term Tafel from other market competitors and seeks to defend its dominant position legally, funded by donations. The economic market behaviour of foodbanks is seen in their desire for market penetration (the logics of efficiency, growth logic), product differentiation (additional purchasing of goods), service differentiation based on a copy of the idea of different kinds of banks (foodbanks, animal banks, culture banks, eye-glass banks, medicinal banks and so on), specification of target groups (children's foodbanks, old-age pensioners' foodbanks, mobile foodbanks in rural areas), as well as quality management and professionalisation. As an enterprise within the economy of poverty, foodbanks now imitate the predominant economic rationality on every level from local, situational practice to long-term strategy. This style of reasoning means that thought and behavioural patterns are adopted from the economy without critique.

Based on reliable cooperation with companies (some of which have been secured through exclusive contracts), interests can be synchronised. Foodbanks receive economic support in the way of goods, equipment and services. The product that they offer in return is an improved image of verifiable moral profits for their supporters. The Tafel offers companies a platform for professional public relations through their membership magazine *Feedback*. In the anniversary addition of *Feedback,* the 20th anniversary of foodbanks in Germany was celebrated by presenting all brand names associated with the Tafel with customised promotional messages. For example, the German supermarket chain REWE's slogan was 'We grow daily – and our responsibility along with us', while the wholesale warehouse company Metro Group headlined with 'Think globally, act locally. Inspired shopping.'[13] At the supermarket chain Lidl, one can 'Do great things with one small gesture', while Mercedes-Benz claims that 'Every social movement needs an engine.'[14] Coca-Cola even referenced the foodbanks' slogan, 'Putting food where it belongs', in its trademark phrase 'Because a drink belongs to your meal.' The partnership with Coca-Cola in particular is exemplary for constant synchronisation within the economy of poverty. While, according to Coca-Cola, foodbanks are fulfilling an important societal task, the group is also flattered to be an official foodbank partner. This is very convenient for Coca-Cola's image and entails the expansion of the company's target group downwards, since Coca-Cola 'is for everyone'.

An even more significant aspect is the general attitude of foodbanks. Their criteria for success is based on a bin ideology – which refers to an increase in the amount of saved and transported food – as well as a membership ideology – which refers to an increase in the number of foodbank users and the detection of new target groups for an ever-increasing number of foodbank locations. Germany's national foodbanks have become monopolists on the market of helpfulness, and, using genuinely economic logic, have either been driving similar institutions from the market or have reduced their competitors' ability to emerge as moral enterprises. All in all, foodbanks behave like enterprises, following a strict economic logic of growth and market displacement. This growth logic is based on a fundamental paradigm shift that has gone almost completely unnoticed by the public. At the beginning of the foodbank era (1990s), the mission statement of foodbanks was to redistribute extras, and although the food that they distributed was still edible, it was actually no longer acceptable for retail. Since 2005, the number of foodbanks has increased, following a set of neoliberal welfare and labour market reforms under Germany's then chancellor, Gerhard Schröder. In the wake of Schröder's reform package, unemployment in Germany reached its post-war high in 2005, when over five million Germans were unemployed. If we look at the ways in which donation-funded food acquisition and marketing campaigns to obtain food donations have come to replace the collection of surplus food from markets, the foodbanks' mission seems to have shifted to an aspiration of replacing what is lacking, rather than redistributing a surplus. This not only means an expansion of the food supply, but also announces a logic of growth, since, in principle, everything can be declared as lacking.

Conclusion: the expansion of the profit zone

One can only ask what the forms and consequences of the expansion of an economy of poverty are. Numerous forms of informal economy activity (Wagner et al, 2013) and the black market must also be accounted for in the field of the economy of poverty, because great profits can be gained in these areas. Many fields in which direct conditions of exploitation exist (low-paying jobs, prostitution, strategic use of temporary employment) also fall into the area of an economy of poverty. In the sector of an economy of volunteers and helpers, numerous phenomena await, such as paid volunteer positions, artists working as unpaid social workers, or corporate volunteering. New phenomena are created in the sector of the donation economy (Müller, 2005), such as the intentional over-production of commodities as a strategic tax-saving model: the extra commodities are then directly transported to the foodbanks, without even having passed through supermarkets, and are officially labelled as donations. As the existence of foodbanks, and therefore of poverty, is a prerequisite for this tax-saving model, in the future this model should be regarded as a classical example of the economy of poverty.

Poverty is a fictitious commodity (Knorr-Cetina, 1998; Polanyi, 2014) because the treatment of poverty follows the logic of privatisation. The crucial thing about the transformation of poverty into a fictitious commodity is the fact that, after this process of transformation has been completed, poverty relief is transliterated from a passive to an active strategy and is thus made compatible with allocatable moral, ecological and health standards, among other societal norms. This global value chains rationale illustrates the new expectations of commodities. Rational calculations are no longer enough in a society of the spectacle. Instead, commodities must have some type of *moral* content (Stehr, 2007, p 297). It is precisely this expansion of economic behaviour on a moral basis that becomes the breeding ground for moral enterprises like foodbanks. However, the expansion of the profit zone is tremendous. Poverty in the form of a fictitious commodity within the economy of poverty is a phenomenon that must be examined further and in more detail particularly in other fields such as the medical exploitation of the poor in reality TV-shows or the emergence of products especially designed for the poor.

Notes

[1] A Hartzer is a person who receives unemployment benefits of the lowest bracket, called Hartz IV. Popularly, the term is associated with a lack of willingness to work, rather than with the structural problems that prevent increasingly large numbers of unskilled Germans from gaining access to the job market.

[2] German foodbanks are either member of charity organisations (for example, Caritas or Diakonie) or organised as local associations. Most of the foodbanks in Germany are also members of the federal association of German foodbanks.

[3] According to the German foodbank founder Sabine Werth, foodbanks make an effort to 'relieve some of the pressure within the system' (Werth, 2009, p 255).

[4] See Gerd Häuser (ex-president of the Tafel) in an edition of the association's member magazine *Feedback*: 'In times of increasingly depleting *resources* … responsibility and conservation of valuable natural *resources* is becoming of ever greater importance, in order to ensure that the lives of following generations will not be compromised. Important steps in achieving this goal are (ecological) foresight and social engagement.… The foodbanks and their partners within the industry, commerce, society and politics … will continue to do all they can to keep impeccable food from landing in the waste bin.… The foodbanks have created a balance.… And the environment wins at the same time: there is less rubbish and important *resources* are spared' (Hartmann, 2013, p 59, emphasis added).

[5] Other members of this alliance are initiatives such as food sharing or the food-saver website www.lebensmittelretten.de, which are gaining popularity among consumer-conscious citizens.

[6] In September, 2011, the Tafel won the sustainability award ECOCARE, in the category of Technology/Process. A German food journal and three food industry trade fairs sponsor this award.

[7]   In the social studies book *People and Politics* in the German state of Thuringia, one finds the following statement: 'With that, the foodbanks help economically disadvantaged people make ends meet during difficult times and give them motivation for the future – at the same time, they prevent valuable food from landing in the rubbish bin' (Schreier, 2012, p 109).

[8]   In January 2014, *Spiegel Online* published an article that illustrated that an increasing number of students receive food from foodbanks. In order to reduce levels of inhibition among users, a foodbank in Münster contemplated opening a foodbank directly on the campus of the local university (*Spiegel Online*, 2014).

[9]   Approximately 500 quotes from those suffering from poverty were put into the first person plural and consolidated. The partially drastic semantics that were used were put into a continuous text and organised in sequences, complying with the demand for plasticity, complexity and urgency of an 'option for the poor' (Sedmak, 2005, p 3).

[10] For critique, see Collins (2007) or Muehlebach (2012).

[11] For a detailed critique of the false self-attribution of 'social movement', see Selke (2013b).

[12] Examples of this symbolic recognition are the different kinds of merits (such as the Order of Merit of the Federal Republic of Germany) that are awarded to foodbank volunteers.

[13] REWE has significantly integrated the foodbanks into its corporate social responsibility strategy, and reports on its engagement for the foodbanks in respective reports. Additionally, REWE is responsible for the periodic 'One more' campaign in which customers of the (US-American inspired) supermarket chain are invited to purchase extra groceries in the form of non-perishable foods in order to donate them to the foodbanks at the cash register, preferably from the REWE line of products. The Metro Group pays the rent for the Tafel's Berlin office as well as the salaries of its regular employees.

[14] Lidl introduced a deposit-bottle campaign in which customers could donate used bottles to the Tafel. In Germany, costumers pay a deposit of 0.25 euro for each bottle. The refrigerated vehicles of the foodbanks that are members of the Tafel e.V. are from Mercedes Benz.

References

Becker, J. and Gulyas, J. (2012) 'Armut und Scham - über die emotionale Verarbeitung sozialer Ungleichheit', *Zeitschrift für Sozialreform*, 1, 83-99.

Bell, D. (2000) *Ethical Ambition. Living a Life of Meaning and Worth*, New York, NY: Bloomsbury.

Bourdieu, P. (1983) 'Forms of Capital', in J. C. Richards (ed) *Handbook of Theory and Research for the Sociology of Education*, New York, NY: Greenwood Press: 241-258.

Brewer, J. (2013) *The Public Value of Social Sciences*, London: Bloomsbury Publishing.

Bröckling, U. (2007) *Das unternehmerische Selbst. Soziologie einer Subjektivierungsform*, Frankfurt: a.M., Suhrkamp.

Bude, H. (2008) *Die Ausgeschlossenen. Das Ende vom Traum einer gerechten Gesellschaft*, München: Carl Hanser.

Collins, P. H. (2007) 'Going Public. Doing the Sociology That Hat No Name', in D. Clawson, R. Zussman, J. Misra, N. Gerstel, R. Stokes and D. L. Anderton (eds) *Public Sociology. Fifteen Eminent Sociologists Debate Politics and the Profession in the Twenty-first Century*, Berkeley, CA: University of California Press: 101-113.

Débord, G. (1996) *Die Gesellschaft des Spektakels*, Berlin: Tiamat.

Distelhorst, L. (2014) *Leistung. Das Endstadium einer Ideologie*, Bielefeld: Transkript.

Enquete-Kommission (1998) *Konzept Nachhaltigkeit. Vom Leitbild zur Umsetzung*, Dokumentations- und Informationssystem für Parlamentarische Vorgänge, [Online] Available at: http://dipbt.bundestag.de/doc/btd/13/112/1311200.pdf [Accessed 17 May 2016].

EU (2007) *Arbeitsdokument über Freiwilligentätigkeit als Beitrag zum wirtschaftlichen und sozialen Zusammenhalt. Ausschuss für regionale Entwicklung*, Bundesministerium fuer Arbeit, Soziales und Konsumentenschutz [Online] Available at: http://bmsk2.cms.apa.at/cms/freiwilligenweb/attachments/6/3/7/CH1058/CMS1292419696384/ep-harkin-papier_%282%29.pdf [Accessed 17 May 2016].

EU (2010) *Entscheidung des Rates vom 27. November 2009 über das Europäische Jahr der Freiwilligentätigkeit zur Förderung der aktiven Bürgerschaft (2011)*, [Online] Available at: www.kontaktstelle-efbb.de/fileadmin/user_upload/4_infos-service/publikationen/Beschluss_EJ2011.pdf [Accessed 17 May 2016].

Fischer, L. (2013) 'Von Müllvermeidung wird kein Mensch satt', *Journal Culinaire*, 3, 129-137.

Forrester, V. (1999) *Terror der Ökonomie*, München: Goldmann.

Göring-Eckhardt, K. (2010) 'Warum sollen Tafeln politisch unterstützt werden?' in S. Lorenz (ed) *Tafel Gesellschaft. Zum neuen Umgang mit Überfluss und Ausgrenzung*, Bielefeld: Transkript: 137-151.

Hartmann, K. (2013) 'Nur ein Heftpflaster', *Enorm*, 1, 56-60.

Häuser, G. (2011) 'Die Wirkung der Tafeln aus der Sicht des Bundesverbandes', in K. Maar and S. Selke (eds) *Transformation der Tafeln. Aktuelle Diskussionsbeiträge aus Theorie und Praxis der Tafeln*, Wiesbaden: VS: 109-120.

Knorr-Cetina, K. (1998) 'Sozialität mit Objekten. Soziale Beziehungen in posttrationellen Gesellschaften', in W. Rammert (ed) *Technik und Sozialtheorie*, Frankfurt a.M.: Campus: 83-120.

Lessenich, S. (2008) *Die Neuerfindung des Sozialen. Der Sozialstaat im flexiblen Kapitalismus*, Bielefeld: Transkript.

Lessenich, S. (2012) *Theorien des Sozialstaats zur Einführung*, München: Junius.

Lorenz, S. (2012) *Tafeln im flexiblen Überfluss. Ambivalenzen sozialen und ökologischen Engagements*, Bielefeld: Transkript.

Lorey, I. (2012) *Die Regierung des Prekären*, Wien: Turia+Kant.

Lutz, R. (2014) *Soziale Erschöpfung. Kulturelle Kontexte sozialer Ungleichheit*, Weinheim und Basel: Beltz Juventa.

Martens, R. (2010) 'Warum sind die Tafeln erfolgreich? Skizze einer gesamtwirtschaftlichen Betrachtung', in S. Selke (ed) *Kritik der Tafeln. Standortbestimmungen zu einem ambivalenten sozialen Phänomen*, Wiesbaden: Verlag für Sozialwissenschaften: 109-128.

Mckenzie, L. (2015) *Getting by. Estates, Class and Culture in Austerity Britain*, Bristol: Policy Press.

Msagd (2009) *Armut und Reichtum in Rheinland-Pfalz*, Ministerium fuer Soziales, Arbeit, Gesundheit und Demokratie, [Online] Available at: https://msagd.rlp.de/fileadmin/msagd/Soziale_Teilhabe/Teilhabe_ Dokumente/Armutsbericht_2009.pdf [Accessed 17 May 2016].

Muehlebach, A. (2012) *The Moral Neoliberal. Welfare and Citizenship in Italy*, Chicago, IL: The University of Chicago Press.

Müller, O. (2005) *Vom Almosen zum Spendenmarkt. Sozialethische Aspekte christlicher Spendenkultur*, Freiburg: Lambertus.

O'hara, M. (2014) *Austerity Bites. A Journey to the Sharp End of Cuts in the UK*, Bristol: Policy Press.

Opaschowski, H. W. (2014) *So wollen wir leben! Die 10 Zukunftshoffnungen der Deutschen*, Gütersloh: Gütersloher Verlagshaus.

Opielka, M. (2016) 'Soziale Nachhaltigkeit aus soziologischer Sicht', *Soziologie*, 1, 33-46.

Pinl, C. (2013) *Freiwillig zu Diensten? Über die Ausbeutung von Ehrenamt und Gratisarbeit*, Frankfurt: a.M., Nomen.

Polanyi, K. (2014) *The Great Transformation. Politische und ökonomische Ursprünge von Gesellschaften und Wirtschaftssystemen*, Frankfurt: a.M., Suhrkamp.

Reidegeld, E. and Reubelt, B. (1995) 'Die Mahlzeitnothilfe in Deutschland. Historische Anmerkungen und aktuelle Situation', *Neue Praxis – Zeitschrift für Sozialarbeit, Sozialpädagogik und Sozialpolitik*, 25, 167-182.

Ritzer, G. (2013) *The McDonaldization of Society*, Los Angeles, CA: Sage.

Roscher, F. (1996) 'Gefährdung von Rechtsansprüchen durch private Wohltätigkeit?' *Info Also*, 3, 147-148.

Schreier, C. (2012) *Der neue Sozialstaat?!, Mensch & Politik. Sekundarstufe 1. Schulbuch aus Thrüringen (9. / 10. Schuljahr)*, Braunschweig: Schroedel.

Sedmak, C. (2005) *Option für die Armen. Die Entmarginalisiuerung des Armutsbegriffs in den Wissenschaften*, Freiburg im Breisgau: Herder.

Sedmak, C. (2013) *Armutsbekämpfung. Eine Grundlegung*, Wien: Böhlau.

Segbers, F. (2010) 'Tafeln in der Wohltätigkeitsfalle', in S. Selke (ed) *Kritik der Tafeln in Deutschland – Ein systematischer Blick auf ein umstrittenes gesellschaftliches Phänomen*, Wiesbaden: VS: 179-198.

Segbers, F. (2013) 'Die Armut der Politik. Das Menschenrecht auf Nahrung – und der Irrweg der Tafelbewegung', *Blätter für deutsche und internationale Politik*, 1, 81-89.

Selke, S. (2008) *Fast ganz unten. Wie man in Deutschland durch die Hilfe von Lebensmitteltafeln satt wird*, Münster: Westfälisches Dampfboot.

Selke, S. (2013a) *Schamland. Die Armut mitten unter uns*, Berlin: Ullstein.

Selke, S. (2013b) 'Umarmter Protest. Tafeln zwischen Charityformat und Bewegungsanspruch', *Forschungsjournal Neue Soziale Bewegungen*, 2, 152-156.

Spiegel (2014) *Armut: Tafel Wattenscheid hat Studenten als Kunden*, Spiegel [Online] Available at: www.spiegel.de/unispiegel/wunderbar/ armut-tafel-wattenscheid-hat-studenten-als-kunden-a-939006.html [Accessed 17 May 2016].

Stehr, N. (2007) *Die Moralisierung der Märkte*, Frankfurt: a.M., Suhrkamp.

Stern (2003) 'Tafelfreuden', *Stern*, 97.

Taz (2014) *Die Hamburger Tafeln sind überlaufen*, Taz.de [Online] Available at: www.taz.de/Umzug-statt-Aufnahmestopp/!131763/.

Wagner, M., Fialkowska, K., Piechowska, M. and Lukowski, W. (2013) *Deutsches Waschpulver und polnische Wirtschaft. Die Lebenswelt polnischer Saisonarbeiter – ethnographische Beobachtungen*, Bielefeld: Transkript.

Werth, S. (1998) 'Die Tafeln in Deutschland', *Forschungsjournal Neue Soziale Bewegungen*, 2, 68-73.

Werth, S. (2004) 'Eine real existierende Utopie - Die Geschichte der Berliner Tafel e.V.', in K. Beuth (ed) *Ins Machbare entgrenzen. Utopien und alternative Lebensentwürfe von Frauen*, Herbolzheim: Centaurus Verlag and Media: 153-161.

Werth, S. (2009) 'Es geht auch anders - Nach der Routine kommt die Vielfalt', in S. Selke (ed) *Tafeln in Deutschland. Aspekte einer sozialen Bewegung zwischen Nachtungsmittelumverteilung und Armutsintervention*, Wiesbaden: VS: 243-257.

Wimmer, W. (2010) *Handeln im Widerspruch. Als Brotverkäufer in der Emmendinger Tafel*, Norderstedt: Books on Demand.

THIRTEEN

Challenges for the struggle against austerity in Britain and Europe

Thomas Jeffrey Miley

We live in a time of unprecedented wealth and opulence, concentrated in very few hands, a plutocratic age. It is also a time of acute capitalist crisis, in which clear signs of systemic irrationality abound. The clearest of these is imminent ecological catastrophe, and the unsustainability of a global political economy that mandates infinite growth but is based on the exploitation of scarce natural resources. Moreover, around the globe, abject misery persists among multitudes, while perpetual war for the sake of perpetual peace surrounds us. Endemic and polarising violence and destruction are careening out of control in the context of the Orwellian 'War on Terror', while civil liberties are slashed, to the detriment of all. Nevertheless, capitalist social-property relations go virtually uncontested, albeit not without exception, but to a degree certainly unthinkable before the end of the Cold War. Our political imagination has been impoverished by the crimes of Stalin and by decades of neoliberal assault. The mantra 'There is no alternative' (Thatcher, 2013) is broadcast ad infinitum, consubstantiated into common sense. Subliminal mind games we are up against, the white magic of Walt Disney and the New Reagan Man.

We have lost our faith in a viable and desirable alternative to the existing social order. And make no mistake, resistance requires faith – faith that resistance is not futile; faith that resistance will not make things even worse. Our conviction in the emancipatory outcome of – especially *anti-capitalist* – political struggle has been shaken to its foundations. It's not just that faith in the inevitable victory of socialism over barbarism has vanished, it's much worse than that. The very distinction between the two has been thrown into question by the millions who perished in the gulags, not to mention the axe in Trotsky's skull.

In turn, the crisis and collapse of the Soviet Union – and with it, the death of the state communist ideal – has triggered a crisis of social democracy as well. The model of 'social democracy' – a model even embedded in the constitutions of many European states – gives way nearly everywhere to the logic of austerity and the mandate of neoliberal reform (Streeck, 2014). The model of social democracy, like that of representative democracy more generally, developed originally 'neither out of the positive tendencies of capitalism, nor as a historical accident'. Rather, it was 'forged out of the contradictions of capitalism' (Therborn, 1977, p 35). An historic class compromise was behind its institutionalisation – the fruit of long, hard, often extra-legal and bloody struggles on the part of the organised working class, not to mention the bad conscience of a capitalist class ashamed of its own complicity in and eager to avoid a repetition of the polarising dynamics that had culminated in the death and destruction of the two world wars.

The descent from social democracy

It is too often forgotten that the so-called 'golden age of capitalism' in Europe was built on the ashes of a devastated continent. From barbarism to social democracy, one could describe the trajectory of its ascent; from social democracy to barbarism, one can describe the trajectory of its demise. The pivot point, in retrospect, was the breakdown of the Bretton Woods system,[1] after which the macro-economic leverage of individual nation states to pursue Keynesian 'social-democratic' formulas for securing full employment and progressive redistribution, and for fending off crises via counter-cyclical demand management, have been rendered decreasingly effective, even dismissed as obsolete. Embedded institutional arrangements rarely crumble overnight; certainly, social democracy has not. The descent from social democracy has occurred in fits and spurts, at best, with uneven results, no doubt, but everywhere the general trajectory is the same: that of descent, or better yet, retreat. As David Harvey (2005) has observed, 'one condition of the post-war settlement in almost all countries was that the economic power of the upper classes be restrained and that labour be accorded a much larger share of the economic pie' (p 15). But since the breakdown of Bretton Woods, such restraint has given way to a frontal upper-class assault.

An upper-class assault on social democracy – this is how best to understand the policy regime and institutional re-equilibration characterising the capitalist state in the period of neoliberal hegemony. Harvey (2005) has perspicaciously defined the neoliberal state as 'a state apparatus whose fundamental mission is to facilitate conditions for profitable capital accumulation on the part of domestic and foreign capital' (p 7). Neoliberalism can be seen as a hegemonic bloc united around a utopian project and dominant ideology. Again, in Harvey's words:

> Neoliberalism is in the first instance a theory of political economic practices that proposes that human well-being can best be advanced by liberating individual entrepreneurial freedoms and skills within an institutional framework characterized by strong private property rights, free markets, and free trade. The role of the state is to create and preserve an institutional framework appropriate to such practices. (Harvey, 2005, p 2)

In Europe, Great Britain has led the way in the neoliberal assault. The result has been a radical and rapid upward redistribution of economic resources, indeed, a reversal of the 'golden age' trend of declining inequality, a massive re-concentration of wealth in the hands of the few. A comparison between Great Britain, at the vanguard of the retreat, and Sweden, much closer to the rearguard, proves most revealing in this regard. As a report recently published by the Equality Trust (2011) emphasises, in the 1960s, 'Sweden and the UK had similar levels of income inequality'. However, by 2005, 'the gap between the two had increased by 28%'. In fact, in Britain, like the United States, 'since the 1980s income inequality has increased substantially and has returned to levels not seen since the 1920s'. Moreover, in Britain, as elsewhere, this growth in inequality 'has been driven by the top 1% of wage incomes'. Finally, such already-shocking figures, which are based on standard household surveys, 'underestimate income inequality by as much as 10 percentage points, due to the under-representation of the top 1% of incomes' (Equality Trust, 2011, p 1). Nor do they even mention other assets besides income contributing to wealth – the super-rich are quite adept at simultaneously flaunting and hiding all of them.

The numbers in Britain are indeed most disturbing. According to a report published in *The Guardian*, 'in 2008, the top 10% of income earners get 27.3% of the cake, while the bottom 10% get just 2.6%' (Toynbee and Walker, 2008). Moreover, things are certainly getting worse. Whereas 'twenty years ago the average chief executive of a FTSE 100 company earned 17 times the average employee's pay; now it is more than 75 times'. Likewise, whereas '[i]n 1977, of every £100 of value generated by the UK economy, £16 went to the bottom half of workers in wages; by 2010 that figure had fallen to £12, a 26 per cent decline'. To make matters worse, '[b]etween 1997 and 2008, the proportion of personal wealth held by the top 10% swelled from 47% to

54%'. As if that weren't bad enough, evidence abounds of tax evasion and tax fraud on a massive scale on the part of the super-rich, which of course goes unpunished. In fact, 'tax consultant Grant Thornton estimated that in 2006 at least 32 of the UK's 54 billionaires paid no income tax at all' (Toynbee and Walker, 2008).

Not surprisingly, as the upper classes in most of the rich countries get an ever larger share of the economic pie, they are also ever more out of touch with the lives of ordinary people. Britain again distinguishes itself at the vanguard of this disturbing trend. In 2008, Polly Toynbee and David Walker (2008) 'conducted interviews with partners in a law firm of international renown and senior staff from equally world-famous merchant banks'. The salaries of the law partners ranged from £500,000 to £1.5m per year, 'putting them in the top 0.1% of earners in the UK, while the merchant bankers ranged from £150,000 up to £10m'. They posed a simple question to their sample of these elite income earners: 'How much would it take to put someone in the top 10% of earners?' Their answer: £162,000. In reality, in 2007, the figure stood at a mere £39,825. 'The group found it hard to believe that nine-tenths of the UK's 32m taxpayers earned less than that.' Likewise with the poverty threshold: when asked where this was located, the lawyers and bankers estimated the threshold to be £22,000. 'But that sum was just under median earnings, which meant they regarded ordinary wages as poverty pay' (Toynbee and Walker, 2008).

But if Britain is at the vanguard, it is certainly not alone. Piketty (2013) has documented in exhaustive detail the extent of the disturbing trends in inequality across Europe and the United States, while Branko Milanovic (2012) has called attention to a more general, equally disturbing, trend that spans the globe. Milanovic (2012) warns against the danger to social and political stability posed by the 'crowding out of national middle classes' in the process of creating a global middle class, a process that entails the destruction of the social bases for democratic accountability at the level of the nation state, thereby facilitating the emergence of a 'global plutocracy' (p 16). The nation state is far from obsolete, but its democratic character is being regressively transformed, and progressively hollowed out. The deregulation of global financial flows, the transnationalisation of global commodity chains, the liberalisation of the terms of global trade, and the imposition of structural adjustment policies in exchange for bail-outs in crisis-ridden countries across the globe: the combined effect of these interrelated developments has been an outflanking of the nation state's capacity to effectively regulate and tame market force.

The late, great democratic theorist, Robert Dahl (2000), pointed out the tensions and trade-offs between scope and voice in attempts to exercise collective, democratic control. The smaller the community, the larger the voice of any individual or sub-group of citizens. But conversely, the larger the community, the greater the scope of control. The nation state can no longer control and tame the effectively organised, cohesively coordinated forces of global capital. The Marxist notion of the structural dependence of the state on capital would seem vindicated at last.

Capitalism versus democracy

The elasticity and expansive capacity of capitalism, its ability to survive and adapt, to co-opt and incorporate opposition, was long underestimated by revolutionary critics of all persuasions on the anti-capitalist left, this is no doubt true. However, these same revolutionary critics were nevertheless right to insist on a fundamental contradiction between the logic of capitalism and the goal of social emancipation – a contradiction that arguably cannot be erased, and certainly was not erased, but was only rendered insidiously invisible during the decades of hegemony of social democracy. Indeed, the models of neoliberal capitalism, social democracy and state socialism all share one crucial feature: they are based on and provide institutional guarantees for the perpetuation of hierarchical, authoritarian social relations. The social-democratic compromise, it is too often forgotten, was but a compromise, never a panacea. The social rights guaranteed by the welfare state, the de-commodification of basic material needs, the provision of public goods such as free healthcare and free education for all citizens, certainly contributed to an expansion of options and resources available for most individuals, and in this respect can be said to have had a democracy-enhancing effect. But these same social rights were achieved and provided through the expansion of vast bureaucratic state hierarchies – a paternalistic state, rendering its services to a pacified citizenry; a state that could intervene to ameliorate the effects of capitalist social-property relations, but at the expense of burying forever the now-forgotten dream of workers' control over the means and ways of subsistence and production.

As the young Marx warned, the improvement of the conditions of workers should not be confused with the goal of social emancipation. Even a 'forcing-up of wages' would mean 'nothing but better payment for the slave, and would not conquer either for the worker or for labour their human status and dignity' (Marx, 1978 [1844], p 80).

Such status, such dignity, would seem to require collective, democratic control over the conditions of production and reproduction, too. In this respect, the common conflation between 'representative democracy' and 'democracy tout court' is most lamentable and contentious. The restriction of democratic voice and accountability to the domains of the legislature and executive, its exclusion from other institutions with direct impact on the lives and wellbeing of citizens, seems arbitrary, if not outright contradictory, and is certainly very difficult to justify on democratic grounds. Indeed, in no less than Robert Dahl's estimation: 'If democracy is justified in governing the state, it must also be justified in governing economic enterprises; and to say that it is not justified in governing economic enterprises is to imply that it is not justified in governing the state' (Dahl, 1984, p 56).

Given the concentration of power and resources in the hands of so few, one could argue that contemporary representative democracies would be more accurately described as oligarchies than as democracies, at least as these terms have been long understood. For example, in Aristotle's classic treatment of the subject, democracy is defined as a constitution in which 'the free-born and the poor control the government – being at the same time a majority' (Politics, 1290b). This is distinguished from oligarchy, in which 'the rich and better control the government – being at the same time a minority' (Politics, 1279b). As Ellen Meiksins Wood (1995) has rightly reminded, in this classic definition, '[t]he social criteria – poverty in one case, wealth and high birth in the other – play a central role…. In fact, they outweigh the numerical criterion' (p 220). Only very recently was the long-established definition of democracy revised and its social content erased. Indeed, in William Robinson's (1996) judgement, the origins of this conceptual transformation can be located with precision:

> [t]he redefinition of democracy, of the erasure of its social content, can be seen, symptomatically, in the influential work of Joseph Schumpeter. In his 1942 study, *Capitalism, Socialism, and Democracy*, Schumpeter rejected the so-called 'classic theory of democracy' defined in terms of 'the will of the people' and the common good'. (p 51)

The conventional insistence on the intrinsic link between democracy as a form of government and substantive social equality, the link between political equality and material equality, has never fully been erased, and informs and fuels the widespread disenchantment with the practices of government in most ostensibly 'democratic' countries, among the general population and expert analysts alike.

Recently, for example, the prominent American political scientist Daron Acemoglu characterised the pathologies of the American policymaking process, its capture by powerful 'special interests', and the tendency for material inequality to bleed into political inequality, along the following suggestive lines:

> When economic inequality increases, the people who have become economically more powerful will often attempt to use that power in order to gain even more political power. And once they are able to monopolize political power, they will start using that for changing the rules in their favour. And that sort of political inequality is the real danger that's facing the United States. (Cited in Garofalo, 2012)

The danger posed by this state of affairs is dual for the 'democratic' system: it leads to increasingly endemic patterns of institutionalised corruption, which in turn leads to ever greater levels of citizen alienation from and disenchantment with the system, a vicious cycle. Notably, in Britain, like in the United States, indeed across the north of Europe, such disenchantment is more frequently capitalised by right-wing populist critiques of the 'establishment', more effectively channelled into right-wing, xenophobic nationalist utopian projects than in an emancipatory direction. Witness the rise of the right-wing populist UK Independence Party, or for that matter, the election of Donald Trump as US president.

The roots of populist reaction

There are many reasons why the winds of the gathering populist storm seem to blow in a decidedly reactionary direction. Some of these relate to the profound transformations that have taken place in the social structures of so-called 'advanced capitalist' countries in the context of globalisation. With the transnationalisation of global commodity chains, the industrial working class proper has largely relocated to places around the globe where production is much cheaper and where living standards are much lower. The dialectic of capital versus labour first diagnosed by Marx in the middle of the 19th century has not been suspended, though it may appear as such through the methodologically nationalist blinders of those seeking to understand political and economic developments in any one country or group of countries without locating them in broader global context. However, if the dialectic has not been suspended, it has been radically transformed by globalisation, in terms highly favourable to the ever-more cohesively coordinated global capitalist class, since the institutions of resistance to global capital, of collective democratic control, remain largely confined to the arena of the nation state. Meanwhile, the control of multinational corporations over institutions of global governance such as the International Monetary Fund and the World Bank is almost total, and mechanisms of accountability to the global demos over which they govern are almost non-existent.

This is the structural kernel of truth behind Thatcher's (2013) self-fulfilling prophesy that 'There is no alternative.' The institutions of collective resistance to the tyranny of untamed and unfettered market relations have been outflanked. As Samuel Bowles and Herbert Gintis (1998, p 15) have warned: '[t]he global integration of national economies has rendered the level of output in each country increasingly sensitive to world-wide demand conditions and to the competitive position of each economy and less dependent on the domestic distribution of income'. This global triumph of capital has triggered in many instances a race to the bottom for workers, especially for workers in the rich countries, where living standards are high, workplace and environmental regulations most frequently more stringent, and labour therefore expensive in relative terms. The collective leverage of workers in the rich countries has thus been weakened. This is a structural reality that would stack the decks against the prospects of taming market forces and exercising collective control, even if workers were united and committed to resistance at the level of the nation state, which they are not.

Working people are divided both across nation states and within them. At the level of the nation state, within the rich countries, class politics have not vanished, but they have been reconfigured, in most divisive and insidious terms. Class antagonisms certainly remain, but more often than not, they are directed at the 'undeserving'. Britain again distinguishes itself in this regard. Indicative of this is a 2013 study by Beedell and colleagues (UWE Bristol, 2013) into the attitudes of residents of deprived areas of Bristol, which found that working-class communities direct their resentments against vulnerable groups who they believe benefit from state favouritism, rather than against the rich. The groups particularly targeted for scorn and hostility included unmarried mothers, disabled people living in social housing, and people given help after leaving prison.

How can we explain the direction of these resentments, the tendency to target the most vulnerable, to label them 'undeserving', to transparently blame the victim? The social-psychological dimension of this reaction needs to be addressed, a task rendered all the more difficult by the prevalence of crude utilitarian assumptions underpinning many social-scientific treatments of class and of the political economy more generally. A more complex social-psychological hermeneutic allows us to identify and diagnose pathological processes of 'venting' and 'projection' at work.

The great Irish writer James Joyce (2016) captured the tragic dynamic and vicious cycle of victimhood at work in the phenomenon of 'venting' quite succinctly in his classic short story, 'The Counterparts', included in *Dubliners*. The story recounts a day in the life of an alcoholic scrivener named Farrington. Joyce describes with precision and detail a series of humiliations Farrington endures over the course of his day, first at the hands of his boss and later by his acquaintances at the pub. The blows to his sense of dignity are palpable, and the account of his foibles invokes much empathy for him in the reader. But the story ends with Farrington returning home, down and despondent, to find that his wife has gone to chapel rather than stay home and make him dinner. So Farrington tells his youngest son, Tom, to make him dinner, but the boy lets the fire in the kitchen go out. At this point Farrington explodes into rage, and begins to beat Tom viciously with his walking stick, while the boy cries for mercy. Many a child, many a woman, has found themselves in Tom's shoes, abused and victimised by a victim. This is what 'venting' is all about – the propensity for victims of systemic violence and humiliation to take out their frustrations and resentments not on their perpetrators, who are stronger, but on others, whom they find close at hand, and who are weaker.

Then there is the matter of projection. The distinction between the 'deserving' and the 'undeserving', so salient in neoliberal discourse, resonates among many workers. How could such a discourse not resonate among workers, given the centrality of industry, discipline and frugality as key virtues within the capitalist cultural system, as Jeffery Paige (2000, p 12) reminds us? The elective affinity between capitalism and the work ethic has been reinforced in the neoliberal era across the rich countries, in both Protestant and post-Christian, secular guise. The working classes are much more exposed to the psychic fear of falling out of the ranks of the respectable and deserving than are the well-off. The moral worth of the well-off, in accordance with capitalist values, is 'ultimately demonstrated by worldly success – the accumulation of property'. By extension, capitalist virtues such as industry and frugality are 'automatically associated with the possession of property'. By contrast, for the worker, 'the accumulation of property is precisely what is denied by the alienation of abstract labour', even though 'the requirements of disciplined work and moral purity are at least as strong if not stronger' (Paige, 2000, p 12). Given the ubiquity of poverty, drudgery and 'unfreedom' in even the most 'advanced' of capitalist societies, and in lieu of a social theory to explain the persistence of such misery, the 'work ethic' provides the hermeneutic key for unlocking the mysteries, and explaining away the negative aspects, of the workings of capitalism. These negative aspects come to be seen 'as the result of the moral and spiritual failings of individuals – the sin, indulgence, idleness, baseness and evil that has caused people to fall into these despised roles' (Paige, 2000, p 12).

For workers subjected to the ever-present threats of poverty, drudgery and unfreedom, their virtue according to this narrative is almost always in question – thus, the psychic pressure and temptation among workers to project these heightened fears and doubts about one's own worth on to others, the 'undeserving', the 'leeches', the 'scrounges', especially in times of increasingly precarious and scarce employment. What is sadder still is that even those targeted by such attacks often come to believe their attackers. Indeed, there is much evidence of a good deal of self-loathing, an acute sense of shame, among those most in need. This sad trend has been well documented by, among others, Sarah Greenwood in Chapter Nine of this volume.

Of course, systemic pressures on the psyche are never felt directly; instead, they are always mediated. And in Britain, the mass media – especially the tabloid press – play a particularly nefarious role in poisoning the ideological climate by targeting vulnerable groups and perpetuating myths about them as leeches and scroungers. In this respect, though support for many aspects of the welfare state, including crucially the NHS, remains relatively robust in Britain, the declining rate of support for unemployment benefits is most revealing. Between 1983 and 2011, the proportion of the British population registering agreement with the proposition that 'unemployment benefits are too high and so discourage work' increased rather dramatically, from around one third of the population to over 60%. Conversely, over the same period, the proportion registering agreement with the more empathetic, obverse proposition that 'unemployment benefits are too low and so cause hardship' fell from over 50% to a mere 20% of the British population (NatCen Social Research, 2011).

It is plausible to assume that this stark hardening of attitudes towards unemployment benefits and their recipients has something to do with the myths that abound about the benefits system – myths perpetuated precisely by the tabloid press, in collaboration with right-wing demagogues. The prevalence of such myths in Britain has been well documented. A 2013 survey commissioned by the Trades Union Congress (Grice, 2013) found widespread misconceptions about welfare and especially unemployment benefits among the British public. For example, when asked to estimate the proportion of the entire welfare budget dedicated to benefits for the unemployed, on average people put the number at fully 41%, although the actual figure that year was a mere 3%. Even more disturbingly, when asked to estimate the proportion of the welfare budget that is claimed fraudulently, on average people guessed 27%, though the Conservative–Liberal Democrat coalition government itself put the figure at a miniscule 0.3%. Similarly, when asked to estimate the proportion of those claiming Jobseeker's Allowance for more than a year, on average people guessed fully 48%, though the actual figure was only 27.8% (Grice, 2013). Such systemically distorted perceptions, no doubt, work to exacerbate the fault line between the 'deserving' and the 'undeserving', between 'hardworking' and 'non-working' poor.

But it will not suffice to blame the prevalence of such myths on the tabloid press alone. The mass media only exacerbate the problem of the broader absence of a counter-hegemonic narrative potent enough to combat the ascendant, increasingly unfettered reign of idolised 'market forces' (except, of course, when big banks go under). An even greater responsibility for the absence of a counter-hegemonic narrative is born by the establishment political parties on the left who long ago abandoned explicit appeals to working-class identity in favour of narratives about and appeals to 'middle-class' sensibilities. Thus was the working class discursively deconstructed, as Adam Przeworski and John Sprague (1988) have emphasised. Or, to put the point in terms more friendly to positivist verification, thus was the salience of working-class identity diminished, and its power to influence political behaviour weakened. When we add to the mix the defeat and retreat of the unions, the sparsity of counter-hegemonic narratives begins to make more sense still. To make matters worse, discursive appeals to 'working-class' identity did not only ever have to compete with, nor did they only give way to, appeals to abstract 'middle-class' subjects. Instead, they always had to compete with, and have increasingly given way to, specific narratives appealing to and legitimating hierarchies not only of class, but also of gender, race, creed and nation.

Fear of the 'feral underclass'

The festering chauvinism reflected and propagated by the refusal to come to terms and condemn the colonial past and its continuing legacy underpins the ideological efficacy of divisive ethno-nationalist and neo-racist narratives across austerity Europe. Scarcely concealed, coded racist language abounds in the terms of public discourse. In the UK, such racist reflexes could be detected in mainstream discussions of the August 2011 riots that broke out in Tottenham and spread to several other London boroughs and urban centres across England, triggered by the death of Mark Duggan, who was shot by the police. In one infamous exchange on the BBC, historian David Starkey responded to evidence of participation by 'whites' in the disturbances by lamenting that such 'whites have become black', denouncing the 'destructive, nihilistic gangster culture … that has become the fashion' (BBC, 2011). Nor was Starkey alone in framing the terms of debate in 'culturalised-racist' terms, although he was widely chastised for having been too explicit. Conservative politicians picked up on his cue nevertheless, and coded race language proliferated in official condemnations of the events. According to the then Secretary of State for Justice, Kenneth Clarke, what was most 'disturbing' about the riots was 'the sense that the hardcore of rioters came from a *feral underclass*, cut off from the mainstream in everything but its materialism' (Clarke, 2011, emphasis added). The London mayor, Boris Johnson, introduced another adjective to this loaded description, referring to the rioters as a 'feral criminal underclass' (Henley, 2011).

The adjective 'feral' has clear racist connotations. Its multiple meanings include, according to the Oxford English Dictionary: 'existing in a wild or untamed state'; 'having returned to an untamed state from domestication'; and 'of, or suggestive of, a wild animal; savage' (Henley, 2011). But even more central to the terms of the conservative blame game is the noun used by both Clarke and Johnson: namely, the 'underclass'. Iain Duncan Smith, who has been dubbed 'the Tory party's social policy guru', pointed the finger at a 'menacing underclass' that has allegedly emerged, 'a new generation of disturbed and aggressive young people doomed to repeat and amplify the social breakdown disfiguring their lives and others round them' (Easton, 2011). The former Prime Minister David Cameron, for his part, diagnosed the main cause of the riots to be 'a complete lack of responsibility, a lack of proper parenting, a lack of proper upbringing, a lack of proper ethics, a lack of proper morals', emphasising the need to correct these behavioural defects through ratcheting up discipline in schools and through making sure that the welfare system 'does not reward idleness' (Easton, 2011). The concept of the 'underclass' can be traced back to the work of the sociologist Gunnar Myrdal in the 1960s, but it was not popularised until the Reagan era by Charles Murray, the co-author of the infamous book *The Bell Curve: Intelligence and Class Structure in American Life* (1994). Murray has been a central figure in developing the academic version of arguments about the so-called 'culture of poverty' – arguments in which the term 'underclass' has figured prominently. He has been influential on both sides of the Atlantic, having introduced the concept to debates in Britain in a visit to the country in the late 1980s (Black's Academy, 2002).

Not surprisingly, the term has been the subject of significant contention in social-scientific circles. Gans and Wacquant have been among the most vocal in critiquing the concept, both pointing to the ways in which it has come to be used as little more than a code word to refer to 'poor inner-city blacks' (Wikipedia, 2016). Indeed, Julius Wilson, who had used the term in his influential 1987 book *The Truly Disadvantaged*, later came to disavow it because of the 'moral and ideological baggage' that had come to be associated with it, and has argued that it should be abandoned and substituted with the allegedly more neutral term 'ghetto poor'. More generally, strong reservations abound within the social-scientific community about using a term widely seen to blame the victim and to 'stereotype the poor as authors of their own misfortune' (Lawson et al, 2000, p 219).

Moral and ideological baggage and victim-blaming notwithstanding, the concept of the 'underclass' does make some sense in both empirical and theoretical terms, albeit for reasons different from the ones adduced by Murray and his Tory fans. Olin Wright, for example, has linked the concept to the distinction between exploitation and oppression, arguing that an 'underclass can be defined as a category of social agents who are economically oppressed but not consistently exploited within a given class system' (Olin Wright, 1994, p 48). This distinction is important insofar as, 'from the point of view of the rationality of capitalism', at least, 'the underclass consists of human beings that are largely expendable' (Olin Wright, 1994, p 48). There is thus a cruel logic underlying the injustices of systemic discrimination, police harassment and mass incarceration. Inversely, there is a logic to responses of 'criminality' and of rioting as well. Since members of the 'underclass' do not have 'the capacity to disrupt production through control of labour' (that is, to strike), their 'main potential power against their oppressors comes from their capacity to disrupt the sphere of consumption, especially through crime and other forms of violence'

(Olin Wright, 1994, p 48). The terms of class struggle salient in the contemporary debate have thus shifted – away from the binary of 'working class versus capitalist class', toward an alternative binary of 'middle class versus "underclass"', with all the racialised baggage this latter binary entails.

Xenophobia and the War on Terror

The vacuum left by the deconstruction of working-class identity, and of the concomitant de-politicisation of the working class, has provided the opportunity, indeed the conditions of possibility, for right-wing populist demagogues to succeed in their divisive appeals to the nation. In the past decade, such demagogues have proven alarmingly adept at setting the agenda and framing the terms of public debate, and at fuelling fears and animosity towards those deemed 'foreign', imagined as intrusions, invasions, even contaminations that have infiltrated the body politics, with migrants, Roma, black people and Muslims being targeted most viciously. The so-called 'refugee crisis' both exposed and exacerbated this disturbing trend of an increasingly toxic ideological climate in Europe, a climate that poses a formidable obstacle to responsible action on the part of European leaders, by triggering the fear that should they behave responsibly, in accordance with humanitarian values, they will be held accountable, punished at the polls. The predictable blowback of 'terrorist' attacks on the streets of European capitals, attacks conceived by their perpetrators as payback for the death and destruction wrought by member countries of the North Atlantic Treaty Organization in their never-ending War on Terror in the Middle East, intoxicates the atmosphere still more, further conjuring a climate of collective hysteria. Thus far, EU policymakers have focused their attention and resources nearly exclusively on the construction of a militarised fortress capable of 'weathering the storm', and diverting the 'flows' of refugees and other migrants. This has occurred alongside a Patriot Act-style[2] slashing of civil liberties and the implementation of surveillance strategies aimed at preventing 'terrorist' acts.

Such policies may be electorally expedient, but they are extremely short-sighted and ultimately counterproductive. Much more energy and attention needs to be paid to putting out the flames; as long as the Middle East remains engulfed in conflict, people will try to flee. And as long as acts of war, easily interpreted as aggression, are being committed by European powers in the Middle East – especially given the colonial legacy reflected in the collective memories and multiple loyalties among Europe's own systemically discriminated and relatively marginalised indigenous Muslim minorities – the potential for terrorist blowback in Europe will certainly remain high. Indeed, a spiralling, dialectical dynamic of violence and repression both at home and abroad continues to gain momentum.

It is, of course, important not to exaggerate the extent of the problems posed by asylum seekers and terrorist attacks on European soil. Compared with the near neighbourhood, the European Union has vastly more resources and currently hosts only a very small portion of global refugees. It also remains among the safest places in the world in terms of the risk of violent death. Indeed, the fact that the so-called refugee crisis and the risk of terrorist attacks are so closely associated in the European press and public debate is itself partly an indicator of the extent of xenophobia and especially of Islamophobia intoxicating public opinion throughout so much of contemporary Europe. Though it also partly reflects a semi-conscious recognition on the part of European citizens that the two 'problems' come from the same 'root' cause – the ongoing catastrophe in the Middle East.

Of course, the panic over refugees and the demonisation of Europe's Muslim minority cannot be separated from the broader poisoning and polarising of the ideological climate wrought by the persistent and widespread anti-terror propaganda used to justify and mobilise public support for aggressive foreign policies in the Middle East. As if the damage done in terms of suffering and civil liberties by perpetual war and the expansion of an ever vaster surveillance apparatus were not bad enough, profligate spending on chaos-inducing wars and police-state spying systems just goes to show that when it comes to national security, the rules of austerity evidently do not apply. The night watchman state of classical liberal theory has thus taken a blatantly tyrannical turn in the age of the catastrophic War on Terror and the obsession with national security. In Britain perhaps especially, the night watchman who guards the fortress with ever-more sophisticated instruments of surveillance seems eve-more validated in the terms of public discourse, while simultaneously, the nanny state, ever-more austere, seems to fall into ever-greater disrepute. The once-hegemonic social democratic image of the state as caregiver, and as provider and guarantor of social rights, has been emasculated and delegitimised, refashioned into the image of an enabler, a nanny on whom the leeches would suck.

An emancipatory alternative?

But all hope is not lost. The neoliberal project of transforming all social relations in the image and likeness of the market, in pursuit of the mighty dollar, is a massively destabilising one. This is the case since it causes immense amounts of social suffering for those at the bottom, even in rich countries, but especially in 'developing' ones around the globe. The much-touted 'end of history' did not bring with it the reign of justice or perpetual peace; instead, it brought calamity and perpetual war. In a word, globalised neoliberalism, combined with a global war on terror, does not make for a stable equilibrium. And where there is instability, there is both risk and possibility. There are sparks of resistance in Europe and even in the United States. There have been brief episodes of collective resistance capable of catching the public's attention (such as the international Occupy, Spanish Indignados and French Nuit debout anti-austerity movements, for example), and significant electoral challenges to establishment party politics have even emerged on the left (such as Jeremy Corbyn in Britain, Bernie Sanders in the US, Syriza in Greece, and Podemos in Spain). But everywhere these challenges face similar formidable obstacles for effecting social change. Among the most formidable of these we see the failure of such movements (with the partial exception of Syriza) to resonate beyond a core of university-educated, mostly white, mostly young, mostly secular activists – their failure to take root among the very segments of society most marginalised and oppressed by the tyrannical status quo. The '1% versus 99%' framing might have proven more credible had the movement that introduced this alternative binary not been protagonised by people so much closer to the first percent than to the 99th. The last shall be first.

Moreover, as the partial exception of Syriza makes abundantly clear, it is one thing to win an election, another to make an effective break with neoliberalism. The latter would require both much higher degrees of transnational coordination and solidarity, and much higher levels of willingness to sacrifice and struggle for the sake of an uncertain future on the part of the general public. But make no mistake: such resistance is necessary, in Europe and around the globe. Indeed, if we are to avoid an apocalyptic outcome, if we are to escape the fate of annihilation of the dreams of all the generations that have come before us, not to mention those of our children and our children's children who have not yet been born – if we are to secure the survival of the collective consciousness of the human race – we must somehow muster the courage to struggle against the unsustainable and tyrannical global order. It is as urgent as it is difficult that we wrest control from the corporate criminals and military thugs whose greed, gluttony and rapaciousness are tyrannising the vast majority of humanity and threatening life on the planet. It is high time for global oligarchy to give way to global democracy. It is, after all, humanity's last chance.

Notes

[1]　As Geoffrey Ingham (2008, p 50) stresses, 'the Bretton Woods international monetary system, which operated between 1945 and the early 1970s, attempted to control international speculative markets in currency and money-capital in order that the democracies could make good the wartime promises to maintain full employment'. Moreover, as he also stresses, 'the disintegration of the Bretton Woods system of exchange controls' would open the floodgates for vastly 'increased international capital flows and currency speculation', which together constitute 'arguably the main factors in economic globalization and place constraints on domestic economic and social policies' (Ingham, 2008, p 235, fn.13).

[2]　For the nefarious effects of the Patriot Act on civil liberties in the US, see Cole et al (2006) and Greenwald (2015). For the civil liberties and surveillance situation in Europe, see De Goede (2008) and Wright and Kreissl (2014).

References

BBC(2011) 'England Riots: "The Whites Have Become Blacks"', Says David Starkey', *BBC News*, [Online] Available at: www.bbc.com/news/uk-14513517 [Accessed 18 May 2016].

Black's Academy (2002) *Theories of Poverty: The Underclass. Charles Murray – the Underclass in Britain*, [Online] Available at: www.Blacksacademy.net/content/3254.html [Accessed May 18 2016].

Bowles, S. and Gintis, G. (1998) *Recasting Egalitarianism: New Rules for Communities, States and Markets*, London: Verso.

Clarke, K. (2011) 'Punish the Feral Rioters, but Address Our Social Deficit Too', *The Guardian*, [Online] Available at: www.guardian.co.uk/commentisfree/2011/sep/05/punishment-rioters-help [Accessed 18 May 2016].

Cole, D., Dempsey, J.X. and Talanian, N. (2006) *Terrorism and the Constitution. Sacrificing Civil Liberties in the Name of National Security*, New York, NY: The New Press.

Dahl, R. (1984) 'Democracy in the Workplace: Is It a Right or a Privilege?' *Dissent*, 3, 54–60.

Dahl, R. (2000) *On Democracy*, New Haven, CT: Yale University Press.

De Goede, M. (2008) 'The Politics of Presumption and the War on Terror in Europe', *European Journal of International Relations*, 14, 1: 161-185.

Easton, M. (2011) 'England Riots: The Return of the Underclass', *BBC News*, [Online] Available at: www.bbc.co.uk/news/uk-14488486 [Accessed May 18 2016].

The Equality Trust (2011) *Income Inequality: Trends and Measures*, [Online] Available at: www.equalitytrust.org.uk/sites/default/files/research-digest-trends-measures-final.pdf [Accessed 18 May 2016].

Garofalo, P. (2012) *MIT Economist: Income Inequality is Crushing the Middle Class' Political Power*, Think Progress, [Online] Available at: https://thinkprogress.org/mit-economist-income-inequality-in-the-u-s-is-crushing-the-middle-class-political-power-b9298307f1dc [Accessed 16 May 2016].

Greenwald, G. (2015) *No Place to Hide: Edward Snowden, the NSA, and the U.S. Surveillance State*, London: Picador.

Grice, A. (2013) 'Voters "Brainwashed" by Tory Welfare Myths, Shows New Poll', *The Independent*, [Online] Available at: www.independent.co.uk/news/uk/politics/voters-brainwashed-by-tory-welfare-myths-shows-new-poll-8437872.html [Accessed 18 May 2016].

Harvey, D. (2005) *A Brief History of Neoliberalism*, Oxford: Oxford University Press.

Henley, J. (2011) 'The F-Word That's Suddenly Everywhere', *The Guardian*, [Online] Available at: www.guardian.co.uk/theguardian/2011/sep/06/use-of-feral-suddenly-everywhere [Accessed 18 May 2016].

Ingham, G. (2008) *Capitalism*, Cambridge: Polity.

Joyce, J. (2016) *Dubliners*, Gutenberg, [Online] Available at: www.gutenberg.org/files/2814/2814-h/2814-h.htm [Accessed 18 May 2016].

Lawson, T., Jones, M. and Moores, R. (eds) (2000) *Advanced Sociology through Diagrams*, Oxford: Oxford University Press.

Marx, K. (1978 [1844]) 'Selections from the Economic and Philosophic Manuscripts of 1844', in R. C. Tucker (ed) *The Marx-Engels Reader*, New York, NY: Norton and Company: 79-91.

Milanovic, B. (2012) *Twenty Years of Globalization: National and Global Inequalities, 1988 and 2008*, World Bank Group, Available at: http://siteresources.worldbank.org/INTPOVRES/Resources/477227-1173108574667/hsbc_short.pdf [Accessed 18 May 2016].

Murray, C. and Herrnstein, R. J. (1994) *The Bell Curve: Intelligence and Class Structure in American Life*, New York, NY: Free Press.

NatCen Social Research (2011) *Poverty and Welfare Data Tables*, NatCen Social Research, [Online] Available at: http://natcen.ac.uk/media/137640/poverty-and-welfare-data-tables.pdf.

Olin Wright, E. (1994) *Interrogating Inequality: Essays on Class Analysis, Socialism and Marxism*, New York, NY: Verso.

Paige, J. M. (2000) *Abstract Subjects: 'Class', 'Race', 'Gender', and Modernity*, Unpublished Manuscript: University of Michigan.

Piketty, T. (2013) *Capital in the Twenty-First Century*, Harvard, MA: Harvard University Press.

Politics (1279b) *Aristot. Pol. 3.1279b*, Perseus Digital Library, [Online] Available at: www.perseus.tufts.edu/hopper/text?doc=Perseus%3Atext%3A1999.01.0058%3Abook%3D3%3Asection%3D1279b [Accessed 18 May 2016].

Politics (1290b) *Aristot. Pol. 4.1290b*, Perseus Digital Library, [Online] Available at: www.perseus.tufts.edu/hopper/text?doc=Perseus%3Atext%3A1999.01.0058%3Abook%3D4%3Asection%3D1290b [Accessed 18 May 2016].

Przeworski, A. and Sprague, J. (1988) *Paper Scissors. A History of Electoral Socialism*, Chicago, IL: University of Chicago Press.

Robinson, W. (1996) *Promoting Polyarchy*, Cambridge: Cambridge University Press.

Streeck, W. (2014) *Buying Time: The Delayed Crisis of Democratic Capitalism*, London: Verso.

Thatcher, M. (2013) 'The Iron Lady: Margaret Thatcher's Linguistic Legacy', *OxfordWords Blog*, [Online] Available at: http://blog.oxforddictionaries.com/2013/04/margaretthatcher/ [Accessed 16 May 2016].

Therborn, G. (1977) 'The Rule of Capital and the Rise of Democracy', *New Left Review*, 103, 3-41.

Toynbee, P. and Walker, D. (2008) 'Meet the Rich', *The Guardian*, [Online] Available at: www.theguardian.com/money/2008/aug/04/workandcareers.executivesalaries [Accessed 18 May 2016].

UWE Bristol (2013) *UWE Researchers Say Benefits Cuts Agenda Breeds Working Class Resentment*, UWE News Release, [Online] Available at: https://info.uwe.ac.uk/news/uwenews/news.aspx?id=2523 [Accessed 18 May 2016].

Wikipedia (2016) *Underclass*, Wikipedia.org, [Online] Available at: https://en.wikipedia.org/wiki/Underclass [Accessed 18 May 2016].

Wilson, J. (1987) *The Truly Disadvantaged: The Inner City, the Underclass and Public Policy*, Chicago, IL: The University of Chicago Press.

Wood, E. M. (1995) *Democracy against Capitalism*, Toronto: York University Press.

Wright, D. and Kreissl, R. (eds) (2014) *Surveillance in Europe*, London: Routledge.

Part IV
Situating solidarity in perspective

FOURTEEN

Individualism and community in historical perspective

Jon Lawrence

Across the western world, social theorists and commentators tell us that everyday life has become selfish and atomised; that individuals live only to consume; that ideas of community and social solidarity have lost their purchase. Influential social theorists like Zygmunt Bauman argue that we have entered a new age of 'Liquid Modernity' in which we have all been reduced to isolated individuals obsessed by our 'solitary individual fears' (Bauman, 2000). Similarly, Robert Putnam has captured the attention of politicians and policymakers worldwide with his bleak assessment of social fragmentation, of a world where everyone goes 'bowling alone' (Putnam, 2000). In Britain, we are surrounded by talk of the collapse of community and the broken society, and by think tanks and government departments constantly hatching new ways to rebuild what they have come to call our social capital. From both left and right, people argue that to halt this inexorable slide towards social disintegration we need to breathe new life into collective identities such as community and class, which supposedly once acted as a bulwark against the tide of selfish individualism. Political projects like Philip Blond's 'red Toryism' and Maurice Glasman's 'blue Labour' offer explicitly backward-looking programmes that champion the revival of face-to-face community as an alternative to the fragmentation they attribute to modern-day liberal individualism (Blond, 2010; Glasman et al, 2011). More radical voices call for the revival of class politics as the only way to halt our inexorable slide towards an atomised, free-market dystopia (Jones, 2011; Dorling, 2014).

But we should be wary. The social transformations of the past half century have brought enormous gains in terms of personal freedom. The social pressure to conform to external norms of behaviour – the pressure, as Jeanette Winterson puts it, to be normal rather than happy – has weakened across the western world (and beyond) in the past half century, eroded both from within and without (Winterson, 2011): from without, by increased mobility, new mass media and the hollowing out of patrician power in state and church, and from within, by rising expectations of life driven by direct personal experience – by people seeing others forge lives not just different from, but palpably better than, the life proscribed by custom and habit (Hoggart, 1995). Many have seized the chance to live life on their own terms, even more have come to believe, as Selina Todd reminds us, that, at a minimum, their children should have the chance to do so (Todd, 2005; Todd and Young, 2012). But it is too easy to equate this revolution in expectations – this broadening of the scope for personal freedom and self-expression – with a rejection of community and social solidarity. The changes of the past 50 or 60 years have been more complicated than that, and we need to break away from simple narratives that chart a relentless journey away from community towards individualism and social anomie.

Contrary to many preconceptions, most people's lives are socially *more* connected today than 70 years ago. Most people have more leisure time, more mobility, more ways to communicate and more space (and inclination) to entertain each other at home, as well as more money to socialise outside the home. Community does not just survive, it flourishes, but because it often takes new forms – less localised, less formal – it is too swiftly dismissed by pessimistic social commentators fixated on an idealised model of true community: place-based and face to face like the pre-modern village, or its supposed 20th-century urban equivalents like that portrayed in early episodes of Granada Television's soap opera Coronation Street, first broadcast in 1960. But as Peter Willmott recognised by the 1980s, community can take many forms besides the classic territorial model that he and Michael Young had celebrated in their famous study of post-war Bethnal Green (Young et al, 1957). Willmott argued that interest communities and communities of attachment, though spatially more fluid, could be no less important, or 'real', for their members (Willmott, 1989). Similarly, the sociologists Liz Spencer and Ray Pahl have argued that it is vibrant friendship networks that provide the social glue of modern life – what they call its 'hidden solidarities' (Spencer and Pahl, 2006). They stress the importance of *personal* communities, and insist that just because modern technologies allow these to be more dispersed than in previous generations, we should not conclude that these communities are less meaningful to people, or less potent as bulwarks against social atomisation, or that place no longer matters – Pahl acknowledges that the local remains one of the vital dimensions through which social connection can flourish (Pahl, 2005; Spencer and Pahl, 2006). But we should celebrate the fact that new technologies, from the car and the telephone to web-based social networking, have made it easier to sustain relationships rooted in genuine affection rather than simply in proximity. Community has changed rather than diminished.

So why are we so wedded to the idea of social fragmentation and the collapse of society? Perhaps we are simply hard-wired to think in terms of 'paradise lost' – after all, despite the secularisation of public life (Brewitt-Taylor, 2013), the powerful narrative of the Fall runs deep in our culture. For at least two centuries, cultural critics like Coleridge, Ruskin and T.S. Eliot have been comparing their own fragmented, hedonistic and selfish times with an earlier age of social harmony and community (indeed a medievalist colleague assures me that the ageing Bede took a similar view of developments in Anglo-Saxon England in the early *eighth* century). We also tend to romanticise local, face-to-face forms of community at the expense of other types of social relationship, glossing over the darker side of *forced* community.

Up until the Second World War, most British people may have been obliged by economic necessity and overcrowding to live on intimate terms with their neighbours, but privacy was jealously guarded. People generally feared the prying eyes and malicious tongues of neighbours, as acquiring a bad name could make it difficult to secure credit or even employment within one's locality. As a consequence, relations with neighbours were often wary. Many lived by the maxim 'we keep ourselves to ourselves and then you can't get into trouble', as a Bermondsey labourer explained to the famous New Zealand anthropologist Raymond Firth when they met in 1948 (Firth, 1956, p 34).

Even those who socialised more freely tended to do so in the street, over the garden fence or down the pub, not just for practical reasons of space but because there were strong taboos around allowing strangers into the home to know your business. In *The Uses of Literacy*, his famous study of urban working-class culture, Richard Hoggart stressed the insistence on the privacy of home, arguing that it arose mainly from a fear of mean-minded gossip. According to Hoggart, 'The hearth is reserved for the family, whether living at home or nearby, and those who are "something to us"' (1981 [1957], p 20). The wider community must be kept at bay despite thin party-walls: 'you can shut the front door, "live yer own life", "keep y'self to y'self"' (Hoggart, 1981 [1957], pp 34–5; see also Langhamer, 2005).

Of course, Hoggart was himself an elite cultural critic, drawing on his upbringing in working-class Leeds to construct his own version of a declinist narrative (Collini, 2008). But it *is* possible to find evidence of how ordinary people viewed their own lives, including the changing nature of community in the decades since the Second World War.

Perhaps the richest sources of such vernacular or everyday social science are the original field notes of sociological and anthropological community studies. From the 1940s, English social scientists began, for the first time, systematically to study ordinary people. The age of the community study was born.

In recent years, historians and social scientists have begun to recognise the enormous potential of these sources (Savage, 2005, 2010; Todd, 2008, 2014; O'Connor and Goodwin, 2013; Lawrence, 2014). They can offer us unparalleled access to the worldview of men and women who would otherwise have left little or no written record. It becomes possible to write a new type of social history: one in which ordinary people's thoughts and feelings *at the time* take centre stage – where they become the experts on their own lives. We get to understand how people made sense of historical change as it unfolded, but just as importantly we get to understand how they felt about the intimate social relationships that structured their life – how they felt about family, friends and neighbours. In so doing, we can begin to challenge many of the cruder assumptions about the collapse of community and the triumph of individualism that dominate contemporary debate.

Surviving testimony suggests that Hoggart was broadly right to insist that ties to family were generally closer than ties to neighbours, but it is nonetheless easy to romanticise the cohesiveness of the extended family, to assume that it is only in recent decades that people have felt free to choose their favourite relatives and disregard the rest. In practice, even in districts that would be held up as the epitome of traditional face-to-face community, people often lost contact with their siblings, let alone their aunts and uncles, and a significant minority openly acknowledged a complete breach with close blood relations (Lawrence, 2016). It is too easy to forget that our forebears often had good reason to want to escape the constraints of close-knit community in the decades after the Second World War. They were not simply hoodwinked by planners and advertisers peddling false dreams of suburban domesticity. Yes, they wanted better homes, with more space and modern facilities, but many also wanted the chance to withdraw from *forced* sociability – to live (and socialise) on their own terms, with the family and friends of their choosing. Crucially, they wanted to live their lives free from the close supervision of neighbours and older relatives who traditionally upheld conformity to established social norms.

Significantly, as prosperity increased and overcrowding diminished in the later 20th century, so taboos around socialising within the home began to weaken. People had less need to hide their poverty, or their domestic sleeping arrangements (always one of the most sensitive issues for those fearful of malicious gossip). But this apparently small-scale shift in popular custom was driven by much more fundamental social changes. In her book *Family Secrets*, Deborah Cohen explores how, during the second half of the 20th century, the determination to protect domestic privacy mutated into a more powerful assertion of the right to live as one wished, in public as well as in private (Cohen, 2013, p xvi). What ultimately defeated the tyranny of mean-minded gossip was not atomisation and the retreat into private life, but rather peoples' growing refusal to accept that there was only one right way to live.

These are changes that should not, and probably cannot, be reversed. The political implications of this are profound, but they are too often ignored. We have to start from where people are, not where we would like them to be. In particular, people are radically disengaged from the idea of class as politics, even if it remains commonplace, at least in Britain, to deploy the language of class as a powerful way to understand (and critique) social inequality (Skeggs, 2004; Jones, 2011; Savage, 2015). Many also feel profoundly disengaged from community – but here disengagement is tinged with regret. The trope of lost community is as much part of everyday speech as it is of elite commentary (Phillipson et al, 2001). But we should not take this longing at face value – people may sincerely wish to feel more connected to those around them, but few would willingly surrender the right to live as they choose. Rather, we should read the widespread nostalgia for community as powerful evidence that people want to find a way to reconcile personal freedom – the right not to have to conform to the expectations of strangers (or indeed of family) – with a deeper sense of social connection.

We need to be mindful here that liberal individualism is not a recent implant to British popular culture. Its roots lie deep in the Reformation (at least for those of indigenous Protestant descent). Mike Savage has written eloquently of the 'rugged individualism' at the heart of British shop-floor culture in the post-war period (Savage, 1999), and political historians have recognised that independence was the central trope of Victorian popular radicalism (Vernon, 1993; Lawrence, 1998). But until the 1950s and 1960s, the more radical implications of liberal individualism were kept in check by powerful counterveiling pressures. The economy might be viewed as a natural terrain for the pursuit of individual ends, but other facets of social life remained strongly structured by corporate identities rooted in place, creed and voluntary association, and by the elaborate social theatre of the British class system with its complex performances of deference and paternalism (Newby, 1977; Lawrence, 2011).

I would suggest that we have not *become* individualist in recent decades – rather some of the more important communal facets of our society and polity have been hollowed out, leaving individualistic impulses less constrained. But to understand what this means to people, we also need to stop seeing individualism and communitarianism as crude dichotomies. Ordinary people are not social theorists and they can, and do, happily live with the contradiction of being a bit of both. Indeed, most want to find new ways in which to reconcile personal freedom and social connectedness in a world where corporate identities have declined, and mobility has loosened ties to place.

We cannot ignore the major social and cultural changes of recent decades, but nor should we assume that their meaning is self-evident. Increased levels of physical and social mobility, and the emergence of the normative two-income (and no-income) household, have altered the raw material from which imagined communities of belonging can be constructed (Anderson, 1991; Pahl, 2005). And in one key measure – the proliferation of the one-person household – everyday life has become objectively more atomised, not just in Britain but across the western world. People are now far more likely to live alone than earlier generations. In Britain, the number of people living alone has doubled since 1974 and now represents approximately one fifth of the adult population, or 7.6 million adults (ONS, 2015). Nearly a third of all separate households now consist of a single adult.

This has had many social consequences, including greatly increasing the demand for housing. The UK population has doubled since 1901 and the housing stock has nearly quadrupled (up from 7.7 million to 26.2 million separate dwellings), but still the country has a severe housing shortage (ONS, 2011). Up until the 1970s, it remained customary for adult children to live with their parents before marriage (and sometimes beyond); divorce and separation were less common, and the elderly were less likely to continue living alone when widowed. Today, large numbers of adults live alone from choice – it is one of the markers of an affluent society with strong welfare that so many people feel free to make this choice. In Sweden, an incredible 48% of households consist of a single adult living alone (Eurostat, 2015). But again we should not leap to conclusions about what this *means*: living alone can be associated with social isolation, but it can also be a lifestyle choice for people deeply connected with friends and family by other means.

We also need to recognise that government policies can accentuate potential social fault lines, notably those between the 'hardworking' and the 'non-working' poor, where both political rhetoric and the operation of welfare rules has helped to exaggerate the differences between households that may live side by side (Pahl, 1984; Jones, 2011). In recent decades, we have also witnessed the gradual erosion of public spaces that can help facilitate forms of social connection operating on a broad, inclusive plane. Across the country, local libraries, which could act as hubs for their neighbourhood, are being closed to save trifling sums. And apart from public parks and gardens, most local leisure services are now run as businesses geared to the maximisation of private profits rather than public benefits. Indeed, public space itself is increasingly being redefined as corporate space, with not just new shopping centres, but whole streets and squares being designated as private so that developers can control how the public may use them. These are trends that, if un-resisted, will certainly impoverish the meaning of community for future generations.

But if these changes are important, it is nonetheless imperative that we resist the temptation to theorise the fate of community from common-sense readings of our own lives. Academics, journalists and public commentators typically experience much greater levels of social and geographic mobility than the population as a whole. A study in 2001 found that only 12% of university graduates lived in the local authority where they had been born compared with 44% of the national population (Gregg et al, 2001, p 8). Mobility and rootlessness is by no means a universal experience. How else can we explain the fact that nearly half of all school-age children are still cared for by extended family members on a weekly basis (Rutter and Evans, 2013), or the fact that one major study found approximately two thirds of grandparents living within ten miles of their grandchildren (Griggs, 2010)? Family is not as dispersed or dead as many assume.

Similarly, the claim to have been born and bred in a particular locality remains an important marker of identity for many, although it is by no means the only way in which loyalty to place can be expressed. Sociologists increasingly stress the importance of 'elective belonging', where connection to place is seen as an extension of a sense of self – an expression of identity (Savage et al, 2005; Phillipson, 2007). Many value where they live precisely because it offers a sense of community that they believe improves their quality of life. The interview transcripts from Yvette Taylor's study of women's lives in north-east England provide a good example. Speaking in 2007, Elisabeth, a social worker who had grown up in a poor Durham mining village – supposedly the epitome of tight-knit neighbourhood – said: 'I love [XXXX], I think it's a fantastic place. And in the north east of England, I wouldn't want to live anywhere else. It's just very different from where I was brought up. It feels more like home than anywhere I've lived, really' (cited in Taylor, 2012, interview 013).

However, not everyone feels able to construct a stable, self-affirming *elective* community. Many find their present lives wanting when measured against the remembered community of their youth. This is by no means a new phenomenon – Michael Young's field notes from Bethnal Green record older residents complaining bitterly about the loss of community in the East End since the inter-war years, and we find similar sentiments in Raymond Firth's field notes from Bermondsey in 1958, and in Rosser and Harris's account of their 1960 survey of Swansea (Young Papers, Acc. 1577, cases BG31 & BG26; Firth Papers, 3/1/13 [Part 1]; Rosser and Harris, 1965). There is likewise a powerful sense of nostalgia for lost community that runs through many recent social surveys. And while there is evidence that this feeling is often strongest among older residents, especially those who feel that familiar localities are changing radically around them, it is by no means confined to these groups (Phillipson et al, 2001; Charles and Davies, 2005; Savage et al, 2005).

Notably, other respondents in Taylor's study of women from north-east England expressed very different sentiments from those of Elisabeth. The following testimony from Jill is fairly typical:

> The community I grew up with. That isn't there anymore. That's where you left your back door open and your granny fetched you up, that doesn't happen. Not in my experience. In all of my married life, that hasn't happened but it did in my youth. I think people live behind … I can honestly say I don't know the names of anyone in our street except the next-door neighbours. After twelve years; that's sad! (Cited in Taylor, 2012, interview 019)

Jill's sense of loss doubtless reflected real changes in her life, and in the lives of her neighbours. When she was growing up, in the 1950s, it was still relatively unusual for married women, especially those with young children, to work. Most now do so. Partly because of the abolition of controlled rents in the 1980s, people also move more frequently. Jill had lived in many different parts of the North East during her adult life, and joked that she now lived the wrong side of the Tyne – that is on the southern, Durham side – whereas she had grown up north of the river.

In general, we need to recognise that children may experience community very differently from adults. People may show kindness to children while ignoring, or even ostracising, their parents. As we grow older, there is also the strong impulse to feel nostalgic about our own childhood. In many ways we are psychologically primed to exaggerate the strength of community in the past. This may help to explain why people have been doing so for generations – why an imagined golden age of community has always seemed to lie in the recent past.

In Jill's case, it is also striking that she does in fact feel close to her immediate neighbours. She and a neighbour even organise an informal job share as receptionist for a company based on their street. Not for her the radical rupture between home and work. But this lived community barely registers; Jill focuses instead on the lost community of her childhood. Arguably, it is from her early memories that she can most easily weave a vision of community that resembles the close-knit, face-to-face community portrayed not just by influential thinkers like Michael Young, but also by mainstream popular entertainment from *Coronation Street* to *Call the Midwife*, a BBC drama series about midwives working in London's East End in the late 1950s and early 1960s.

The other great change of recent years has been in the world of work. Manufacturing has collapsed as a source of employment – falling from 45% to 9% of the workforce in the past 50 years and taking with it many of the archetypal (male) working-class jobs of the 20th century, such as miner, steelworker and shipbuilder. We have also seen important shifts in the *nature* of employment. In 1975, Britain had 1.9 million self-employed workers. Today the figure is almost five million (ONS, 2014). At the same time, short-term contracts, agency work and casualisation have become the norm for many still in paid employment. As Mrs Miller, an accounts clerk from Luton, explained in 1996:

> That's the way the world's going now, everybody's on contracts.... It's easier from the company's point of view because they don't need to pay sick pay and there's no redundancy involved should you finish ... I personally think that's the way the world's going, job wise. (Cited in Dean and Melrose, 1999, interview 037)

Today, the archetypal working-class worker is mobile and socially isolated: the trucker or the 'white van man', not the miner.

But if lives have been individualised, it does not follow that values have too. People's behaviour may be shaped by the external realities of the market, but their values are much less malleable. The powerful sense of lost community is itself evidence of this resistance to atomisation. And if most people yearn to be both radically free *and* socially connected, the challenge for politicians is to develop a vision of the future that recognises that individualism and community need not be polar opposites – a vision capable of reconciling this urge to be both free and connected. But how, one might ask, can one reconcile these arguments with the recurrent images of urban anomie and alienation that regularly assail us across the mass media? Aren't scenes of shoppers fighting over electrical goods in the Christmas and Black Friday sales proof positive that people have been reduced to atomised, selfish consumers, happy to elbow old ladies and abuse staff in a desperate bid to grab a bargain? Certainly that was how most journalists explained the unruly scenes that surrounded the hype of Black Friday flash sales in November 2014. Shoppers were denounced as animals and barbarians. In *The Guardian* Barbara Ellen drew unfavourable parallels with 'footage from troubled countries of crowds of people desperately fighting to get to the front after an airdrop of food and provisions' (Ellen, 2014), and across the media commentators concluded that the engulfing tide of selfishness and greed had reached a new high, and that another nail had been driven into the coffin of 'civilisation'.

Doubtless, some people behaved badly, but is such behaviour really unprecedented, and should it be used to diagnose the ills of an entire society? Not only is English history littered with scenes of looting and crowd violence, but we need to recognise that Black Friday was a carefully stage-managed phenomenon. We have become used to relying on poor-quality mobile phone footage to view scenes of spontaneous public disorder, but media professionals were out in force for Black Friday 2014. The whole event was a giant publicity stunt. Most of the more anarchic scenes took place in the early hours of the morning because retailers had fuelled the hype about massive, one-off discounts by choosing to open their doors at midnight. They also made it clear that stock was strictly limited – if you wanted to grab a bargain, you would have to queue into the night and sharpen your elbows. Writing in the *Sunday Telegraph*, Jane Llewellyn Smith was convinced that most people were fighting to buy things they 'already own, or do not need', but, after six years of falling living standards, hardship seems a more plausible explanation (Llewellyn Smith, 2014). It is striking that across the country disturbances were concentrated in areas of deprivation, including north London, Manchester and Glasgow.

In many ways, the whole phenomenon of Black Friday is just another example of stage-managed poverty porn. Since the heated debates about the supposedly pernicious influence of affluence in the late 1950s, it has been fashionable to argue that people (for which read *other* people) are locked on a treadmill of hedonism and consumption – that they are lost to the pursuit of more and more stuff in the vain hope that this will bring not just happiness, but also social approval. This is the central proposition of Avner Offer's excoriating study *The Challenge of Affluence*. Offer mostly blames politicians and economists for the western prioritisation of growth and consumption over happiness, but he also indicts the public for being seduced by false wants, and for being more interested in the approval of others than in their own wellbeing (Offer, 2006). It is a common view – though very few of us would accept that *we* care more about status than practicality and usefulness. Our wants are rational and true; only other people's are irrational and false. I need an expensive German car for its safety, reliability and (if I am honest) its speed; you want one to show off (Trentmann, 2016).

But when ordinary people talk about their possessions, or about the things they would like to own, two qualities are repeatedly stressed: practicality and sentiment. The anthropologist Daniel Miller calls this 'the comfort of things' – what we care about are objects that make our lives better and objects that carry sentimental meaning (usually as symbols of our relationships with other people, living or dead (Miller, 2008). Nobody claims to want to keep up with the Joneses, even if they are happy to believe it of others. But large numbers do remain sensitive about others judging them by their possessions. On Tyneside in the late 1960s, workers talked about avoiding driving to work from fear that their mates might think they were showing off (Brown, 1969, Box 1, File 3, p 34). Similarly, at almost any point in the 20th century, one could find women talking about the importance of having clean nets, not just as outward symbols of respectability, but as a way of ensuring that their neighbours could not pass judgement on their possessions (or lack of them).

Even behaviour that may appear to be all about asserting status often turns out to be designed to protect people from the judgement of others. I had always assumed that people bought private (that is, personalised) car number plates to show off, and doubtless some do, but a quick search of motorists' web forums shows another side. As one site puts it: 'If you have a vehicle that is in good condition but is maybe getting on in years, why let your neighbours know how old it is?' (www.nationalnumbers.co.uk). Certainly, £100 plus VAT, the going rate for a basic dateless plate, represents a tiny fraction of the depreciation hit from buying a new car every year. So if you care whether your neighbours will judge you by the car you drive – and many people clearly do – it is a rational (and cheap) way to navigate Offer's challenge of affluence.

But as we have seen, there is nothing new about the wish to keep one's business from the neighbours. Domestic privacy has long been jealously guarded. In fact, the direction of change has been towards greater sociability and openness in recent decades. Old taboos around allowing non-family members, including neighbours, into the home have loosened, and greater mobility has enabled people to develop wider circles of friends and acquaintances (the doubling of female paid employment since the 1950s, so often held up as corrosive of community, has been an important factor broadening social networks, increasing the range of social contacts from which people can construct personal communities).

At the same time we need to recognise that local, face-to-face community is far from dead. Many people never move far from their place (and family) of origin, and even those who do often compensate for a sense of rootlessness by identifying strongly with their new communities of choice. In addition, sport, hobbies, leisure and religion all offer people new communities of taste or belief that can provide a powerful sense of belonging and social connection. In all these areas, increased prosperity, greater leisure time and the radical transformation of communication technologies in the digital age have combined to make it easier for people to sustain meaningful social networks based on personal choice rather than propinquity. True, these personal communities are therefore by definition looser than the idealised, village-like community of our imagination, but in a sense that is the point – few of us want to live under the watchful eye of Lynda Snell, the forbidding owner of Ambridge Hall in the long-running BBC radio series The Archers.

These looser forms of social connection are no less meaningful to people, and no less potent as barriers to anomie and social disintegration. They provide the hidden solidarities that help to bind modern societies together, preventing them from descending into atomised clusters of self-absorbed individuals heedless of their fellow man and woman (Spencer and Pahl, 2006). It is time that we recognised the power of these hidden solidarities to transcend the trap of narrow individualism. It is also time that we stopped trying to recreate historic forms of face-to-face community that our forebears often had good reason to escape, and instead started to nurture and develop the forms of community that exist all around us, and that offer our best hope of resisting the forces of atomisation within our culture.

References

Anderson, B. (1991) *Imagined Communities: Reflections on the Origin and Spread of Nationalism*, New York, NY: Verso.

Bauman, Z. (2000) *Liquid Modernity*, Cambridge: Polity.

Blond, P. (2010) *Red Tory: How Left and Right Have Broken Britain and How We Can Fix It*, London: Faber and Faber.

Brewitt-Taylor, S. (2013) 'The Invention of a "Secular Society"? Christianity and the Sudden Appearance of Secularization Discourses in the British National Media 1961–4', *Twentieth-Century British History*, 24, 327-350.

Brown, R. (1969) *Shipbuilding Workers on Tyneside, Modern Records Centre*, Warwick: MSS.371/shipbuilding.

Charles, N. and Davies, C. A. (2005) 'Studying the Particular: Illuminating the General: Community Studies and Community in Wales', *Sociological Review*, 53, 672-690.

Cohen, D. (2013) *Family Secrets: Living with Shame from the Victorians to the Present*, London: Penguin UK.

Collini, S. (2008) 'Richard Hoggart; Literary Criticism and Cultural Decline in twentieth-Century Britain', in S. Owen (ed) *Richard Hoggart and Cultural Studies*, Basingstoke: Palgrave Macmillan: 33-56.

Dean, H. and Melrose, M. (1999) 'Poverty, Wealth and Citizenship: A Discursive Interview Study and Newspaper Monitoring Exercise, 1996', [data collection], UK Data Service. SN: 3995, http://doi.org/10.5255/UKDA-SN-3995-1 [Accessed 30 December 2015].

Dorling, D. (2014) *Inequality and the 1%*, New York, NY: Verso.

Ellen, B. (2014) 'The Black Friday shopping scrums are so shaming', *The Guardian*, [Online] Available at: www.theguardian.com/commentisfree/2014/nov/30/black-friday-shopping-frenzy-shameful [Accessed 30 December 2015].

Eurostat (2015) *Statistics Explained: Household Composition Statistics*, European Commission, [Online] Available at: http://ec.europa.eu/eurostat/statistics-explained/index.php/Household_composition_statistics [Accessed 30 December 2015].

Firth Papers (No date) *Sir Raymond Firth Papers*, London: London School of Economics Library Special Collections.

Firth, R. (1956) *Two studies of kinship in London*, London: University of London, Athlone Press.

Glasman, M., Rutherford, J., Stears, M. and White, S. (eds) (2011) *The Labour Tradition and the Politics of Paradox*, Oxford and London: The Oxford London Seminars.

Gregg, P., Machin, S. and Manning, A. (2001) 'Mobility and Joblessness', *NBER Working Paper*, Cambridge, MA: NBER.

Griggs, J. E. A. (2010) '"They've Always Been There for Me": Grandparental Involvement and Child Well-being', *Children & Society*, 24, 200–214.

Hoggart, R. (1981 [1957]) *The Uses of Literacy: Aspects of Working-Class Life*, London: Penguin.

Hoggart, R. (1995) *The Way We Live Now*, London: Chatto and Windus.

Jones, O. (2011) *Chavs: the Demonization of the Working Class*, London: Verso.

Langhamer, C. (2005) 'The Meanings of Home in Postwar Britain', *Journal of Contemporary History*, 40, 341–362.

Lawrence, J. (1998) 'Speaking for the People Party, Language and Popular Politics in England, 1867–1914', Cambridge: Cambridge University Press.

Lawrence, J. (2011) 'Paternalism, Class and the British Path to Modernity', in S. Gunn and J. Vernon (eds) *The Peculiarities of Liberal Modernity in Imperial Britain*, Berkeley, CA: University of California Press: 147–164.

Lawrence, J. (2014) 'Social-Science Encounters and the Negotiation of Difference in early 1960s England', *History Workshop Journal*, 77, 215–239.

Lawrence, J. (2016) 'Inventing the "Traditional Working Class": a Re-analysis of Interview Notes from Young and Willmott's Family and Kinship in East London', *Historical Journal*, 567–593.

Llewellyn Smith, J. (2014) 'Why does Sales Shopping Turn us into Barbarians?', *The Telegraph*, [Online] Available at: www.telegraph. co.uk/finance/newsbysector/retailandconsumer/11262420/Why-sales-shopping-turns-us-into-barbarians.html [Accessed 30 December 2015].

Miller, D. (2008) *The Comfort of Things*, Cambridge: Polity.

Newby, H. (1977) *The Deferential Worker: A Study of Farm Workers in East Anglia*, London: Allen Lane.

O'connor, H. and Goodwin, J. (2013) 'The Ethical Dilemmas of Restudies in Researching Youth', *Young*, 21, 289–307.

Offer, A. (2006) *The Challenge of Affluence: Self-Control and Well-being in the United States and Britain since 1950*, Oxford: Oxford University Press.

ONS (2011) *Social Trends 41: Housing*, Office for National Statistics, [Online] Available at: www.ons.gov.uk/ons/rel/social-trends-rd/social-trends/social-trends-41/housing-chapter.pdf [Accessed 30 December 2016].

ONS (2014) *Persistent Poverty in the UK and EU: 2014*, Office for National Statistics, [Online] Available at: www.ons.gov.uk/peoplepopulationandcommunity/personalandhouseholdfinances/incomeandwealth/articles/persistentpovertyintheukandeu/2014 [Accessed 17 August 2016].

ONS (2015) *Families and Households*, Office for National Statistics, [Online] Available at: www.ons.gov.uk/peoplepopulationandcommunity/birthsdeathsandmarriages/families/bulletins/familiesandhouseholds/2015-11-05 [Accessed 30 December 2015].

Pahl, R. (2005) 'Are All Communities in the Mind?' *Sociological Review*, 53, 621-640.

Pahl, R. E. (1984) *Divisions of Labour*, Oxford: Blackwell.

Phillipson, C. (2007) 'The "Elected" and the "Excluded": Sociological Perspectives on the Experience of Place and Community in Old Age', *Ageing and Society*, 27, 321-342.

Phillipson, C., Bernard, M. and Phillips, J. (2001) *Family and Community Life of Older People: Social Networks and Social Support in Three Urban Areas*, New York, NY: Routledge.

Putnam, R. D. (2000) *Bowling alone: the collapse and revival of American community*, New York, NY: Simon and Schuster.

Rosser, C. and Harris, C. (1965) *The Family and Social Change: a Study of Family and Kinship in a South Wales Town*, London: Routledge and Kegan Paul.

Rutter, J. and Evans, B. (2013) *Improving Our Understanding of Informal Childcare in the UK*, London: Daycare Trust.

Savage, M. (1999) 'Sociology, Class and Male Manual Work Cultures', in J. Mcilroy, N. Fishman and A. Campbell (eds) *British Trade Unions and Industrial Politics: Volume Two: the High Tide of Trade Unionism, 1964-79*, Aldershot: Ashgate: 23-42.

Savage, M. (2005) 'Working-Class Identities in the 1960s: Revisiting the Affluent Worker Study', *Sociology*, 39, 929-946.

Savage, M. (2010) *Identities and Social Change in Britain since 1940: The Politics of Method*, Oxford: Oxford University Press.

Savage, M. (2015) *Social Class in the 21st Century*, London: Penguin.

Savage, M., Bagnall, G. and Longhurst, B. (2005) *Globalization and Belonging*, London: SAGE.

Skeggs, B. (2004) *Class, Self, Culture*, London: Routledge.

Spencer, L. and Pahl, R. E. (2006) *Rethinking Friendship: Hidden Solidarities Today*, Princeton, NJ and Oxford: Princeton University Press.

Taylor, Y. (2012) *From the Coalface to the Car Park? The Intersection of Class and Gender in Women's Lives in the North East, 2007-2009 [data collection], UK Data Service. SN: 7053*, UK Data Service Discover, [Online] Available at: http://dx.doi.org/10.5255/UKDA-SN-7053-1 [Accessed 4 January 2016].

Todd, S. (2005) *Young Women, Work, and Family in England, 1918-1950*, Oxford: Oxford University Press.

Todd, S. (2008) 'Affluence, Class and Crown Street: Reinvestigating the Post-War Working Class', *Contemporary British History*, 22, 501-518.

Todd, S. (2014) *The People: the Rise and Fall of the Working Class, 1910-2010*, London: John Murray.

Todd, S. and Young, H. (2012) 'Baby-boomers to "Beanstalkers": Making the Modern Teenager in Postwar Britain', *Cultural and Social History*, 9, 451-467.

Trentmann, F. (2016) *Empire of Things: How we became a World of Consumers, from the Fifteenth Century to the Twenty-First*, Allen Lane: Penguin.

Vernon, J. (1993) *Politics and the People: a Study in English Political Culture, c. 1815-1867*, Cambridge: Cambridge University Press.

Willmott, P. (1989) *Community Initiatives: Patterns and Prospects*, London: Policy Studies Institute.

Winterson, J. (2011) *Why be happy when you could be normal?* London: Jonathan Cape.

Young, M. D., Willmott, P. and Studies, I. O. C. (1957) *Family and kinship in East London,* London: Routledge and Kegan Paul.

Young Papers (No date) Acc. 1577. Bethnal Green Survey, Cambridge: Churchill Archive Centre.

FIFTEEN

Aiming for reconnection: responsible citizenship

Christopher Baker

At the heart of this chapter is a deceptively simple thesis – namely, that in the context of an increasingly post-secular and post-welfare/austerity public sphere, the motivating energy of beliefs, values and attitudes (what I will later expand on as spiritual capital) comes more into the frame as a key conceptual framework for both analysing current political and citizenship trends and projecting future policy trajectories. Concrete actions in terms of volunteering and other forms of engagement (the 'what') have always been directly shaped and brought into being by principles, commitments and beliefs that shape our ethical orientation in the public sphere (the 'why').

However, for reasons of historical and philosophical development in the West, the 'why' in the form of individual beliefs, values and attitudes has traditionally been viewed with suspicion as a threat to a universally recognised, and therefore coherent and fair, narrative of the public sphere and its rules of engagement. For both ideological and cultural reasons, it was deemed both appropriate and desirable that when it came to organising or policing the western public sphere, the 'what' should be disconnected from the 'why'; that personal beliefs (especially those of a religious nature) should be subsumed within loyalty to abstract entities and principles (such as the nation/welfare state or justice).

However, I argue that we (at least in the West) have arrived at a political, cultural and social nexus of events and trends where it is indeed no longer possible (or indeed desirable) to disconnect the 'why' from the 'what'; that in terms of helping to build a vibrant, resilient, participatory (and therefore more democratic) public sphere, the motivating and energising capital of beliefs, values and attitudes needs to foregrounded and harnessed in the service of 'what' (after Featherstone et al, 2012) I shall call a 'progressive localism'. Key to my proposed methodology for developing a 'responsible citizenship' in an era of austerity will be to look at how faith groups are modelling the generative power of spiritual capital to other forms of capital (such as social, human and economic) in a post-welfare policy landscape. We can prove that the demonstrable power of religious-based social capital can only be enhanced if one allows the 'why' and the 'what' 'to be reconnected – if the spiritual is reconnected to the civic and the political.

But in order to argue the importance of the concept of spiritual capital for these debates into responsible citizenship, it is crucial to take it one step further. And that is to remove it from the specific milieu of faith groups, even though these are obvious and resilient repositories in which it operates, and to open it up as a potential lever of progressive politics in groupings and individuals outside the faith sector. In order to show how the present *Zeitgeist* (which includes the post-secular, and resistance to austerity as well as other elements) is currently reshaping notions and performances of citizenship, it is necessary to outline briefly some preceding historical models and understandings from which a new model might emerge. I call this historical legacy the Rawlsian dispensation.

Notions of citizenship: Rawlsian/Kantian, communitarian/ republican and radical democratic

The notion that we have entered a post-ian dispensation is not that novel or radical. There has been a steady stream of critiques of Rawls' notion of the public sphere and his duties of citizenship, which were first articulated in *A Theory of Justice* (1973, p 4) and then subsequently finessed in *Political Liberalism* (1993). The fundamental tenet of the Rawlsian public sphere is the idea of justice, which is located and expressed within the concepts of liberty and equality. Individual liberty, said Rawls, has to be held within a system of equal liberty for all. His idea of equality is more nuanced. It does permit inequality, but only in cases where such inequalities would benefit all citizens. It was the idea of justice that Rawls saw as being a legitimate and sustainable way of managing the growing diversity of the public sphere (what he called 'reasonable pluralism' (1993, p 188). This diversity in the public sphere was not manifested so much in multiple ethnicities and lived cultures, as in ideas and beliefs. Rawls referred to these fundamental ideas and beliefs, held by individual citizens, as 'comprehensive doctrines' (1993, p 13). The art of creating a virtue of this diversity, while protecting the autonomy of the individual citizen and preventing unmanageable dissent, was to find a universal doctrine that would be a point of compatibility (or 'overlapping consensus') with most reasonable philosophical and religious worldviews. This universal doctrine for Rawls was the idea of justice, or what he calls 'the public conception of justice' (1973, p 5).

This in turn requires the idea of a well-ordered state that distributes reasonable equality and liberty in honour of the political idea of justice. Rawls (1973) defines it thus:

> .... [The state] is not only designed to advance the good of its members, but is also effectively regulated by a public conception of Justice. That is ... a society in which 1) everyone accepts and knows that others accept the same principles of justice and 2) the basic social institutions generally satisfy and are generally known to satisfy these principles. (1973, p 5)

Within such a society, Rawls maintains that 'the general desire for justice limits the pursuit of other ends' (1973, p 5). The main criticism of Rawls' ideas of citizenship and the state is that of idealism and idealisation (Brown, 2003, p 11). Rawls' principles of justice rely on a cognitive framework that most average citizens would struggle to comprehend. Rawls tries to distinguish between what he calls the 'freestanding condition' of justice (that is, a universal and autonomously derived ideal) and the basic structure restriction (in other words, what social institutions and citizen cooperation can actually deliver) (Neufeld, 2013, p 781). Even so, it has been calculated that even on the basis of very generous estimates, only around 12% of the voting population in the US would be capable of conforming to the Rawlsian template of a good citizen (Brown, 2003, p 14).

Other critiques of Rawls' concepts of citizenship have also emerged from proponents of what has become known as the communitarian approach, including Charles Taylor, Alasdair McIntyre, Michael Sandel, Michael Walzer and Benjamin Barber (Coulter, 2013, p 14). The main critiques of this school are the individualism and neutrality associated with the rights approach formulated by Rawls and more neoliberal developers of political liberalism like Robert Nozick (1974). Nozick stressed that the basis of political liberty began with the right to possess property, rather than the right to the redistribution of wealth by the state advocated by Rawls. According to Coulter, both Rawls and Nozick focus on what the individual citizen derives from the political order and society, rather than what he or she contributes. For them, 'there is a priority of *rights* of the individual over any *good life* that might be proposed. Related to this individualism, they argue that the state must be neutral with respect to any version of the good life that might be proposed' (Coulter, 2013, p 13, emphasis added). Under pressure from earlier critiques, Rawls underscores in his later work the importance of citizens possessing desirable qualities (for example, the virtues of civility, tolerance, reasonableness and a sense of fairness [1993, p 194]). Essentially, however, his model of citizenship contends that the citizen accepts the validity of the universal notion of justice and thus displays loyalty to those political and state institutions that exist to uphold those rights associated with it.

In the light of this liberal normativity towards rights, the citizen is seen as 'antecedent, individuated or unencumbered' (Sandel, 1982, p 4). They are entities or monads that exist prior to a communitarian identity; they are abstracted from the community from which they come and into which they could continue to have an impact. The countervailing concept to the 'unencumbered selves' proposed by the communitarian school therefore is that of the 'situated self' (Coulter, 2013, p 15).

Certain facets of citizenship follow on from this proposal. First, citizens now see themselves as individuals who do have moral obligations to their fellow citizens, and in general will see this as a positive state of affairs. This behaviour is 'rational' in the sense that all citizens belong to a social order in which they are interdependent and in which their fates are intertwined. To hold the view that citizens are not morally bound to each other fatally undermines the notion that citizens can and should form cohesive solidarities, stable movements and parties within the liberal public sphere (Kartal, 2001, p 114). At the heart of a fragmented ideology of the citizen lies a dysfunctional and fragmented view of the social order, which is hobbled by what Mouffe (1991) calls a 'radical indeterminacy', which thus makes a 'substantive common good' impossible to nurture or discern (1991, p 74).

Linked to this political assertion of the situated rather than the unencumbered citizen, is the disavowal of the idea of the neutral public sphere. There are two objections to this. The first is the now-familiar critique bequeathed by post-modern ethnography – that there is no such thing as the view from nowhere. The avowed Kantian liberal position of prioritising neutrality has its own genealogical epistemology, which prioritises patriarchal and secularist norms, and covert ideas of the good (Galston, 1991, p 79). The second is that any political economy based on the notion of the unencumbered self promotes a limited reading of the public sphere. A broader account better reflects embodied, rather than abstracted, diversity, and endorses the idea that individual and communities should be allowed to propose their own visions and versions of the common good.

Chantal Mouffe formulated this influential model of citizenship, which she calls the radical democracy tradition. This emerged from her desire to create a new model that combines the best traditions and instincts from both the Kantian/liberal and communitarian approaches. She agrees with the critiques of the communitarian school that the liberal tradition needs to reinsert an ethical and values-laden framework into the idea of citizenship. Without what she calls 'the absolute need to re-establish the lost connection between ethics and politics' (Mouffe, 1991, p 75) civic activity will be devalued and citizen loyalty and participation in the public sphere will be lost through a perceived lack of legitimacy. Mouffe thus aspires to reconceive a modern concept of citizenship that is able to '... formulate the ethical character [of the citizen] in a way that is compatible with moral pluralism and respects the priority of the right over the good' (1991, p 75).

Her model of citizenship thus introduces the notion of ethico-political values, which ensures that the notion of citizenship is not over-essentialised. Rather citizenship becomes a principle that affects 'the different subject positions of the social agent' and allows for the expression of a plurality of allegiances (Mouffe, 1991, p 79). However, despite this valorising of diversity there is still a need to corral these plural allegiances into a coherent narrative as an expression of loyalty to the *respublica*. The *respublica* is an idea Mouffe borrows from Oakeshott (1991), who in turn rehabilitates it from the late Middle Ages. The *respublica* is a group of citizens defined by a shared civil discourse, a discourse that is mediated through rules and norms of conduct that help to create a common bond and public concern.

Mouffe and Oakeshott both stress that this bond should incorporate a 'moral' dimension; not in the sense of a comprehensive doctrine, imposed from the top down, but a shared and bespoke form of moral consciousness and decision making that emerges, as it were, from within the life of the *respublica*. It emerges, says Oakeshott, from a dialectical concern that 'reflects the promotion of all interests, the satisfaction of all wants and the propagation of all beliefs' provided they are 'in subscription to conditions formulated in rules indifferent to the merits of any interest in truth or error of belief' (that is, the concept of justice, and its twin poles of equality and liberty) (Oakeshott, 1991, p 172). Thus Mouffe's notion of ethico-political values distinguishes between passive observance to moralistic comprehensive doctrines and more proactive engagement and sifting of ideas and actions within a framework of principles.

Mouffe is also keen to critique Oakeshott's over-smooth conceptualisation of the *respublica*, which she says reflects an innate conservatism. The civic sphere is not made up of a single we, but is in reality far more likely to reflect a dynamic that separates the we from the they or the Other. The realism of a contested public or civic sphere means adopting a more agonistic notion of pluralism, civic identity and engagement. Mouffe wants to preserve this notion because it is often in assertive and revolutionary ethico-political movements expressing the principles of equality and liberty (for example, rights of recognition and inclusion on the part of gender, sexuality, class, ethnicity and so on) that the radical forms of democratic expression and impact are seen.

So some aspects of Mouffe's model of radical democratic citizenship I warm to. I affirm her idea that citizenship is a process of becoming – of acquiring a clear sense of identity as a citizen. I welcome her idea that this becoming is intimately linked to the expression and deployment of ethico-political values and concern. In keeping with a post-modern sensibility, she says that the basic principles of equality and liberty, bequeathed by Kantian liberalism, can only come alive when citizens are allowed to interpret these ideals performatively in different contexts and collectivities. Her vision of a radical and participative citizenship in an agonistic and contested public sphere is a dialectical one; a performative ethico-politics brings alive and puts into effective use the deep traditions of secular liberalism. The aim of her model is to '... use the symbolic resources of the liberal-democratic tradition to struggle for the deepening of the democratic revolution, knowing that it is a never-ending process' (Mouffe, 1991, p 81).

However, there are shortcomings in Mouffe's model that hamper its effectiveness as a model for the present age. First, it relies on abstract conceptualisations that require prior knowledge of western historical and intellectual norms. Much of the description of her model is taken up with extrapolating Latin terms like *universitas, societas* and *respublica*, and the subtle nuances between them. Although she sees these words as 'discursive surfaces' (Mouffe, 1991, p 81), her discourse never strays into the empirical, but remains at the level of the abstract. If the *respublica* is to be negotiated across plural dimensions and worldviews, without being controlled from the top down, then it is not at all clear how this happens in practice.

Second, the radical democratic citizenship model is still blind to its own normativity. Like Rawls, Mouffe claims that her model uses concepts like equality and liberty in a neutral fashion that does not rely on the substructure of a truth claim for its validity. But this normativity is not neutral. It contains a specifically western and secularised genealogy that sees any form of belief or truth claim as a prescribed form of knowledge that is partial, selective and irrational. It certainly does not reflect the post-secular turn in global society that I refer to later in the chapter.

Although displaying some awareness and critiques of Rawls' neo-Kantian liberalism, I contend that Mouffe's model is not sufficiently post-Rawlsian to resonate with the emerging epoch and its *Zeitgeist*. I shall now extrapolate the elements of the new *Zeitgeist* with reference to the central motif of the Great Reconnection following from the Great Disconnection. Within this motif I explore ideas of the post-secular, cosmopolitanism, spiritual capital and progressive localism. I then offer two case studies of spaces of ethico-political convergence that offer insight into these new performances and expressions of citizenship, before making some concluding remarks.

The post-secular and cosmopolitanism

These two major conceptual frameworks help to articulate and define the new social, cultural and political *Zeitgeist* into which our discussion about modern citizenship is located. Both ideas have been expanded and developed by the Marxist and post-Marxist social theorists Jürgen Habermas and Ulrich Beck, who share a large theoretical body of knowledge with Mouffe, but who take that tradition into more radical territory. In particular, they acknowledge the re-emergence of globalised religion as a powerful cultural and political actor in the 21st century and they are interested in how religious discourses, practices and imaginaries both shape, and are also shaped by, the public sphere.

It was Jürgen Habermas who first coined the term 'post-secular' in the early 2000s. Since then it has become a much debated and contested term, with some traditional social science perspectives objecting to its linearity (that is, the implication that western society has moved decisively from a secular dispensation to a religious one), while others suggest that it is the neoliberal demand for religiously based goods and services to take up the provision of welfare abandoned by the retrenching state that is creating a market in religious interest (Beckford, 2012; Lancione, 2014). To be fair to Habermas, he is not suggesting either. Rather he is proposing that the West in particular enters into a new moral and political imagination that is capable of accepting and deploying the diversity and plurality of the public sphere for inclusive and progressive outcomes, rather than utilitarian and individualistic ones.

His critique of the social foundations of the liberal democratic state are both empirical and moral. Empirically, he reflects on the rise of religion in Europe following the collapse of the Soviet Union, and the new globalised phenomena associated with the rise of both conservative Islam and Pentecostal Christianity. In the light of this fact, he says, it is no longer fair under the traditional rules of engagement of a one-size-fits-all secular public sphere that religious citizens should be expected to occlude their identity or mask their discourse in the public sphere. This is because secular citizens are not required to do the same. The liberal democratic state, Habermas (2005, 2006) argues, is failing to uphold its foundational obligation to provide equality and liberty by creating, in effect, a two-tier system of citizenship.

What is required instead, he argues, is that all citizens recognise the truthfulness and integrity of their comprehensive worldviews by making the strenuous effort not simply to tolerate, but to understand in a self-reflexive way, the nature and impact of each other's beliefs. The epistemological neutrality of the state is preserved and upheld in terms of its public business (for example, official neutrality applies in the case of elected politicians and important holders of office and policy). However, the long-term future of the liberal democratic state will, thinks Habermas, depend on:

> ... whether secular and religious citizens, each from their own respective angle, are prepared to embark on an interpretation of the relationship between faith and knowledge that first enables them to behave in a self-reflexive manner toward each other in the political public sphere. (2006, p 20)

His *moral* critique of the liberal democratic state is even more far-reaching. With the development of neoliberal capitalism, he says, the Enlightenment virtues of rationality, autonomy and the right to private property (as a utilitarian means of redistribution of wealth) have become distorted and decoupled from the moorings of ethical and moral thought. The consequent stress on individualism as a social and cultural norm hollows out the basis of solidarity and mutuality on which fundamental concepts of justice depend. Religion, suggests Habermas (2010), creates therefore an indispensable source of moral and ethical wellsprings by which the liberal democratic state justifies its own ontological commitment to the concepts of equality and liberty. Without this depth of commitment and vision, the liberal democratic state will be unable to appeal beyond the materialistic present in its engagement with its citizens. The sources of legitimacy for the existence of the nation state and what it claims to do in the name of its citizens become wafer-thin and unsustainable. This is because the claims of the nation state are, says Habermas, dependent on 'autochthonous world views or religious traditions' (that is, self-generating and original), which themselves reflect 'collectively binding ethical traditions' (2005, p 339).

While a co-writer of Habermas (2010) would use the language 'hollowed out' (p 33) to describe the impact of neoliberal capitalism on the Enlightenment tradition of modernity, Beck's (1995) analysis operates at an altogether more existential level. He refers to modernity putting itself at risk, by creating, in the constant search for new markets and financially based products, a global system that is now too interconnected and increasingly unaccountable to legal scrutiny or democratic mandate. The risks generated by this increasingly unaccountable and interconnected system emerges from the fact that the number of unintended consequences far exceed the intended ones (Beck, 1999). This creates a scenario where even well-intended and progressive actions can get lost and diverted within circuits and feedback loops. A particularly acute example of this is climate change, a phenomenon Beck anticipated back in the 1980s. He pointed out that a wilful disregard for the environmental side-effects of aggressive acquisition and development would quickly reach a tipping point whereby a complex set of chain reactions would be set in place that would defy the ability of either the nation state or the market to control or resolve. These chain reactions would prove to be an existential threat to the flourishing and progressive development of global society. Beck (1995) also predicted similar outcomes created by the increasing financialisation of social goods by the market and the distribution of what he called financial 'bads' (rather than financial goods).

He goes as far as calling this risk society a form of modernity – or what he calls Modernity 2. Modernity 1 is the modernity of the western Enlightenment, which he defines as 'ends–means rationality, interests, classes, the market, science and socially-constructed "nations" which distinguish themselves from other nations and welfare states' (Beck, 2011, p 76). A key assumption within this modernity is predictability – namely, the unshakeable correlation between cause and effect, research and truth.

Accelerating from the end of the 20th century into the 21st is Modernity 2.0. This is modernity as globalisation that intensely and vigorously attacks all barriers and hierarchies erected under the auspices of Modernity 1. 'It refers to the erosion of clear boundaries separating the markets, states, civilisations, cultures, and the lifeworlds of different peoples and religions, as well as the resulting worldwide situation of an involuntary confrontation with alien others' (Beck, 2011, p 74). In other words, predictability has been replaced by unpredictability. Beck develops the political impacts of his analysis with three striking assertions. The first is that the rise of globalised religion in the 21st century is due precisely because it fits so well within the de-territorialised and rootless spaces generated by Modernity 2. Religion, says Beck, has always held within itself the idea that we are global citizens of heaven and communicates this idea through the symbolic richness of its liturgy; religious citizens, he says, always have the choice *not* to be held back or weighed down by 'the ballast of the modern nation state' (Beck, 2011, p 178).

Second, he asserts that a modernity that is always putting itself at risk requires the active moral and civic intervention and contribution of religion, which has hitherto been invisible, but is now a strategic and visible force in the world that can create a new more balanced and sustainable modernity – a Modernity 3.0 perhaps. He writes:

> It is hardly possible to overestimate the potential of religions as cosmopolitan actors – not just because of their ability to mobilise billions of people across barriers of nation and class, but because they exercise a powerful influence on the way people see themselves in relationship to the world. Above all they represent a resource of legitimation in the battle for the dignity of human beings in a civilisation at risk of destroying itself. (Beck, 2011, p 198)

But in order for religion to rise to the challenge of discovering the influence of its own 'political power' in an inclusive and uniting way, it needs to encourage its global followers to act in a 'cosmopolitan' manner. And this is the third element of Beck's analysis of his 'two modernities' thesis – namely, his juxtaposition of what he calls a 'cosmopolitan vs a universalism' imagination.

Beck highlights the fact that both violence and tolerance are historically endemic within religion. Religion, he says, responds to change and diversity in one of two ways. One is universalism (which is really only a form of fundamentalism) that insists, usually through the use of coercive violence, on a single narrative and identity to which everyone else must to varying degrees conform (Beck, 2011, p 178). Or, he says, religion can, and historically has, turned its face towards cosmopolitanism which he describes thus:

> The cosmopolitan vision is based on the actually existing historical impurity of world religions: the recognition that they are intertwined, that they are both one and the same. Learning to see and understand themselves through others' eyes does not mean that religions must sacrifice their own special nature, nor does it mean that they must all merge in a decadent value neutral secular relativism. On the contrary they enrich their own religiosity, mutually reinforce one another, and in this way they can practice and develop anew the public role of religion in the postsecular modern era. (Beck, 2011, p 178)

It is this notion of intertwined fates and genealogies, implies Beck, that lies at the heart of a cosmopolitan perspective and is the basis for shared action in the public sphere. Although he has stressed the importance of religious social actors rising to the norms and challenges of a cosmopolitan perspective, it is also clearly a challenge and choice confronting all social actors, irrespective of religion or no religion. The idea of intertwined fates and genealogies is an essential component of the Great Reconnection that I propose is the new *Zeitgeist* in which debates about the nature and form of modern citizenship need to take place.

Progressive localism and spiritual capital

The purpose of these two elements of a post-Rawlsian *Zeitgeist* is to link the rather abstract formulations associated with the post-secular and cosmopolitanism with more grassroots activity in civil society. The concepts of progressive localism and spiritual capital are bridging concepts that frame what is happening in localities and are explored in the context of my case studies.

Progressive localism

Progressive localism is a concept that has emerged from a Marxist critical geography tradition. Although it is closely tied to a public policy initiative in the UK (that is, localism), its juxtaposition with the word progressive takes it into a broader framework for evaluating new forms of civic engagement and citizenship. David Featherstone and colleagues (2012) are highly critical of the idea of localism or at least the way that the concept is currently deployed by the UK government. The policy of localism is enshrined in the Localism Act 2011, which was brought into being by the UK Conservative–Liberal Democrat coalition government of 2010-15. It exists '... to devolve power from central government to individuals, communities and local councils' (HM Government, 2010, p 7). Its central idea is therefore the decentralisation of state-provided goods and services (especially in health and social care, housing and education) from central government to the local community. Under this shift, local communities, in partnership with local authorities, are now responsible for handling budgets, delivering services and taking into local control former state assets (such as buildings) and planning responsibilities.

Featherstone et al (2012) identify contrasting visions of localism. The first they define as austerity localism. This refers to the government's deliberate and purposeful decision to cut the budgets of local authorities and other public bodies as a form of budgetary rebalancing. The depth of austerity cuts (typically 65% cuts to local authority budgets over a 10-year period) goes well beyond what might be called savings or cost cutting. While masked in a rhetoric of empowering local communities and freeing them from the predatory machinations of a meddling and intervening state, the real intent is aimed at fundamentally restructuring the contract between the state and its citizens. Thus Featherstone and colleagues maintain that localism is '... part of a broader repertoire of practices through which the government has constructed the local as antagonistic to the state and invoked it to restructure the public sector' (Featherstone et al, 2012, p 178). This involves '... attacks on public bureaucracies and collective entitlements through the "now familiar repertoire of funding cuts, organisational downsizing, market testing and privatisation"' (Featherstone et al, 2012, p 178).

Progressive localism, on the other hand, is a concept that seeks to tap into the genuinely empowering potential of the idea of localism – namely the creating of robust, resilient and flourishing localities. Featherstone and colleagues are keen to arrive at a definition that brings together the different facets and dimensions historically associated with practices of effective community empowerment. Their definition is therefore complex and multi-dimensional, but it is worth quoting in full:

> [Progressive localism] ... suggests community strategies that are outward looking and that create positive affinities between places and social groups negotiating global processes. [These processes] are expansive in their geographical reach and productive of new relations between places and social groups. Such struggles can ... reconfigure

existing communities around emergent agendas for social justice, participation and tolerance. (Featherstone et al, 2012, p 179)

There are a number of elements here that are worth unpacking because they represent important dimensions of the type of responsible citizenship I am seeking to recalibrate for a post-Rawlsian dispensation. First of all, the word progressive is stripped back to its simplest definition. It is not used in the sense of liberal or elitist, but simply means being outward looking. The opposite of this term would be regressive, which would in this context mean inward looking. Thus the implication of this concept is that a prerequisite for flourishing localities is the presence of social actors, groups and institutions that are outward looking – that is, prepared to work alongside other outward-facing institutions and identify common areas of engagement regardless of worldview or belief.

This identification of common agendas and areas of engagement is then broken down into a series of key components. First is the idea of creating positive affinities between places and social groups negotiating global processes. Notice here the use of the word affinities. It implies a loose and pragmatic network of social actors united by a common cause. Joining an affinity group suggests aligning oneself to a group where loyalty is based on shared ideas rather than on predetermined characteristics. It also has a more organic quality than a more formal word like partnership. The subtle implication of the word affinity is that we have moved beyond the policy world of top–down partnerships managed by local authorities into a more fluid set of self-selecting spaces of action and engagement.

Next, these new affinities are expansive in their geographical reach and productive of new relations between spaces and groups. Here we have a strong indication that the shift towards a progressive politics involves crossing into new territories and spaces of engagement that overlay, or in some cases, transcend the old cartographies of bureaucratic demarcations (such as parish or local authority boundaries). Old top-down notions of hierarchy and place are being subverted by the restless fluidity of Modernity 2 and new relations between different groupings and different places are being reconfigured and reimagined all the time.

So the idea of progressive localism brings a considerable sense of dynamism to the hitherto rather static and essentialised reading of the public sphere. But while the concept of progressive localism is good at describing new potential frameworks and mechanisms for a dynamic reading of modern citizenship, it does not really address the issue of *motivation*. So why might citizens be impelled to seek new affinities and expanded geographical boundaries by which to better express their understandings of responsible citizenship? Is there a wider and deeper turn in public life that is contributing to these new civic and political arrangements?

Spiritual capital

To answer these questions, I turn to my final category. The concept of spiritual capital, as I now deploy it, helps provide the missing link that explains the search for the Great Reconnection that I suggest is a major component of the contemporary *Zeitgeist* that is shaping our ideas of citizenship. It also contributes to a deeper and more nuanced reading of progressive localism. My use and understanding of spiritual capital emerges from research undertaken by the William Temple Foundation in the early 2000s into the contribution of church groups to urban regeneration in areas of post-industrial blight in south and east Manchester.[1] We were interested not only in the contributions made by faith groups in these communities, but also in what they understood by the term itself. As a rule, the visions for regeneration offered by the churches tended to focus more on the importance of process as well as the product – on the means as well as the ends. Thus, for example, regeneration:

- focuses on transforming people personally and spiritually, as well as improving their area physically;
- values personal stories, especially about how individual regeneration occurs;
- believes implicitly or explicitly that God is at work within regeneration and civil society;
- involves an acceptance that there is considerable and strong emotion experienced and expressed when working for healthy communities (for example, anger, frustration, cynicism, weariness, fragility) and an acknowledgement of the importance and significance of feelings;
- introduces the values of self-emptying, forgiveness, transformation, risk taking, and openness to learning;
- begins with the intention of accepting those who have been rejected elsewhere (Baker and Skinner, 2006, p 7).

What emerged from the Foundation's data was that a vision for spiritual and emotional regeneration was integral to the church groups' engagement in the civic and public life. So in trying to capture the overlapping contributions of churches and other faith groups to regeneration, the Foundation used social capital theory, which by then had become the defining policy framework for UK-based public policy.

The Foundation's research suggested that, as a contribution to social capital, faith groups like churches provide both religious and spiritual capital. Religious capital is 'the practical contribution to local and national life made by faith groups'. Spiritual capital, meanwhile, '*energises* religious capital by providing a theological identity and worshipping tradition, but also a value system, moral vision and a basis of faith' (Baker and Skinner, 2006, p 7, emphasis in original). Religious capital is the 'what': the concrete actions and resources that faith communities contribute. The 'why' is spiritual capital: the motivating basis of faith, belief and values that shapes these concrete actions. And where public policy insisted on separating the 'what' from the 'why' of these faith groups by ruling out acknowledgement of their beliefs and values, we said that the demonstrable power of religious-based social capital would only be enhanced if you allowed the 'why' and the 'what' to be reconnected.

However, as intimated at the start of this chapter, it is crucial to go one step further if spiritual capital is going to be a key component of civic reconnection. If the concept of spiritual capital highlights the motivating energy of our beliefs, values and worldviews that orientates us as citizens in a certain way in the public sphere, and influences the way we contribute to social capital, spiritual capital is not the sole preserve of people who label themselves religious or belong to religious communities. Secular or non-religious beliefs and worldviews (in other words, secular spiritual capital) are also significant, potentially generative sources of social capital (Baker and Miles-Watson, 2008). The debate about the socially generative role of secular spiritual capital has barely begun.

So in my view, there is a clear link between progressive localism, spiritual capital and radically responsible citizenship. Key to this link is the theme of reconnection – of crisscrossing geographical cultural and bureaucratic boundaries in the search for new partners and spaces of authenticity where citizens can reconnect their politics and economics with a deeper sense of ethical engagement and a values-based approach and vision for change and transformation.

However, because of the depth of diversity that now confronts us, it is clear that the desire and search for reconnection will increasingly involve crossing ideological and epistemological barriers as well. The challenge, as well as the opportunity and invitation from within the post-secular public sphere, is to experiment and occupy both new intellectual and political spaces, offering both intellectual and emotional hospitality to others, but from within the wellspring of our own values and beliefs. This wellspring of values and beliefs I have called spiritual capital. In all scenarios of cosmopolitan ethics, I suggest, we invest our spiritual capital with and alongside others for the sake of making an intervention for change, but also so that our own wells can be replenished.

Two case studies: a Muslim foodbank and a local currency

I now offer two case studies that I think express the new spaces, processes and imaginations associated with the emergence of radically democratic but also deeply ethical expressions and subjectivities of citizenship that are being shaped by the post-secular public sphere. The first case study revolves around a recently opened Muslim-run community food project in the London Borough of Brent called Sufra. Sufra is a polyphonic Middle Eastern word that has connotations of tablecloth, dining room and space of hospitality. Ninety per cent of the people who access the service are non-Muslim. Sufra's first client was a young man named Stephen, who, on being given a bag of food, had no idea how to cook it. This led Sufra to run a 10-week cooking course for its clients that is now an accredited training scheme for 16- to 25-year-olds (25 people have found work as a result). Sufra runs a vegetable box scheme – providing fresh produce at wholesale prices – and a food-growing project. Fifty per cent of Sufra's funding and resources comes from other faith groups, including the local Catholic church and Jewish community, as well as a multi-faith workforce including people from non-religious backgrounds. Meanwhile Sufra volunteers are trained by staff from the council's housing department to offer advice on housing needs – something 'never seen before' in Brent, and a 'radical' change from the status quo. Sufra was also a venue for pre-election hustings in 2015 where the issues of food poverty and homelessness were centre stage. Sufra's Director, Mohammed Mankami, says the project feels like the end of the road for many who step across the threshold for the first time, but he wants it to be the start of a new journey. Sufra also aspires to be an organisation where people of different beliefs and worldviews can 'take part in social action together, fundraise together, and share resources together' to create what Mankami calls a 'sustainable common purpose' (William Temple Foundation, 2015).

The second case study concerns a local currency called the Bristol Pound, initiated by an Anglican priest, Chris Sunderland. His purpose for establishing a local currency was 'to give people a taste of a different form of money, that was embedded in the local economy and could produce a new values-led community of exchange' (William Temple Foundation, 2015). These values were based on a deeply held organising principle: namely that global economic and political systems need to reflect the moral imperative to develop what Sunderland calls a 'sustainable relationship with creation' (William Temple Foundation, 2015). Prior to the formal launch of the Bristol Pound, Sunderland had been involved in many related grassroots and community-based initiatives, including setting up a community called Earth Abbey and converting a vicarage garden into a community food-growing project. He was also an instigator of a city-wide scheme, Chooseday, which encouraged car owners to leave their cars at home in order to reduce pollution levels in Bristol and the surrounding area. During the course of these many initiatives, Sunderland found himself working naturally with many other social activists and citizens whom he described as 'having a spiritual heart, but who were also suspicious of formalised Christianity' (William Temple Foundation, 2015).

The mission statement for the Bristol Pound is 'We need to do a currency that is city-wide and uses both electronic and printed media' (William Temple Foundation, 2015). This idea, in the words of Sunderland, grew a team of like-minded citizens around it, both people from traditional faith backgrounds and those who would define themselves as having no religion. After three years' gestation, including a validation process with the Bank of England, the Bristol Pound was launched in 2012. Currently 700 businesses and 1,300 individuals are part of the scheme and 30,000 Bristol Pounds were exchanged over the 2014 Christmas period. Further initiatives include the launch of a new cooperative scheme called Real Economy. This scheme aims to bring Bristol citizens into touch with local producers to encourage the uptake of fresh food consumption at wholesale prices through the encouragement of buying groups able to order using a bespoke webtool.

Conclusion

What we observe within these two case studies are some of the salient features of a post-Rawlsian concept of responsible citizenship. Where once there was an expectation that citizenship could be rationalised into a form of individualised cognitive assent to universalist conceptual frameworks based on notions of justice, equality and liberty, we now see different elements and drivers at play. What these two case studies hint at is a new social and political hinterland created by what I suggest is a new *Zeitgeist* based on the desire for reconnectivity after 40 years of neoliberalised imaginaries and assumptions of monadic disconnectivity. This desire to reconnect at both a community and an ethical level, I suggest, is partly driven by the deepening inequality and lack of hope created by what many see as a punitive and regressive focus on deep and sustained austerity. However, as I have suggested in the social theory analysis of Habermas and Beck, these policy drivers are part of a wider and more complex framing of macro-drivers including the re-emergence of religion into a post-secular public sphere, and the realisation of the depth of the moral as well as the political crisis presented by the new risk modernity. Beck's typology of a cosmopolitan moral and political imaginary based on intertwined fates is a challenge that is understood and felt by many across a wide spectrum of belief and ideological positions.

So in these case studies we see the emergence of what Cloke and colleagues refer to as new spaces of convergence (Cloke et al, 2016, p 2). One of these spaces is a foodbank. The other space is 'an idea' that has produced multiple practical responses (including a local currency). Both spaces were originated by individuals profoundly shaped and motivated by their beliefs, values and visions of transformation (what I refer to as spiritual capital). What characterises these spaces is a radical hospitality and commitment to practically living out an ethic of care and dignity for both human and non-human actors. The clear moral frameworks characterising these spaces have attracted other social actors from a variety of political, epistemological and ontological positions, which has created added value in terms of problem-solving capability, insight and shared resources. Key to the success of these projects has not been to secure an intellectual agreement. Rather, what has attracted others to join is the pragmatic and practicality of *ethics in action*. The attraction to the space is primarily performative and affective.

Both case studies have developed a form of non-hubristic leadership that has encouraged reflexivity alongside performativity, so that people can make the connections for themselves between their own spiritual capital and the contributions to social, economic and human capital that they are making. In other words, there is a hermeneutical revolution with respect to the Rawlsian notion of citizenship. In this model, citizens express loyalty to pre-loaded beliefs about the structure of the world through their actions. In my model, citizens grasp the meaning of concepts like justice, equality and liberty through the lived experience of putting into practice their spiritual capital in what, thanks to the intense globalisation processes associated with Modernity 2, are increasingly post-secular spaces and affinities of progressive, as well as potentially regressive, localism.

Along with Mouffe's radical democracy model, I share an understanding that new subjectivities of engaged (as opposed to passive) citizenship emerge alongside performative practices. As Mouffe reflects, citizens do not simply exist as pre-packaged entities, but emerge and are refined by the direct application of ethico-political concerns in dialectical conversation and engagement with deeper moral principles. I hope that I have expanded on, added nuance to and grounded this insight in the light of the current *Zeitgeist*.

Mouffe's model, I think, challenges mine to constantly address the issue of power dynamics and incorporate clear analysis of cycles of oppression and inequality. As citizenship migrates primarily from an *institutional* model to one based on *affinity*, there is a danger that issues of power will receive insufficient attention. These and other questions need to be rigorously explored and upheld if my proposed model of citizenship is to fit more closely with the current *Zeitgeist* and help call it to account.

Note

[1] *Regenerating Communities – A Theological and Strategic Critique* (2002-05) conducted for the Church Urban Fund. These findings are primarily documented in Baker (2009).

References

Baker, C. (2009) *The Hybrid Church in the City – Third Space Thinking*, London: SCM Press.

Baker, C. and Miles-Watson, J. (2008) 'Exploring Secular Spiritual Capital; An Engagement in Religious and Secular Dialogue for a Common Future', *International Journal of Public Theology*, 2, 442-464.

Baker, C. and Skinner, H. (2006) *Faith in Action – The Dynamic Connection between Religious and Spiritual Capital*, Manchester: William Temple Foundation.

Beck, U. (1995) *Ecological Politics in an Age of Risk*, Cambridge: Polity.

Beck, U. (1999) *World Risk Society*, Cambridge: Polity, Blackwell.

Beck, U. (2011) *A God of One's Own*, Cambridge: Polity.

Beckford, R. (2012) Public Religions and the Postsecular: Critical Reflections. *Journal for the Scientific Study of Religion*, 51, 1-19.

Brown, E. (2003) 'Rawls and the Duty of Civility', in S. Gorman (ed) *Locations of the Political*, Vienna: IWM Junior Visiting Fellows Conferences: 1-18.

Cloke, P., May, J. and Williams, A. (2016) 'The Geographies of Food Banks in the meantime', *Progress in Human Geography*, 1-24.

Coulter, M. (2013) *What is needed in a Citizen: Citizenship and Western Political Philosophy*, Grove City, PA: Grove City College

Featherstone, D., Ince, A., Mackinnon, D., Strauss, K. and Cumbers, A. (2012) 'Progressive Localism and the Construction of Political Alternatives', *Transactions of the Institute of British Geographers*, 37, 177-182.

Galston, W. A. (1991) *Liberal Purposes: Goods, Virtues, and Diversity in the Liberal State*, Cambridge: Cambridge University Press.

Habermas, J. (2005) 'On the Relation between the Secular Liberal State and Religion' trans Matthias Fritsch', in E. Mendieta (ed) *The Frankfurt School of Religion – Key Writings by the Major Thinkers*, New York and London: Routledge: 339-348.

Habermas, J. (2006) 'Religion in the Public Square', *European Journal of Philosophy*, 14, 1-25.

Habermas, J. (2010) 'An Awareness of What is Missing', in J. Habermas, N. Brieskorn, M. Redre, F. Brieskorn and J. Schmidt (eds) *An Awareness of What is Missing*, Cambridge: Polity: 15-24.

HM Government (2010) *Decentralisation and the Localism Bill – an essential guide*, HM Government, [Online] Available at: www.gov.uk/government/uploads/system/uploads/attachment_data/file/5951/1793908.pdf [Accessed 23 August 2016].

Kartal, F. (2001) 'Liberal and Republican Conceptualisations of Citizenship: An Enquiry', *Turkish Public Administration Annual*, 27-28, 101-130.

Lancione, M. (2014) 'Entanglements of Faith: Discourses, Practices of Care, and Homeless People in an Italian City of Saints', *Urban Studies*, 51, 3062-3078.

Mouffe, C. (1991) 'Democratic Citizenship and the Political Community', in M. T. Collective (ed) *Community at Loose Ends*, Minneapolis, MN: University of Minnesota Press: 70-82.

Neufeld, B. (2013) 'Political Liberalism and Citizenship Education', *Philosophy Compass*, 8/9, 781-797.

Nozick, R. (1974) *Anarchy, State, and Utopia*, Oxford: Basil Blackwell.

Oakeshott, M. (1991) *On Human Conduct*, Oxford: Oxford University Press.

Rawls, J. (1973) *A Theory of Justice*, London: Oxford University Press.

Rawls, J. (1993) *Political Liberalism*, New York, NY: Columbia University Press.

Sandel, M. J. (1982) *Liberalism and the Limits of Justice*, Cambridge: Cambridge University Press.

William Temple Foundation (2015) *Building a Politics of Hope. Report of Conference Proceedings 24 February 2015*, William Templeton Foundation, [Online] Available at: http://williamtemplefoundation. org.uk/wp-content/uploads/2015/01/Politics-of-Hope_Event-Report.pdf [Accessed 25 October 2015].

SIXTEEN

Conclusion: citizenship, community and solidarity at the end of the welfare state

Jan-Jonathan Bock and Shana Cohen

In May 2016, a revealing encounter took place at the Social Democratic Party's (SPD) conference on social justice in Berlin. The party leader, Sigmar Gabriel, discussed labour conditions with a female cleaner, Susanne Neumann. In front of hundreds of SPD members and dozens of television cameras, Neumann attacked precarious working conditions. She told Gabriel that the SPD had become unelectable for many working-class voters because of Chancellor Gerhard Schröder's labour market deregulation and crippling welfare cuts in the early 2000s. She called for the neoliberal reforms to be reversed. "You changed the law so that people can be hired on short-term contracts," she accused Gabriel, "and in my sector, everyone is on short-term contracts now. People don't get a chance." She elaborated:

> "These guys get a six-month contract. If they have to take any sick leave, or if someone tells their boss that they are union members, or if they ask for overtime pay, the contract is not extended. Young people start their working lives with these short-term contracts. That means that no landlord lets you rent a flat; you don't get a bank credit to purchase anything and design your home. We are being domineered, and it creates frustration and anger. So why should I vote for a party that caused this situation and doesn't have any solutions?"

Neumann accused the SPD of promoting a two-tier system that creates a hierarchy between workers on open-ended contracts and those on short-term ones. She disclosed that she would have to take early retirement soon, because of cancer. After 38 years of work, Neumann revealed, she will receive a monthly pension of 725 euros (around £600 sterling in mid-2016):

"If I didn't have my husband, I would have to ask the job centre for a top-up. That basically means stripping naked. 'How big is your flat? How much do you have in savings?' In Germany's constitution, it says that human dignity is sacred. But I have worked hard my entire life – I never took any money from the state. Then you get into that kind of situation, because of illness, and the state does not support you."

Gabriel barely featured in the exchange. It was apparent that the audience's sympathies were with Susanne Neumann. The party leader seemed irritated when the cleaner received loud applause for her suggestion that the SPD leave the grand coalition government with the conservative CDU. The scene was striking. The SPD appeared taken aback and bewildered by Neumann's account, as if she were an exotic visitor from another world: a struggling working-class person. The SPD leadership was confronted by those crippled by its neoliberal reform agenda, from which the party had failed to distance itself in the post-Schröder era: cuts to welfare, labour market deregulation, smaller pensions, short-term contracts and harsh sanctions. Neumann was sporting short hair and a colourful t-shirt. Her account of working-class life in the age of SPD social reform clashed with Gabriel's elegant suit and suntan, seated on stage in what was intended as a carefully crafted political spectacle. Neumann was angry with the SPD. She had once even joined the Left Party in protest against the neoliberal welfare and labour market reforms under Schröder.

As we have shown in the introduction to this volume, Schröder's neoliberal reform projects alienated many Social Democratic Party voters, who sought an alternative in the newly founded Left Party, or abstained from voting. In 2015, Angela Merkel's decision to offer shelter to hundreds of thousands of war refugees intensified the debate about a sense of disenfranchisement among many Germans, who were themselves struggling with the repercussions of welfare cuts, rising house prices, small pensions and precarious labour conditions. In response to Merkel's humanitarian approach, a right-wing populist party, the Alternative for Germany (AfD), became established, unprecedented in post-war Germany's political landscape. Since Germany's election system, unlike the UK's, is based on proportional representation, new parties can emerge relatively quickly. Growing disenchantment with elites and their political decisions was discussed across the country (Ackner, 2016). The debate coined a new term, the *Wutbürger* (the anger citizen): he, less frequently she, protests in squares and streets, rages online and in newspaper comment sections, and punishes the traditional political elites through support for populist platforms in the voting booth. The *Wutbürger's* political leanings are ambiguous, but nostalgia for the past and hostility towards Muslims, migrants and refugees distinguish anger citizens from the internationalist, progressive and socially liberal Indignados, Occupy, or 99% movements. The latter have also called for an end to austerity, but at the same time demand wealth transfers to the south, global justice, and respect for religious, cultural or sexual minorities (Graeber, 2012; (Ancelovici et al, 2016) – issues about which the *Wutbürgers* care little. They are predominantly furious about losing safety and privileges (see also Kimmel, 2013).

One particularly noticeable platform for the expression of *Wutbürgers'* political and social ideas has become the Pegida movement, which has spread from the East German city of Dresden across the country, and even into other European countries (Pegida UK had a stronghold in Birmingham). In Dresden, the Patriotic Europeans against the Islamisation of the West (Pegida is the German acronym) started their weekly marches in October 2014. However, fear of Islamic culture was predominantly an umbrella term to unite a heterogeneous group of people. Participants carried posters and signs protesting against a range of issues, from social benefit cuts over supposed American warmongering in the Middle East to migration; many demanded closer ties with Russia (Vorländer et al, 2016). In Dresden, tens of thousands of people participated during the movement's peak in 2016. Pegida became an outlet for anger, specifically for people from Dresden's rural hinterland, battered by post-reunification economic decline. Many East Germans have lamented the loss of employment, self-esteem, pensions and state protection in the wake of reunification with West Germany in 1990. This is why hostility to the government's support for Muslim foreigners was particularly strong in Germany's formerly socialist regions, but similar expressions of discontent could be found in the country's post-industrial and struggling rural zones in general.

Before observing one Pegida rally in Dresden in February 2016, Jan Bock spoke with Frank Richter, the head of the State of Saxony's Office for Civic Education, about the Pegida movement and the sociology of its participants. "When I spoke to Pegida supporters," Richter explained, "one of them said to me: 'It's all nice and well what you are saying, Mr Richter, but I will keep on marching with Pegida until the state finds me a job and I get a wife.'" Richter elaborated that many women had left Dresden's hinterland as a result of economic decline, creating a noticeable male surplus with few employment opportunities. In Saxony's rural regions, stretching from Dresden to the borders with

Poland and the Czech Republic in particular, Richter continued, administrative reforms have merged municipalities and administrative districts to such an extent that the only relic of state organisation in many towns or villages is the local bus stop. The intersection of private affairs with demands on the state might be especially prominent among East Germans, for whom universal employment, secure pensions and state protection were part of the political ideology, if not of everyday reality, during 40 years of socialism. Beyond Saxony, however, the success of Pegida groups has also revealed West Germans' demands for more active public institutions that ought to support citizens with challenging personal circumstances. The mid-2010s were marked by the rise of the *Wutbürger*, who received much media coverage and analysis. Pegida movements, the AfD, and numerous online platforms and social media sites have created an angry, alternative public sphere for resentful citizens, challenging mainstream media and political discourse.

That is why, when Susanne Neumann expressed her anger at Sigmar Gabriel and the SPD at the party's conference, attacking short-term contracts, precarious employment and the betrayal of working-class solidarity, she appeared as the typical *Wutbürger* – bitter, angry and frustrated. In fact, however, Neumann was an invited speaker at the conference because she had recently abandoned the Left Party. Instead, she had joined, of all political forces, the SPD. She made it clear that the Social Democratic Party was still important for working-class Germans, even though it was languishing at an all-time low in the polls. If the SPD disappeared, Neumann said, the consequences would be devastating for workers. She wanted her anger to become a wakeup call: "The party has declined so much that I had to ask myself: should I not become involved to change things?" Following energetic applause, she added: "Ordinary people, working-class people, have to be represented better; they have to speak up and to join groups and committees." Despite her frustration with social democratic politics and her difficult personal circumstances, Neumann did not join other *Wutbürgers*, romanticising the past and deriding political elites as hopelessly remote. Instead, she chose engagement in the party she still believed ought to represent working-class interests and deliver social justice.

Emergent citizenships in crisis-ridden Europe

What has happened to citizenship in Germany and the UK – and to ideas of what it means to be a citizen – during an era marked by downward pressure on wages, labour market flexibility that requires hire-and-fire employment models, the push for self-reliance, and the reduction of both universal benefits and, in particular, supportive intervention for vulnerable individuals and groups? How have local, perhaps previously uninvolved, citizens, as well as long-term activists, faced with growing social need and poverty in their own neighbourhoods, responded to transformations of welfare regimes and public sector retreat? In the process of helping those rendered vulnerable and insecure by welfare reforms and extreme flexibility in the job market, have these activists, and local s more generally, pursued new forms of community belonging and social solidarity? Have they thereby also developed a new type of 'social citizen' that, in essence, offers a contradistinctive trend to the angry citizen?

Economic pressures and the concomitant ideology of the non-interventionist state – at least in the fields of welfare and social justice (Wacquant, 2009) – have produced new visions of what it means to act politically as a citizen in Europe. As mentioned above, the anger citizen became prominent in the mid-2010s, with marches, protest parties and anti-establishment aggression. In Europe, a spectacular demonstration of such emergent visions of national politics was the UK's referendum on European Union (EU) membership in June 2016. The Leave camp predominantly characterised the vote as dividing the UK into removed, upper-class elites, protecting their privilege in the South East, on the one hand, and the rest of the country, with its battered former working-class strongholds, where labour and hope had become sparse, seeking an escape from decline, on the other, thus manipulating a sense of disenfranchisement (Lanchester, 2016). As more experts on the economy, finance, politics, or European history sought to convince voters to remain, the polls swung to Leave. Commentators suggested that telling those struggling with long-term unemployment, steep house prices, declining social services, urban decay, health surgery queues and underperforming schools that leaving the EU would hit the economy – and thus make their lives materially more insecure – did not have the desired effect:

> Making economic arguments to voters who feel oppressed by economics is risky: they're quite likely to tell you to go fuck yourself. That in effect is what the electorate did do the almost comical cavalcade of sages and bigshots who took the trouble to explain that Brexit would be ruinous folly: Obama, Lagarde, the IMF [International Monetary Fund], the OECD [Organisation for Economic Co-operation and Development], the ECB [European Central Bank],

and every commentator and pundit you can think of. (Lanchester, 2016, p 4)

In this interpretation, the anti-EU vote was a manifestation of anger and frustration. The debates surrounding the referendum gave attention and coverage to Britain's equivalent of the *Wutbürgers* and its influence on Europe's political landscape. Neoliberal austerity politics has not simply reduced people's capacity to consume material goods and plan their economic future, but also transformed understandings and practices of what it means to be a political subject, and how one ought to confront political power. The experience of frustration regarding what Neveu (2000) has called vertical citizenship – that is, how citizens encounter public institutions – has shaped new practices of horizontal citizenship – how citizens construct possibilities for action by relating to one another directly and through emergent forms of associationism. Investigating these properties of citizenship, the contributors to this volume have shown that the notion does not refer to a straightforward bundle of legal rights and obligations by virtue of holding a modern state passport, which would be the definition of formal citizenship, but rather to substantive, social citizenship, understood as participation in public affairs and attempts to shape social reality (Glick Schiller and Caglar, 2008).

This quieter, less aggressive citizenship emerged alongside the *Wutbürger* across Europe in response to economic pressure and neoliberal statehood: community activism aimed at producing neighbourhood solidarity through understanding, thus confronting hardship, stigma and exclusion. Contributions to this volume have traced manifestations of such civic engagement. Susanne Neumann resents SPD deregulation and neoliberalism, which also affect her personally. However, instead of angrily waving placards, she is pursuing concrete ways of changing policy and providing life chances, as do many of the people portrayed by our practitioners in their chapters. Our book explores how the people who have come to practise this kind of horizontal citizenship under austerity and economic pressure experience their work, and how academics reflect on its repercussions for Europe's social democracies. Contributors have examined how activism that challenges policies can exist beyond angry protest and populist extremism, namely in grassroots forms of positive citizenship that seek to generate solidarity.

Across the UK and Germany, as our chapters have shown, austerity has caused new struggles, exacerbating the uncertainty and sense of precariousness characteristic of late modernity anyway (Beck, 1992; Hage, 2003; Abélès, 2010; Nowotny, 2016). Cuts to state spending and welfare provisions during the first two decades of the new millennium, intensified after the 2008 global financial crash, have not alone caused the emergence of new kinds of citizenship. There have been other factors: rising economic inequality (Piketty, 2014); the declining faith in economic actors to provide quality goods and services for citizens, rather than enrich shareholders (Mayer, 2013); distrust in the political class to represent the interests and serve the needs of the general public, not just economic elites (Crouch, 2004); and uncertainty that the current economic model, which fails to deliver sufficient, purposeful employment, will change to benefit the majority (Mason, 2015). Despite their already apparent and dramatic social consequences, the detrimental political ideologies of neoliberalism and austerity continued across much of Europe in the 2010s (Crouch, 2012; Blyth, 2013; Stewart and Knight, 2016). Jeff Miley, in Chapter Thirteen, has called this an 'upper-class assault on social democracy'. Elites protect their spoils by removing their experiences from the lives of the majority, simultaneously cutting back the legal frameworks and protective institutions that used to mediate the impact of economic hardship.

This volume documents attempts of remaking political behaviour when faced with such adverse conditions. Future research will have to investigate whether the quieter and socially constructive practices of citizenship documented here can become as prominent as angry protest movements in shaping media perceptions, national politics, party agendas and public institutions' response to economic pressure. For Germany, the question is whether people such as Susanne Neumann will have the same impact on the trajectory of Germany's Social Democrats as Pegida or the AfD have had on the country's conservative party (CDU), whose grassroots pushed the party leader, Angela Merkel, to strike a contentious deal with Turkey to prevent refugees from coming to Europe. The impact of anger citizens on conservative politics has been unmistakable, particularly concerning issues of migration, religion and integration. Can engaged community actors and social movements do the same for Germany's SPD and for the UK's Labour Party?

Examples from both the UK and Germany have shown that social activism in both countries appears increasingly politicised. Our chapters on the German Tafel foodbank network, for instance, illustrate that social activism is contested on political grounds. While the Tafel founder, Sabine Werth (Chapter Eight), emphasises the network's important social contribution to alleviate hunger and shape emergent forms of understanding across social barriers, her most prominent critic in Germany, Stefan Selke (Chapter Twelve), highlights the Tafel's supposedly detrimental effects: it turns poverty into a private business and reduces the capacity for political action to tackle the root cause of hardship and exclusion. The reliance on public funding has an impact on social initiatives in the UK, too. Grassroots groups are faced with a difficult choice: supporting those left behind by the state, charities fear that their work might become an excuse for further social cuts (see Chapter Seven by Chris Price). In Germany, state welfare offices began to refer benefit recipients to charity foodbanks, wrongly asserting that they were entitled to support, as Sabine Werth reports in Chapter Eight. She expresses frustration that her organisation could become a fig leaf for the small state, and advocates a critical distance to the authorities (see also Milligan and Conradson, 2006). At the same time, the pressure on charitable organisations to professionalise and expand is high. Community work becomes more bureaucratic, because of political constraints. As Michelle Howlin and Paul A Jones argue in Chapter Six, organisations such as credit unions are under pressure to demonstrate success in order to access public funding. This requires them to focus on attracting clients with a regular income rather than economically marginalised populations who might pose a risk. Such requirements might contravene an organisation's aim of providing a universal service or ensuring that vulnerable individuals and families have access to support. More generally, voluntary organisations could become complicit in a social order that relegates responsibility for wellbeing, equality and social justice to private actors, which, in turn, respond to official pressure to perform and select on the basis of profit sector standards. Dedication to the production of solidarity across social divisions is reworked by a market economy logic that requires professionalisation and expansion, which might displace primarily charitable objectives (Smith and Lipsky, 1995; Baines, 2004; Hungerman, 2005; Cunningham and James, 2009). In the end, people in need will be left behind again.

This throws up important questions for future investigation: given these institutional constraints, how much scope is left for activists to demonstrate alternative models of citizenship, concerned with solidarity, community care and belonging, and to use these alternative models to influence not just small-scale realities, but also national trajectories of social policy? Which are the effects of professionalisation and bureaucracy on the resources available for effective political advocacy? In their charitable work, do emergent forms of neighbourhood solidarity and political advocacy simply follow a deliberately neglectful state, compensating for its failures, or do they give rise to autonomous, innovative and attractive forms of citizenship – or both? Our authors have shown that these issues require further analyses.

We need to scrutinise the implications of emergent activism carefully, exploring to what extent emergent types of involved citizenship might play into the hands of a political project that seeks to shift responsibilities for support and care from the state to private persons and communities. Analysing the Italian welfare state since the 1990s, Andrea Muehlebach (2012) has shown that neoliberal politics is accompanied by a strong sense of private duty and moral citizenship practices, which serve to corroborate the privatisation of state functions (see also Harvey, 2005). The country's strong Catholic ethics of care, as well as its communist tradition of solidarity, were instrumentalised by the neoliberal state – championed by the self-made billionaire-turned-Prime Minister, Silvio Berlusconi – to shift public sector responsibilities to private volunteers. Muehlebach suggests that '[h]yperexploitation is … wedded to intense moralization, nonremuneration to a public fetishization of sacrifice' (Muehlebach, 2012, p 7). Many chapters in this volume have also shown that an ethics of social solidarity – Christian and otherwise – lies at the heart of emergent community practices. Stefan Selke suggests in Chapter Twelve that the moral quality routinely ascribed to the work of foodbanks may prevent critical engagement with the implications of expanding social services beyond the state. Further research ought to investigate whether the manipulation of people's desires to do good remains a feature of neoliberal and austerity politics, or whether local forms of citizenship can rework national political trajectories and dominant ideologies by combining the right to access public institutions with private voluntary, or even business, commitment – or whatever negotiations and intersections might exist between the two developments.

More generally, can the local forms of activism evidenced in this book and subjective motivation for community and solidarity, versus solely individual self-interest, lead to a new political agenda? Is it enough that people such as Susanne Neumann or new Labour Party members participate in an existing party to influence its direction, or does there need to be a new framework for policy? Does this framework need to encompass different interaction between those working on the frontline of social services, addressing local need, those in need of services, and policymaking elites? In a short piece that addresses the question of whether the British Labour Party could split, the columnist Aditya Chakrabortty (2016) calls for Momentum's members to look beyond forming a political movement. He writes:

> [I]f Corbyn's Labour and Momentum want to be social movements, let's see them get involved in civil society. How about getting more people registered to vote? Now that access to legal advice and other civil society organisations have been so badly stripped back, let's see Labour organisations help renters in dispute with sharky landlords, or negotiating good collective deals with utility firms. If the future of left politics lies partly in becoming a social movement, that means actually doing stuff.

Practitioners' accounts concerning the ideological assumptions of policy and lived hardship support the case that greater knowledge of, and involvement in, the consequences of welfare reforms would be beneficial. The distance, even antagonism, between the private, public and voluntary sectors constitutes a consistent theme throughout the book, and potentially indicates a new policy agenda.

On a conceptual level, in an era of neoliberalism, solidarity has been left to charities both to define and to practice. On a practical level, charities battle with the repercussions of private sector employment practices and the implementation of welfare reforms, most notably withdrawal of benefits, on a daily basis. A more productive political agenda may be to overcome the gap between sectors, making collaboration among them the core of fighting poverty and promoting social opportunities. Inequality would thus not be a matter of state regulation and income redistribution, or of charities intervening where the state has failed to act, but, rather, a collective responsibility and foundation for thinking about society, community, and other concepts of social ties. Community and individualism, as Jon Lawrence notes in Chapter Fourteen, do not reflect underlying patterns in consumption or lifestyle trends, but remain a complex mixture of desires in different time periods. In this era of emerging post-neoliberalism, the combination should be recognised in policymaking, where the experience of belonging is acknowledged as an important objective (see Chapter Two by Patrick Diamond) and as a process that includes a range of private and public actors. Charities would thus not have to work hard to solicit corporate donations or cultivate government support, or, more specifically, be trapped between zero-hour contracts in the job market and government sanctions when trying to help individual clients. Government policy would outline common goals and shared obligations, combining political mobilisation and social action within an approach to social solidarity that extends beyond one type of actor or a specific social group. This differs from a government consultation exercise with private actors or charities, mostly those operating at a national level and thus with relatively extensive resources, lobbying policymakers. Rather, it assumes collective responsibility across sectors to support individual opportunity and dignity, with representatives from each sector working together to achieve desired change.

References

Abélès, M. (2010) *The Politics of Survival*, Durham and London: Duke University Press.

Ackner, W. (2016) *Warum ich ein Wutbürger bin*, Welt.de, [Online] Available at: www.welt.de/debatte/kommentare/article155713761/ Warum ich ein Wutbuerger-bin.html. [Accessed 10 August 2016].

Ancelovici, M., Dufour, P. and Nez, H. (eds) (2016) *Street Politics in the Age of Austerity – From the Indignados to Occupy*, Amsterdam: Amsterdam University Press.

Baines, D. (2004) 'Pro-market, Non-market: The Dual Nature of al Change in Social Services Delivery', *Critical Social Policy*, 24, 5-29.

Beck, U. (1992) *Risk Society: Towards a New Modernity, translated by Mark Ritter*, London: Sage Publications.

Blyth, M. (2013) *Austerity: The History of a Dangerous Idea*, Oxford: Oxford University Press.

Chakrabortty, A. (2016) 'This is about who gets to define what leftwing politics is and how', *The Guardian*, [Online] Available at: www.theguardian.com/commentisfree/2016/jul/13/labour-split-owen-smith-angela-eagle-jeremy-corbyn [Accessed 30 August 2016].

Crouch, C. (2004) *Post-Democracy*, Cambridge: Polity.

Crouch, C. (2012) *The Strange Non-Death of Neoliberalism*, Cambridge and Malden: Polity.

Cunningham, I. and James, P. (2009) 'The Outsourcing of Social Care in Britain: What does it mean for Voluntary Sector Workers?' *Work Employment & Society*, 23, 363-375.

Glick Schiller, N. and Caglar, A. (2008) 'And Ye Shall Possess It, and Dwell Therein: Social Citizenship, Global Christianity and Nonethnic Immigrant Incorporation', in D. Reed-Danahay and C. B. Brettell (eds) *Citizenship, Political Engagement, and Belonging: Immigrants in Europe and the United States*, New Brunswick, NJ and London: Rutgers University Press: 203-225.

Graeber, D. (2012) *The Democracy Project: A History, a Crisis, a Movement.* New York, NY: Spiegel and Grau.

Hage, G. (2003) *Against Paranoid Nationalism: Searching for Hope in a Shrinking Society*, Sydney: Pluto Press.

Harvey, D. (2005) *A Brief History of Neoliberalism*, Oxford: Oxford University Press.

Hungerman, D. M. (2005) 'Are Church and State Substitutes? Evidence from the 1996 Welfare Reform', *Journal of Public Economics*, 89, 2245-2267.

Kimmel, M. (2013) *Angry White Men – American Masculinity at the End of an Era*, New York, NY: Nation Books.

Lanchester, J. (2016) 'Brexit Blues', *London Review of Books*, 38, 3-6.

Mason, P. (2015) *Postcapitalism – A Guide to Our Future*, London: Allen Lane.

Mayer, C. (2013) *Firm Commitment – Why the corporation is failing us and how to restore trust in it*, Oxford: Oxford University Press.

Milligan, C. and Conradson, D. (2006) 'Contemporary landscapes of welfare: the "voluntary turn"?' in C. Milligan and D. Conradson (eds) *Landscapes of Voluntarism: New Spaces of Health, Welfare and Governance*, Bristol: Policy Press: 1-14.

Muehlebach, A. (2012) *The Moral Neoliberal: Welfare and Citizenship in Italy*, Chicago, IL: The University of Chicago Press.

Neveu, C. (2000) 'European Citizenship, Citizens of Europe and European Citizens', in I. Béllier and T. M. Wilson (eds) *The Anthropology of the European Union*, Oxford and New York, NY: Berg Publishers: 119-136.

Nowotny, H. (2016) *The Cunning of Uncertainty*, Cambridge: Polity.

Piketty, T. (2014) *Capital in the Twenty-First Century*, translated by Arthur Goldhammer, Cambridge, MA and London: Harvard University Press.

Smith, S. R. and Lipsky, M. (1995) *Nonprofits for Hire – The Age of Welfare in the Age of Contracting,* Cambridge, MA: Harvard University Press.

Stewart, C. and Knight, D. M. (2016) 'Ethnographies of Austerity: Temporality, Crisis and Affect in Southern Europe', *History and Anthropology*, 27, 1-18.

Vorländer, H., Herold, M. and Schäller, S. (2016) *Pegida – Entwicklung, Zusammensetzung und Deutung einer Empörungsbewegung*, Wiesbaden: Springer Fachmedien.

Wacquant, L. (2009) *Punishing the Poor: The Neoliberal Government of Social Insecurity*, Durham and London: Duke University Press.

Index